Autobiography
of
a Simple Soul

by **Martha Stevens-David**

3-21-12

TO LOUISE, HOPE MY STORIES MAKE
YOU LAUGH!

THANKS SO MUCH!,

MARTHA

Cover image base from iStockphoto, design by Laura Ashton
Photo credit page 287, Martha Stevens-David
Layout by Laura Ashton, laura@gitflorida.com

Copyright 2011 by Martha Stevens-David

At the specific request of the author, PRGott Books Publishing allowed this work to remain exactly as the author intended, without editorial input. The author assumes sole responsibility for the book's content.

Although some of the stories in this book are true and some of the characters are real, their names (except those of the author's immediate family) were changed to protect their privacy.

First Printing

ISBN: 978-0-9845898-5-2

Printed in the United States of America

PRGott Books Publishing
P O Box 43
Norway, Maine 04268

www.prgottbooks.net

Dedication

I dedicate this short story collection to my husband,
Leo M. David,
without whom, I could never have completed this work.

Contents

Autobiography
of
a Simple Soul

INTRODUCTION

In the seventeen hundreds they came. At first it was but a trickle, but still they came. They came from the North, the East and the South. They were of many different tongues, Indian, French, English, Irish, Scots, German and Italian. They came with all that they owned tied in rolls across their backs or "jist" the very clothes they wore.

They came by boats across the great waters and followed the rivers, the streams and the brooks until they couldn't follow them anymore. They came by horse, mule or oxen, but mostly they came, by placing one tired foot in front of the other, until they reached a destination that met their needs. They followed the narrow trails that the moccasins of the Micmac, the Maliseet, the Penobscot and the Algonquin had made in the forests of Aroostook County.

They braved the hoards of black flies, moose flies, no-see-ems, midges and mosquitoes to follow their dreams to a better place. Some followed the rag-tag army of Benedict Arnold as he made his way up from Houlton through Island Falls, Sherman Station, Patten, Ox Bow, Masardis, Ashland, Portage, Buffalo, Soldier Pond, Winterville, Eagle Lake, Wallagrass to Fort Kent and the very edge of the Saint John River Valley.

These men and woman were a proud and hardy lot. Some were truly dreaming of a better place while others came because they were unwanted in their former lands. They carried surnames like: Young, Howe, Kallock, Cook, Scarlett, Webber, Bell, Cunningham, Holman, Robins, Boswell, Weeks, Wakefield, Littlefield, McDonald, Peterson, Mountain, Page, Burby, Lewin, Goss, Keep, Hawes, Howes, Winslow, Rafford, Crocker, Robinson, Stevens, Foster, Jimmo, Dorman, Sutherland, Pike, Sawyer, Orcutt, McGowen, Holmes, Bragdon, Colbath, McHatten, McCormack, Hews, Davenport, Weaver, Bolestridge, Gilman, Coffin, Rossignol, Bartlett, McNally and Clark.

1

These are my people and my heritage and I am immensely proud of them.

The sky, in Aroostook County, is a sharp, clear blue with large, fluffy white clouds floating lazily across it. The slight breeze is so fresh and clean that the first thing one notices is that it doesn't have any smell at all. The air sweeps across the close-cropped pastures and down through the potato fields with barely a ruffling of the leaves. With the advent of autumn, the wild grasses have turned a deep gold, and their golden stocks contrast deeply with the lush greenness of the potato plants.

The soft droning of bees is all that one can hear as they rush about gathering nectar from the multitude of flowers, which grow in wild profusion as far as the eye can see. The patches of bright orange, red and gold Indian paintbrushes sway to and fro in the gentle breeze like the heads of sleepy children.

Down below Sutherland's hill on the Goding Road, jist outside of Ashland, there is the shimmer of silver as the late afternoon sun is reflected off the slowly moving Aroostook River as it winds its way through "Tha County." If one ventures closer to the river, you can see the ripple of the water, as the numerous schools of fish rise to the surface to feed off the hoards of insects that are floating on it. The slap of a beaver's tail on the water sounds like a cannon's boom in the silent air.

Across the river on the Garfield Side, the stands of Pine, Spruce, Hemlock, Beech and Maple stand straight and tall like sentries in the army of the forest. In the lush coolness, there is evidence of the abundance of wild animals. One can readily see that rabbits, bear, moose, deer, raccoons, muskrats, mink and otter still occupy this vast area. The intermingling calls of blue jays, crows, ravens and woodpeckers echo in the quiet stillness of the fall day.

Off in the distance, you can also hear another sound, the sound of man and his chainsaw as its steel teeth rip through the white meat of the virgin timber. The snarl and smoke of the skidder permeates the air as the huge machine struggles to pull the slaughtered logs up out of a deep ravine.

If you raise your head and look off, in the distance, your eyes will naturally be drawn to the southern horizon. There is an oft-repeated expression "On a clear day, you can see forever." From where our house stood on a high knoll on the Goding Road, we couldn't exactly see forever, but on a clear day we could see the majesty of the snow-capped peak of Mt. Katahdin seventy-five or so, miles to the south.

When winter comes once again to Aroostook County, the harsh realities of living confined, for the most part, in doors for the next six or seven months, is almost too much to bear. Another winter of bone-chilling cold, wet socks, mittens and long underwear are the realities of living in "Tha County." Wet wool, Kerosene and the crackle of the wood burning stove are all too familiar smells and sounds to a true Mainer. This is a season of hardship, suffering and most of all great patience.

For all this, Aroostook County is a place of great beauty too. On nights when the temperature hovers around ten clapboards below zero and wise souls hug the blazing wood stove, outside the Aurora Borealis, with its shimmering bands all the colors of the rainbow, shifts its way across the Northern sky.

As proof that this dance has been choreographed by the "Master Choreographer," the Indians, who are older than time, called this magical event "The Dance of the Heavenly Spirits," and this so aptly describes this atmospheric phenomenon.

At times, the cold is so intense that it completely freezes the sap in the trees, and even the slightest wind will cause the branches to break, sounding like gun shots in the frigid air. Cold sears the tissues of the nose and lungs and compels one to move quickly on their appointed rounds.

Man is completely at the mercy of Mother Nature in this unrelenting season. The morning may dawn bright and clear but within the hour, the sky has turned a dull gray and the wind shifts out of the north with a vengeance. The wind-driven snow comes skittering across the desolate potato fields to pile up in huge drifts across the roads. The only contrast to the barren whiteness is the leafless trees and fence posts as they stand like frozen soldiers in the swirling, drifting snow.

In Aroostook County, in the dead of winter, the roads remain in alternating conditions of either deep-piled snowdrifts or frozen ribbons of steel blue ice. One ventures out of doors only under extreme cases of necessity. To live in this northern environment, year after year, requires not only supreme patience, but also an indefatigable spirit or a combination of both to survive in this "God-forsaken" place.

Visitors, who live in warmer climes, which to us meant any place south of Bangor, often voiced the opinion that "Tha County" must be a wonderful place to live when there is so much snow. Upon hearing this, mother would roll her eyes and mutter a few choice words under her breath and say, "Surely God protects fools and children."

Now that I am grown and have wandered around the world a little, I find that no matter how far one roams, your heart, sooner or later, always brings you home....

THA BOOTS

In 1954 dad fell in love, but the really odd thing about this new-found love affair wasn't that he fell in love with another woman and his strange feelings didn't bother mother one dite. You see, dad fell in love with a pair of hunting boots.

To say that dad was a modest man was the understatement of the year. Dad never outright asked for anything ever and it was always up to mother to ferret out any whims or desires that this gentle man might have wished for or downright coveted. After all, she'd spent many years with the man and got to know him inside and out, so it didn't take two brains to rub together to know when way down deep inside, he really wanted something.

Dad had an older sister Ada and two younger brothers, Herbie and Johnny and it was Uncle Johnny who really caused the problem. Dad was an excellent woodsman, hunter and fisherman and many hunters or fisherman from the cities, who happened to be hunting or fishing in the greater Aroostook County area, would ask dad to guide for them or show them where he caught all the biggest fish. And dad, being the father of eight children, always looked for any chance he could to supplement his meager potato farmer's salary.

Well, the year that dad fell from grace was the year that Uncle Johnny came sailing up from Massachusetts with all the latest hunting gear from "L.L. Beans" in Freeport, Maine. Uncle Johnny was a mailman in Athol and not having any children at that time, he had money to burn and he spent a large part of that largess on all his little whims and needs.

Since we didn't have a phone in nineteen fifty-four, Uncle Johnny had written weeks in advance, to make sure that dad wasn't tied up with anyone else and they could take their annual hunting trip to Moosehead Lake together. Upon receiving his brother's short note, dad came alive.

There was nothing he loved more than to go way out into "God's" wonderland and lose himself in the great north woods and lie in wait for the biggest buck that might wander across his path. Thinking back, now I can understand what it must have been like for him, working all year long with noisy, cumbersome potato farming equipment and then coming home to a house full of eight lively, noisy kids. His spirit must have longed for some peace and quiet and most of all, solitude from time to time.

Saturday arrived and so did Uncle Johnny. We all loved him and not having had any children, he always made sure to bring us some candy or small gifts. He and dad immediately broke open the expensive bottle of Gin that was his gift to his older brother and they shooed us outdoors or upstairs so that they could rehash all the news that had passed since they'd last seen each other.

We girls would always go up to bed, but Walt, Jake and Bub would sneak back down and lay across the steps in the living room to listen to all the stories and profanity streaming from the kitchen story tellers. Upon hearin a long litney of swear words roll off Uncle Johnny's tongue, the three boys would convulse with laughter and invariably one of them would roll off the steps alerting the kitchen storytellers that they were being spied upon. Dad would turn in his chair to see who the offenders were and the boys would be up the stairs and into bed in a heartbeat, settling down amidst bursts of laughter brought on by repeating to each other all the new swear words they'd jist learned.

Finally, as the moon moved into the western part of the hemisphere, dad and Uncle Johnny would stumble off to bed and the house would settle down amidst snores from the older generation of gin drinkers and storytellers.

Morning arrived early and dad, used to getting up at four am every day of his natural life, would slide out of his nice, clean sheets, light his first Chesterfield of the day and head out the kitchen door to the toilet that was located at the far end of our woodshed. After answering nature's call, dad would return to the kitchen where he'd make the coffee and then he'd carry the first cup in to mother who was still in bed. This was a ritual that lasted them all through the days of their married lives.

Uncle Johnny, having spent the night on our old, decrepit couch, would soon be wide awake, especially after having been crawled all over or jumped upon by six or seven rambunctious nieces and nephews. Nursing huge hangovers and wanting to escape all of our noise and commotion, he and dad would scoff down mother's scrumptious biscuits, scrambled eggs and beans and hurriedly pack whatever vehicle they were planning to take into the Maine woods and they'd be off. We children, along with Tippy, our old dog, would chase them up the road or down to the corner of the Goding Road, until the dust or the distance obscured them from our sight. Then, we'd wait for the days to slowly crawl by until dad's old pickup came crawling home, usually with a couple of deer tied to the back.

Nineteen fifty-four was a banner year for hunters and dad and Uncle Johnny managed to get their kill on the third day of hunting season and they were back home before we'd actually missed them. Walt and Jake, upon seeing the kill, clambered all over the pickup to get a better view of the deer and asked a million questions about how dad and Uncle Johnny had gotten them.

Dad sent them on one foolish errand after another jist to have some peace and quiet while he and Uncle Johnny untied their deer and carried them onto the porch where they were hung so that he could skin them and cut them up. The boys would hang on every word of the stories that dad and Uncle Johnny told them and every once in a while, Walt, getting the idea that dad or Uncle Johnny were pulling their leg, would punch Jake in the arm and laugh like hell. Jake, not understanding the joke or why he'd been punched, would punch Walt back and the fight would be on. Dad would reach out and pull them apart with his deer's blood-stained hand and that was the end of the fight.

Anyway, it wasn't too long before dad would have the venison all cut up, packaged and ready for his brother's return to Massachusetts the following morning. But, he'd given mother what he called the "best parts" for her to cook for our supper that night and mother knew how to cook them jist right too.

She'd take the heart and liver, slice them real thin and sauté them in a combination of bacon grease and cow's butter and sliced onions until they were "fall apart" tender and then she'd scoop the meat out of the frying pan and set it aside. Next she'd add the venison that dad had cut into small cubes and cook that slowly in the same juice that the liver and heart had been cooked in. After this meat was done, she'd slide the pan with all the dripping aside to the back of the stove and leave it there while she made the potatoes.

We always thought it odd that our dad, being involved with potatoes all of his life, loved potatoes more than anything and mother knew how to make these to perfection too. She'd boil a big pot full and then drain the boiling water into the sink. Next, she'd pour cream into the pot; add a huge dollop of butter, salt and pepper and mash all of this until there wasn't a lump to be found. Then she'd haul a huge pan of golden baking powder biscuits out of the oven, lovingly put them into a large bowl and place these on the table. She'd already cooked the peas and carrots and jist for added measure, she'd open a jar of her famous beet pickles and a jar of canned fiddleheads, and the feast would begin.

Uncle Johnny, after having eaten until, as he said, his ears popped, would slide his chair back, stumble to the sofa and lie there for a while until he'd recovered enough to eat some more. Every year, we'd wait to see if his ears really popped, but we never got to see them do that and we were always very disappointed.

Then he'd stagger back to the kitchen to eat his fill of mother's blueberry or lemon meringue pie. Dad, never ever having had an appreciation for deserts, would slide that stuff aside and sip on his black tea until he'd digested his food. Mother, having taken his refusal of her lovely pies as a personal affront, would urge Uncle Johnny to eat more and he usually did, and without too much urging either. Dad, always being the taller and leaner of the two, would jist laugh and tell his brother that he'd better watch it, or he'd be too fat to come hunting next year. Uncle Johnny would laugh, pat his already rotund belly and remind his brother that that he was a mailman and he'd walk it all off during the year.

That visit of nineteen fifty-four was the one that caused dad's fall from grace so to speak. On his way up to "Tha County" Uncle Johnny, never the one to deny his baser needs, had stopped off at the famous "L.L. Bean's" store in Freeport and bought all the latest hunting gear that he decided he needed to make it through a week's hunting in Aroostook County. As he later confided in dad, he'd spent a "Christly" amount of money at the store but he felt confident that all of the merchandise was jist what he'd needed for a week in tha north woods.

Upon hearing jist how much money his younger, wealthier sibling had actually spent, dad jist laughed and shook his bald head in wonder. One hundred and thirty-five dollars seemed a terrible amount of money to have spent on clothing for a week in tha woods, especially when all dad earned for a week of back-breaking work in the potato fields was fifty-four dollars a week.

We all gathered around as our uncle pulled package after package out of his suitcase. He'd bought a couple of thick, flannel shirts and he handed them over for mother's inspection and approval. Being a sewer of the finest kind, she examined every minute detail and finally, even she had to admit that they were well-sewn, or nearly up to her demanding standards.

Then he took out a bag filled with three pairs of socks made from one hundred percent lamb's wool from some of Canada's best sheep. This really perked mother's interest because every spare minute of her time and she didn't have much time to spare, with eight kids and a husband always needing something knit, altered, sewn or mended.

Mother grabbed the socks from her brother-in-law and eyed them severely for several long minutes then she turned one inside out and examined it again from the inside. She stretched it out and pulled it sideways to see if the wool had any spring in it and then after turning it to the right side again she said, "Well, they're okay, I guess."

Upon hearing the slight disapproval about his woolen socks in her voice, Uncle Johnny stopped his preening and demanded to know jist what was wrong with them. Mother, never one to hold her "Colbath" tongue, eyed the socks again and said, "Well, if I'da made them, I might have turned tha heels a little better than they did. When you're traipsing all over to hell and gone in tha woods, that seam is going to rub tha hell out of your feet and it ain't going to feel too good when you get blisters on your heels. What with you being a mailman and all that."

Uncle Johnny took his socks back, not quite so in love with them as he'd been when he first handed them over to mother. "After all," he conceded to himself, "a woman who's been knitting ever since the age of nine, would certainly knew her way around socks if she knew anything at all." Rummaging around in another bag, he pulled out a pair of one hundred percent wool pants but this time, he didn't hand them over to mother for inspection.

He held them up in front of him and danced himself around the kitchen, commenting how these sons ah whores ought to keep him warm during a snow storm or a sudden rain squall. Mother, upon hearin this, shifted her eyebrows jist a dite and never said a word. Uncle Johnny upon seeing her reaction, stopped dancin and asked her what was wrong with his new pants. Mother, eyeing the material agreed that it was some of the finest she'd ever seen and then she added, "I don't know, but if it was me, I rather have a lighter pair because you know how wool is, when it gets wet, well, it smells and it takes forever to dry and once it's wet, it's going to hang real heavy on your legs." Mother stopped and lifted her brown eyes and looked at her brother-in-law, waiting for his response.

Uncle Johnny moved his pants away from mother's fingers with a quick snap of his wrists and said, "Jaysus Mona, you sure have a way of taking tha fun out of life!" And with that comment, he shoved his precious pants back into his suitcase and snapped it shut. He still had one large bag from "L.L. Beans" that he hadn't shown us and he reached down, opened the bag and pulled out a pair of brand new boots.

He stood there in the dim light of our kitchen, holding the boots as though they were the most precious things he'd ever owned. And in the kitchen light, the smooth, golden leather on the top part of the boots gleamed as though made of burnished gold. He bent the soles back and exclaimed at how supple the rubber bottoms felt in his hands. He turned them upside down and showed dad how they'd been constructed of the best materials and so carefully sewn that he'd been told that they carried a "lifetime" guarantee from "L.L. Beans."

Finally, he handed them over for dad's inspection. Dad hefted them, all the while examining every detail of the sewing and how they'd been constructed. He commented that they certainly beat what he'd been wearing all of his life, and he lifted one foot and displayed a rundown rubber boot that had seen much better days. He put one of the leather boots down on the floor next to his rubber clad foot and slowly shook his head. Yes sir, they were a mighty fine pair of boots, that's for sure! He picked the boot up and reexamined it all over again. Finally, he handed them back to his brother, agreeing all the while that they were tha best pair of boots he'd ever laid eyes on.

Mother, seein the way dad caressed the boot's leather and the look on his face, knew that he'd fallen in love and like all women the world over who love their men, felt a little pull of her heart strings. And she resolved then and there, even if it took a lifetime, somehow, someway, dad was going to have a pair of "L.L. Bean's" finest hunting boots, even if it killed her!

Uncle Johnny, somewhat mollified by the approval of at least one of his expensive purchases, pulled his old boot off and slid his foot into his new boot. He laced it up a little then he stomped around the kitchen, testing how it felt on his foot. Dad watched him with a detached look on his face and thought to himself that his brother acted jist like a little five year-old boy sometimes.

Dad asked him if the boots weren't jist a dite small and his brother stopped walking and said, "Jaysus Bill, I guess at my age I should know how to buy tha right size by now." And with that, he pulled the boots off and put them back in the bag. That was the end of the fashion parade from Uncle Johnny for the night.

Bright and early the next morning, dad and Uncle Johnny took off for a week's worth of hunting down around the Moosehead Lake region and as they drove away in the still dark dawn, Mother turned, eyed all of us kids, and said one of her famous sayings to no one in particular, "fun," "fun," "fun." And then she turned and went back into the house. It was going to be a long, long week for sure what with no husband, eight kids and no runnin water.

The days drug by and since they'd gotten their deer on the third day, they were back sooner than we'd anticipated and Dad commenced the ritual of many years of being a Maine hunter. Since they'd already gutted the deer in the woods, all that was left was for him and Uncle Johnny to do was to skin dad's doe and cut up the carcass. There was still a lot of work for them to do and while they were getting all this done, mother had her work cut out for her too. She'd washed and sterilized all of her canning jars and lids for the canning process that she knew by heart and she waited impatiently for dad to start sending the meat in to the kitchen.

Since Uncle Johnny had gotten a small buck, he wanted to take the deer back to Massachusetts in the way that most out-of-staters did, on the top of his car with the head pointed forward proclaiming to all, that he "was a great hunter of tha North Maine woods." Dad and the boys helped him carry the buck out to his car and then they tied it to the top of the roof. After that task was done, he turned to dad, gave him a brief hug and climbed into his car. He backed out of our driveway and after turning into the road, he waved and shouted, "See yah next year!" and he was gone. As we watched the dust settle in the dirt road, we all smiled to ourselves because we all knew that no matter where or how far you roam, your heart always brings you home.

Dad walked back to the porch to continue cutting up his deer for mother to can and we had fresh venison for supper that night and dad spent a long time patiently answering all of Bub's, Jake's and Walt's questions about the hunting around Moosehead Lake and how they'd bagged their deer. Finally, mother, seeing that dad was worn out, interceded and sent the boys off so that dad could digest his supper in peace and catch up on the news since he'd been gone.

After dad had a lovely bath in the ancient tin washtub that mother always placed in front of her old Glenwood cook stove in the kitchen, he pulled on his threadbare long johns and stumbled off to bed. As they lay awake discussing the events since he'd been gone, mother, curiosity getting the better of her, casually asked dad how Uncle Johnny's "L.L. Beans'" stuff had worked for him.

Dad, upon hearing her question, let out a loud chuckle and said, "Well, you were right mum and you were right." Upon hearing this conundrum for an answer, she pulled herself up on one elbow and looked at him. "And jist what does that mean?" she asked. "Well," dad said. "You told him that tha way the socks were sewn, they'd rub tha skin right off his heels and you were right. We hadn't been walking along tha wood's trail for more than half an hour before I saw him begin to limp a little. Thinking that he had a rock in his boot or something, I asked him what was wrong. And you know how stubborn my brother is, he wouldn't right out say that tha socks were killin him. Oh no, he lied and said that walking on uneven ground had aggravated his old war injury and that's all he'd say. We must have walked about five miles up hill and down, through mud holes and small streams. I kept thinking that he was going to complain that his new woolen socks were soakin wet but no sir, them boots didn't leak! Not a drop of water! I tell yah Mum, I've never seen a pair of boots like them!"

"Finally, I took pity on him and said that I was tired and that we'd best make camp for tha night. I've never seen a man gladder to sit down in all my life. I waited all night for him to finally admit that his feet were killin him, but he wouldn't. That darn fool even slept with his socks and boots on. I figure that he was afraid to take them off because he knew his feet were so bad that he probably couldn't get them boots back on come mornin."

"Well, tha next mornin he was movin real slow and I asked him if there was something wrong with his boots?" Johnny looked at me and brushed some dirt off the beautiful leather with his fingertips and said, "There ain't nothin wrong with my boots! Why they feel jist like slippers on my feet. Its them Christly socks that have done me in. I've a mind to take them sons-ah-whores off and chuck them in tha friggin bushes!"

"I could see that we were going to have a repeat of the day before and I decided that I jist didn't have tha stomach to watch him hobble around through tha woods all day so I told him that we'd only walk about a mile from camp and wait to see if we could find any signs of deer. Upon hearin my suggestion, he smiled for the first time since we'd left home and I tell yah mum, I felt real sorry for the silly bastid."

"So, I left him at camp, nursing his feet and went to scout tha area. I'd no more gotten away from the camp by about five hundred feet when I saw tha doe and tha buck standing quietly off to tha right of tha trail. I got lucky and with one shot, I took them both down. My only bullet went through the doe's neck and killed the buck too! I couldn't believe my luck. I hurried back to camp and got Johnny to come and help me get tha deer. I felt real bad for Johnny though because he really couldn't walk, all he could do was hobble and we both had to carry our own deer back down the trail to tha truck. To tell you tha truth, I didn't think he was going to make it. Five miles is a long way to walk in the woods when your feet are killin yah." Dad chuckled at the thought of his brother hobbling along in his beautiful "L.L. Beans" boots and friggin Canadian socks, with a deer tied to his back. That was a sight he never thought he'd see in his lifetime.

"Are you going to tell tha boys that you were tha one who shot tha buck?" Dad chuckled and replied, "No mum, let them believe that their uncle really killed tha deer. After all, it's no skin off my nose."

After hunting season drew to a close and dad's routine at the potato house picked up, mother set about finding ways to build up her secret "boots" account. From time to time, she sent us out to pick up bottles and cans along the Goding and Masardis Roads and she'd connive with our Great Aunt Cassie to get us to help her clean out her chicken coop or cow shed. Oh! mothers can think up all kinds of ungodly ways to earn money if they have to.

When spring reluctantly strolled into Aroostook County, mother set about getting dad the boots before fishing season began. We picked rocks, pulled mustard, piled wood and shoveled manure; if there was a chore to be done within ten miles of our country home, we did it.

Finally, mother had the money she needed and after counting it one more time, she sat herself down in dad's place at the head of our old rickety kitchen table and filled out the order form to send away for "tha boots." That done, she shrugged herself into her coat and took us on the two mile round trip walk across a swamp road to her parent's house. Once there, she ditched us with Grammy Colbath and went off with Grandfather in his old pickup to Ashland to get a money order and to mail the boots order down to "L.L. Beans."

Nearly three weeks passed before she received word that a package had arrived at our Grampy Colbath's and once again, she scurried across the swamp to her family home to get the long awaited package. It wasn't too long before she was back with the precious order grasped in her hands.

Mother was beside herself with excitement at the prospect of having kept a secret from dad. She's warned us within an inch of our lives to keep our mouths shut and not tell dad what she'd done. We were so relieved that all the money making jobs were over, but it sure was nice to see her cheeks all pink and her eyes sparkling with excitement.

That night, she out-did herself with our supper. Since dad loved meat and potatoes and would eat them seven days a week if he could, she made a pot roast and when the meat was done, she transferred it to another pot and slid that to the back of the stove. Then she sliced some onions and dropped the slices into the hot meat juice to sauté. When the onions were nice and crispy, she added the sliced potatoes and we had a feast.

Jist as dad's old, green pickup pulled up into the driveway, mother pulled a pan of homemade bread out of the oven and put it on the table. Dad, used to mother outdoing herself with cooking, never even noticed that anything was different. He came in, gave mum a smile, endured all of us kids rushing to greet him and hung his hat on the hook behind the kitchen door.

While he was washing up, mother made a pot of black tea and then we all sat down to eat. As we ate our supper, we never took our eyes off dad, waiting for him to finish. Never a fast eater, he took his time and related all the happenings of the day at the potato house, never noticing that mother had finished her supper way ahead of all of us.

Finally, mother gave Bub a little nod of her head and he shot out of his chair like a rocket to the moon and into her bedroom to get the package. He came running back and shoved it into dad's work-worn hands. Surprised, dad looked at Bub and then at mother who had a tight little smile on her face. "Well, it ain't my birthday and it shore ain't Christmas, so what's this all about?" Mother wasn't going to tell him and she motioned for him to go ahead an open it.

Dad tore open the shipping wrap and as he turned the package around and was able to read the writing on it, his mouth dropped open and his cheeks turned pink with emotion as he recognized what was in the box. He looked up at mother for the longest moment and then the incessant urgings by us for him to open it, got to be too much, so he pushed his plate aside and placed the box on the table.

He slid his bright, blue eyes at all of us gathered around the table and then he said, "There must be some mistake mum, I didn't order any "L.L. Bean" boots!" Upon hearing this, mother's chin shot up and she said, "Well, maybe you didn't, but I did! I saw how much you liked them boots your brother had, so we all saved up and bought you a pair! Now go ahead and open it!"

Dad slid the top off the box and there, nestled between layers of expensive wrapping paper lay his golden boots. Dad slid his work-scarred fingers under one of the boots and carefully lifted it out of the wrapping. It was a thing of beauty alright. It was the exact duplicate of Uncle Johnny's, jist a size bigger. Dad gazed at it in wonder and he had a lovely smile on his face. "How ever did you manage this mum?" he asked but mother didn't answer him. She slid her eyes over all of us and we knew without being told, "Tell him tha truth and you're gonna die!" So all of us kids sat where we were and kept our mouths shut too.

"I saw how you loved the ones that your brother had so I thought you might like to have a pair too. We all worked to save the money to buy them for you and now, why don't you try them on." Dad reached down and pulled off his worn-out rubber boots and after adjusting his woolen socks, he slid his feet into the new boots. He carefully pulled the leather laces tight and tied them. Then he stood and walked around the kitchen. We all watched as he bent forward and then back to see if they gave enough to be comfortable in the arch.

"Well, what do you think?" mother asked. Dad, never the one to ask for anything, was at a loss for words. He sat and began unlacing the boots and after examining them again, he carefully placed them back in the box. "Oh, I think they'll do jist fine mum, but you shouldn't have." "Well, you needed a new pair and God knows, your old rubber ones are beginning tah stink." With that, mother began clearing off the table and dad slid the boot box into her empty chair.

Hunting season arrived again and we all waited with baited breath to see dad go off in his new boots, but it wasn't to be. As he came out of the house to leave, we all gaped in surprise at what he had on his feet. He was wearing the same old rubber boots that he'd worn every year, since we could remember. They were so old that the original green had faded to a sickly, bile yellow and they had been patched so many times that there really wasn't room for another patch.

Mother came out onto the porch to wave goodbye and she too was shocked that he was still wearing his old boots. She stormed off the porch and over to where he was sitting in the truck. "Bill Stevens!" she yelled. "Can you give me a good reason why you ain't wearin them "L.L. Bean's" boots we bought yah?" Dad, seein the light in her brown eyes and fearin a fight, gunned the motor, shifted into reverse and when he'd rolled down the driveway, a safer distance from mother, he yelled out the window, "Now mum, these old boots jist fine, I jist didn't want to ruin them beautiful boots, that's all. Besides, these will last for another year." He gunned the engine, backed down the driveway into the road and was off with a slight wave of his hand, leaving a very perplexed wife in the driveway.

The years slid by and hunting season came and went and dad never did wear his precious boots. This non-wearin of the boots was a long discussed affair at our house especially when once a year, he'd take them down from the closet shelf, open the box, examine them and then he'd rub them with a melted lard, buff them till the leather shone like new and put them back in the box and back in the closet till tha next year.

We never did get to see dad wear them boots that we'd all worked so hard to buy him and when we asked him why, he'd smile a little, slide his blue eyes away and reply, "Well, I've never had anything so special and I jist don't want to ruin them."

We lost dad in 1982 and it was a sad day for all of us to have to let him go. There was some humor in the sad event though, when mother marched into the funeral home with the boxed boots clutched firmly in her hands and insisted that the undertaker put them on dad to be buried in. When a nosey relative finally gathered the courage to ask mother why she'd done that, she turned and said, "Well, he was always saving them for a special occasion and I figured that where he's goin, they'll stay shiny and special forever! After all, you haven't heard that there's any dirt in heaven, now have yah?" And with that she turned and walked away and over to the casket to have a long look at dad one last time….

ALKEY

Alkey swung his legs over the side of the bed and sat-up. He rubbed his hand over the top of his bald head and across his eyes. He squinted at the numerals on the old clock that was sitting on the top of his dresser and seein the time, swore under his foul breath. He pushed himself up off the bed, shuffled over to the open bedroom door where he paused for a moment before proceeding down the long, narrow hallway to the top of the stairs. He listened for a minute to the muted sounds from below, and then he bellowed, "Gaetane! I'm on my way down, and you'd best have my breakfast ready!" With that threat aimed in his wife's general direction, he ambled over to the bathroom door and went inside.

Alkey smiled at himself in the mirror at the thought of his wife scurrying around in the kitchen below. "Have to keep em in-line somehow." He mumbled to himself, as he tried to avoid looking at the reflection of himself in the mirror. When he'd finally gathered the courage, he slid his eyes at the mirror, and he was shocked at what he saw. His hair had receded to a point that he could no longer see any hair, unless he tipped his head way forward. And it was then that he noticed several large, ugly, brown liver spots nestling in the scaly, white skin on the top of his head. "Those weren't there tha last time I looked." He thought to himself.

He turned his head slightly to the left and slid his gaze down until he saw the side of his face. The skin on his puffy, gray face had shifted and now hung in deep folds down along his jaw line and under his chin. His eyes had all but disappeared in the wrinkles, and they weren't the deep, clear brown that they used to be either. Sometime, somehow, somewhere, his eyes had changed color! The "whites" of his eyes had turned a dull yellow with red streaks running through them and his iris were a color that now could only be described as "shitty" brown.

18

Alkey was glad that the mirror was quite small because he had the feeling that if it had been any larger, he would have committed suicide right then and there. He didn't have to be told that the rest of his body wasn't in any better condition than the parts he'd jist seen.

He eased himself down onto the toilet and grimaced as his withered flesh connected with the cold toilet seat. "Fine friggin way to start tha day!" He thought to himself. "Can't piss, can't shit, and can't sleep either!" He tried to block his thought process as his mind automatically began to list the other numerous things that he couldn't do.

Finally, completing his task, he pulled his long johns up and left the room. He could smell the eggs and bacon his wife always cooked for his breakfast as the aroma floated up the stairs from the kitchen below. As he slowly made his way down the cluttered staircase, his bare foot came in contact with a pile of folded clothes that his wife had placed on one of the bottom steps to await her next trip upstairs. His foot caught on the pile, and he tripped. "For good God's sake woman!" he screamed at his wife, "Can't you ever put anything away! What are you tryin tah do, kill me?" With a swift move of his foot, he kicked the pile of neatly folded clothes off the step, and they landed with a swoosh at the bottom of the stairs.

Gaetane, hearing his outraged yell and the immediate sound of the falling clothes, she never even turned around. She kept her back to him as she stood over the stove tending his food. Still breathing heavily from outrage and exertion, Alkey plopped himself down in a rickety chair at the head of the small table and looked around. He'd been born in this house, and it hadn't changed a bit in the last sixty years. Oh sure, it had had quite a few coats of paint, and the wall paper had been changed several times, but the basic structure was still the same.

His wife turned around and looked at him and said the same thing that she had been sayin for the past thirty years. "Alkey, are yah ready tah eat?" He raised his bleary eyes to look at her and a shaft of bright sun light from the window over the sink bored a hole into his retinas. He winced in pain and blotted out the sun with his beefy hand. "What tha hell do you think I'm sittin here for?" He snarled. "My good looks?" She sighed and took her own sweet time as she scraped the eggs and bacon out of the iron frying pan and dumped it on his chipped plate. He looked down at the watery eggs and the limp bacon. "Jesus friggin Christ woman!" He exploded. "Ain't yah never goin tah learn tah cook?" He shoved the plate away and grabbed for the hot mug of coffee. He swilled it down in great gasping gulps and signaled with his empty cup for more. Alkey sat in his chair for a long time as the uneaten eggs and bacon slowly dried up and tried to remember when everything had turned to hell and gone.

He'd been the only child born to his mother late in life and his mother had doted on him until she'd died at the age of eighty-three. No matter what he did or said, she couldn't find anything to criticize about her precious Alkey.

Alkey's French grandfather, Alcid had been a woodsman all his life. On a clear, cool day in early nineteen hundred, he had ambled over the United States border and had never returned to his birthplace in New Brunswick, Canada. He'd settled down in the small town of Sheridan and raised a large family and considered himself lucky to be living in the United States.

Wilfred, Alkey's father, was a decent, hard working man. He'd never gone to school because schooling wasn't deemed important in that day and age. He'd gone to work in the woods with his father Alcid, as soon as his father would let him, at around the age of six. Wilfred's first jobs in the lumber camps, were to take water to the men and to take care of the huge horses that they used to pull the logs out of the woods and back to the sawmill situated on the banks of the Aroostook River in Sheridan.

Wilfred loved his job in the woods of "Tha County." He liked the men too because, being the smallest and youngest, he was treated like the camp pet, but he especially loved the horses! He wasn't intimidated by the huge, muscular beasts in any way. He lugged numerous pails of water to the horses twice a day and in the evening; he brushed every part of them that he could reach until their coats shone like glass in the moonlight. If he turned up missing, he almost always could be found fast asleep, cuddled up in the stall with the huge draft horses. He would scramble all over them and under them, and they'd merely life one tired eyelid, look at the small boy who loved them unconditionally and go right back to sleep.

After Wilfred had grown to be a man, which in those days meant that you had pounded the piss out of your father, usually over some trivial matter, his father had shaken his hand and wished him well. Wilfred, barely fourteen years-old, set out to make a life of his own jist like his father and grandfather had.

He'd met Alkey's mother one Saturday night as she was coming out of the A. & P. Store in Ashland. She was with her family, and Wilfred held the door for them as they were leaving. As they passed by, Wilfred caught a whiff of a "clean" woman, and he liked it. From that day on, every waking moment was taken up by the plan and design of how to meet her again. He took to spending so much time at the A. & P. that folks soon nicknamed him "Mr. A. & P."

It wasn't too long before things took their natural course. After a few months of courtship in secret and a couple of "knee-tremblers" thrown in for good measure, they got married. She was only sixteen, when she'd run off to marry Alkey's father, and she'd been disowned by her family. They were strict Protestants and they felt that she had lowered herself to marry a "Frenchie Frog" or a "Puddle Jumper." as people of French heritage were commonly called back then. In those days, in "Tha County", a girl could come home drunk and that wasn't too bad. Or she could come home drunk and pregnant and that wasn't too bad either, but if a girl came home with a Frenchman... well, that beat all Hell! Her family wasn't any better educated or better off financially than his, but being Protestant, they still considered themselves a cut above everyone else.

On his parents wedding day, her father had packed all of her belongings into an empty pork barrel, took it down to Sheridan to St. Matthews Church and dumped it in the middle of the church-yard. His mother had never gone home again, not even when her father, Winslow Galbraith, lay dying.

They settled down in a small house in Sheridan. The building, which had once been a stable, was long and narrow, and it had a small upstairs room that had been used for storing grain. When Alkey's mother complained that the building still smelled of manure and animals, Alkey's father said that if the smell was good enough for him, then it was good enough for his family and the matter was settled. "After all,"

21

His father said. "There ain't nothin wrong with good old horse shit! It certainly smells a lot better than some of the woodsmen that I've worked with!" Even his mother had to agree that there was more truth to that than poetry. They cleaned the stable from top to bottom and moved in, but the underlying smell of manure was always hanging there in the fetid air.

Alkey's mother was nearly forty when Alkey made his way into the world. She'd long ago given up on the idea that she'd ever have a child, and it was love at first sight when she spied Alkey for the first time. The old midwife eased the large child out of his mother and briskly wiped his face on her soiled apron. The boy squealed in protest, and the midwife had to laugh. "He's only jist arrived and he's already complainin," she said as she handed the child to his mother. Alkey rooted around for his mother's breast, locked his lips and began a good, strong suck. When the midwife interrupted his nursing to place him on the other breast, he emitted a loud squeal of protest, and his mother laughed. She felt a strong surge of love for her only child that was over-whelming. "I'll never let anything happen to him!" she vowed, and that was Alkey's beginning. His mother smothered Alkey with love. She bathed him in it. She wouldn't let anyone, not even his father, touch him. He was hers and hers alone.

Things changed drastically in the Gosselin house once Alkey arrived. His mother took to being a mother with a vengeance. She was going to make up for all the lost years of being childless in one fell swoop! The only mother who could lay claim for "besting" his mother in the care of her child was the Virgin Mary herself.

As Alkey grew, his care was the direct cause of most of the dissention in the Gosselin home. His father, being a devout Roman Catholic, demanded that Alkey be christened in his church, St. Matthews. He christened his son, Alcid Francis Xavier Gosselin. His mother, still true to her Protestant faith, secretly carried the child off to the Seventh Day Adventist Church in Ashland where she'd been christened and baptized him Alton Edward Galbraith Gosselin.

By the time the child was four years-old, his name had been shortened to Alkey, although his mother secretly referred to him as Alton, when his father wasn't around. Alkey was finally weaned, kicking and screaming, at the age of five. The truth be told, his mother would have still been nursing the boy, but Alkey had a mind of his own, and she didn't trust him now that he had his first set of permanent teeth. Alkey grew to be a strong, sturdy child, and his mother puffed with pride if any of the neighbors happened to mention his name in her presence.

Alkey's mother, having never finished her high school education was determined that Alkey would have a fine education, or she'd know the reason why. The time for Alkey to register for school was fast approachin and his mother spent the better part of every night sewing clothes for Alkey. She'd made numerous trips to Ashland to buy the finest materials that she could find at Chasse's Department Store and when it came time for him to go to school, all his fine, handmade clothes were nearly the death of him.

Alkey, at six years-old, was a big, strapping kid. He had his father's black hair and the white, fair skin of his mother. Since his mother didn't speak French and his father only knew a smattering of English, you really couldn't call Alkey bi-lingual. When he spoke, it was usually half in French and half in English.

The local parochial school was run by nuns of the "Order of the Perpetual Light," and was located in the basement of St. Matthew's Catholic Church. It was only a short walk from his home and Alkey could easily have walked to school all by himself, but his over-protective mother wouldn't hear of it.

On the first day of school, she got Alkey up bright and early. She drug the old copper wash tub into the kitchen and set it next to the wood stove.

After she'd filled the tub with water that was jist the right temperature, she dumped Alkey in. She scrubbed him with her homemade soap until what little skin he had left on his body was bright red. Then she dusted him with some of her best talcum powder and proceeded to dress him in the clothes she'd so lovingly sewn. When she was finished, she stepped back to have a look at him.

She gazed in rapture at her son. He was the epitome of perfection! His first pair of long pants had been hand sewn out of soft, brown wool, and his shirt was made out of the finest muslin that she could find at Chasse's. His boots were made of supple, cow's leather and there wasn't a scuff mark on them. She'd combed his straight black hair back from his white brow, and then she placed a small, navy blue sailor's cap on his head. Now he was ready for learnin.

The old nun, Sister Marthe, was ringing the school bell as Alkey and his mother hurried up the dusty path to school. His mother smiled at the nun as she handed her darling boy over to her care. Sister Marthe looked at the exquisitely dressed kid and motioned for him to enter the school. Jist as his departing mother wiped the tears from her eyes and turned around for a last look at her darling, she saw the old nun give Alkey a rough push through the open school room door. Anger surged through her like a bolt of lightning. She didn't like that one bit!

Sister Marthe, unused to seeing such a spoiled, pampered child, propelled the whining boy down the aisle and into a seat. Then, she began speaking to the class in Parisian French. Suddenly, all the kids stood up and began reciting the "Hail Mary". Alkey simply sat where he was and kept swinging his chubby legs back and forth. The toes of his new, patent leather boots were all scuffed as he kept kicking the legs of the seat in front of him. All the other kids whispered and giggled in French as they watched Alkey.

The nun, noticing that Alkey wasn't standing like the others, stepped down off the small platform and marched over to where the little boy was sitting. She grabbed the poor, pampered kid by the nape of the neck and drug him out of his seat and up to her desk. She turned him around and swatted him across the back of his well-combed head with her hand. His large, brown eyes filled with tears at the sharpness of the blow and the shock of not being everyone's darling anymore. All the other kids waited to see what would happen next.

The nun resumed reciting the prayer, and she'd poke Alkey every now and then, to prod him into repeating her words. Alkey was dumbfounded! He didn't know what to do! Finally, the praying was over and the nun shoved him in the direction of his seat, but Alkey, having had enough of education for one day, didn't stop there. He flew down the aisle as fast as his chubby legs would take him and out the schoolroom door. He never stopped running until he rounded the corner for home. His mother was hanging out her wash when she heard him coming up the drive way. Alkey was howling like a dog on a night with a full moon.

She dropped her wash on the ground and rushed to meet him. "Alton, my darling boy!" she exclaimed. "Why are you home so early? Are you sick?"

She plied him with question upon question, but Alkey wouldn't answer. He buried his tear stained face in her skirt and held on to her for dear life. She took him into the house, undressed him and put him to bed. Alkey fell into an exhausted sleep, and this only reinforced her anxiety that he might be sick.

When his father came home that night, his mother told him the story of Alkey's first day of school. Wilfred walked over to the bed and looked down at his pampered son. He prodded Alkey with his finger and demanded to know what had happened. Alkey told him and when his father finally stopped laughing, he shook his head and said, "Why don't you send him to work with me tomorrow and forget this "school" ting. I'll make a man out of him, I tink." But his mother, unwilling to give up her dreams for Alkey so easily, only nodded her head.

The next morning, after his father had left for work at the Sheridan Paper Mill, she drug Alkey out of his nice, warm feather bed, dressed him in the same clothes he'd worn the day before and once again, took him off to school. His mother stayed with him until the nun came out to ring the bell. Then she marched up to the nun and informed her that she didn't want a repeat of the day before. The nun, not understanding a word of English, merely smiled at his mother and nodded her head. Alkey's mother, thinking that the nun had understood, patted Alkey on the back and left him standing there. By now, Alkey knew what was expected of him, and he hurried down the aisle to find a seat. He stood when the other kids stood, and he moved his lips when the other kids did, but he still didn't have a clue about what he was supposed to do.

Finally, after what seemed like a hundred years, Sister Marthe marched to the back of the room and threw open the classroom door. She uttered a sharp command in French and pointed towards the door and all the children hurried out into the school yard. When the last child was outside, she slammed the schoolroom door and locked it behind her.

All the kids gathered around Alkey and some of them poked and jabbed him with their fingers. Others whispered and laughed at him. Jist about the time that he felt his fat little feet edging down the path towards home, one of the older kids came up behind Alkey and knocked his precious hat off his head. Alkey, blind with rage, grabbed the other kid and threw him to the ground. They pummeled each other as they rolled around into the bushes and out. Alkey drew back his fist and whacked the kid in the face. Blood spurted out of his nose and all over Alkey's new clothes.

Scared by all the blood, Alkey climbed off the kid and fell back against the ground. The other kid scrambled to his feet, grabbed his bleeding nose and ran screaming to the school door. He pounded on it until the nun finally opened it up. She listened intently to the other kid's version of the fight for a couple of seconds, and then she hurried down the steps and headed in Alkey's direction.

She didn't say a word to Alkey. She grabbed him by the ear and pulled him over to a small bush. She held him firmly with one hand and with the other; she ripped off a branch. Holding the slender reed in her small, white teeth, she deftly stripped off the leaves. Then she turned to Alkey. She bent him over her knee and the small branch whistled as it cut through the air, landing on Alkey's bottom, and he felt the sting clear through his woolen pants and underwear. Alkey's plump bottom was burning like fire by the time the nun had run out of anger and energy.

Alkey looked through his tears down the road towards home, and it wasn't too long before his feet were also headed in that direction. Jist like the day before, his astounded mother heard him coming long before he arrived. He flew through the door and into his mother's arms, wailing at the top of his lungs! His mother pushed him away and looked at him. His face was dirty and covered with sweat. The only spots that were clean were the two lines his tears had washed as they made their way down his red cheeks. His lovely blue hat was gone, and his once immaculate white shirt was ripped and covered with blood and grass stains. His brown pants were twisted sideways and several of the buttons were missing. His shiny leather boots now looked like they'd been worn by a dozen other kids before him. When he'd finally calmed down enough to tell his mother what had happened, she was outraged! "Well, if that's the way the cachons run their schools, I'll jist have to teach Alkey myself!" she said.

To give her credit, Alkey's mother tried her best, but school jist wasn't for Alkey. As soon as he crawled out of bed each morning, he was out the door and down the road to the mill where his father worked. It wasn't too long before the image of the spoiled, pampered kid was only a figment of his mother's imagination. The first Alkey had disappeared, replaced by a younger version of his father. A version, who cussed, smoked and drank alcohol whenever he got the chance. His, mother, still kept a strong hold on her dream of a "refined" Alkey, but it was never to be. Her Alkey was forever gone, replaced by a swaggering, swearing, man-child.

Sometimes, late at night, when Alkey was fast asleep, his old mother would slip out of her bed and steal up to Alkey's room and look at his sleeping face. It was only then that she saw the son that might have been. Many's the night, unbeknownst to Alkey and his father, she stood over his bed as tears of loss slid down her withered cheeks as she silently prayed for God to have mercy on her little Alton.

The years passed and so did his father, and his mother and Alkey was left to make his way alone in the world. By now he was a grown man and time, and hard living had taken its toll of him. He had all the vices known to man and then some.

Alkey drank to excess, smoked, chased wimmen and generally lived the life of a reprobate. He was well-known to all the local cops and had been known to inhabit the jail at "Tha County" seat in Houlton more than a couple of times.

One night as he was driving down the road to Sheridan, after having had a "few" at Michaud's Restaurant in Ashland, Alkey was pulled over by the local cop. The officer strode up to the window and asked Alkey if he'd been drinking. Alkey grinned, his little shit-eatin grin and shook his head no. The cop looked him over real good and said, "If you aren't drunk, why did you jist go through that stop sign back there?" Alkey looked at the cop and replied, "Well ossifer, I was tryin to stop, but the sign turned red too quick." He spent three days down to the lock-up in Houlton for that wise-assed remark.

Having no "real" education, his jobs when he was lucky enough to have one, were usually menial, minimum wage friggers that didn't last too long. But Alkey soon found a way to land on his feet. He found a woman who'd met life head on and come out a winner. She'd had a husband who had settled every argument with his fists and that was one thing that Alkey didn't do. He talked a good talk and sung a sweet song, and before he knew it, he was a married man. His life, after he'd married Gaetane, took a decided turn for the better.

Gaetane, after having been married to a wife beating alcoholic, thought that Alkey was a king. It didn't matter to her that he didn't work all the much and it didn't matter that he drank, because he didn't abuse her. Alkey couldn't believe his good fortune, it seemed as though his mother had been reincarnated in the form of Gaetane. Finally, there was another woman who loved him, jist the way he was, warts and all.

Gaetane was a hard worker and a good provider and Alkey had never had it so good! He had a hard working loyal, wife. He had money to play with and freedom to do as he pleased, with no questions asked. He spent his days in leisure. He'd roam around town from one nonworking pal's house to another, looking for someone to play cards with, drink with or jist keep him company.

Alkey never really planned to be a business man. You might say that he happened upon the "business" quite by accident. It seemed that because he was the one who never held a full-time job, he was the one who was always available to "run for the rum" every time his pals needed something to drink. Now Alkey may have been uneducated, but he wasn't anybody's fool. It didn't take him too long before he realized that he had the makings of a business. "Demand and Supply." His drunken cronies demanded that he bring them liquor, and he supplied it at a little extra cost. And Alkey's "career" as a rumrunner took off.

It wasn't too long before Alkey was the man everyone called when they needed a little soothin brew. He really did a brisk business during the holidays and had gained quite a reputation as being reliable so, he was always busy deliverin to one person or another. Living in an isolated county like Aroostook, he wasn't bothered too much by the cops either and besides, the truth be told, some of the cops were his best customers.

Gaetane was the kind of woman, who never asked for anything for herself, but there was one thing that she demanded of Alkey and Alkey almost always complied. Gaetane was a devout Catholic, and she demanded that Alkey accompany her to church every Saturday night. If something came up and they couldn't make it to mass on Saturday night at Saint Matthew's in Sheridan, then she and Alkey would drive up the road a few miles to attend Saint Mark's Church in Ashland either Saturday night or early on Sunday morning.

Now Gaetane was no fool, and she knew that Alkey usually made what little money he had from selling bootlegged liquor. She didn't like it, but she knew that she wasn't going to change him, and that was that. She usually looked the other way when a neighbor or friend accosted Alkey for some booze. Alkey, ever the manipulator, would shush the inquirer with a look and then say, "Jeeze Leo, sure would like to help yah change that tire, but I lent my tools to Hampy last week, and he's supposed to return them tomorrow. I can probably help you then. Will that be good enough for you?" The inquirer, hearin the date of the next bootlegged shipment, would nod his head vigorously and the meetin was over. Both men parted with a slight wave of the hand, thinking that they had pulled the wool over Gaetane's eyes, but she wasn't fooled, not one little bit. She'd been married to him far too long to be fooled by a devious husband.

Old Alkey wasn't foolish enough to have his bootlegging equipment at home. The Aroostook River ran along the back of his property and there was a small island out in the middle of the stream that had a deserted fishing shack on it. With a little imagination and a lot of work, he'd appropriated the shack for his own use and now, after several years, he had quite a sophisticated brewery setup out there in the middle of the slow moving stream.

When a batch was about done workin and the brew was lookin pretty good, Alkey would spend a couple of long nights out on the island, gettin the liquor bottled and capped. Sometimes if Alkey was in a drinkin mood and not a cappin one, he'd sample one too many and not get the job done. Other times, he'd forget jist when he'd mixed the batch and commence to cappin the too green mixture, only to be reminded when the entire batch would blow its caps as the pressure increased in the bottles.

In a small community like Sheridan, there isn't too much that passes by unnoticed and everyone, including the law and the priests knew of Alkey's sideline business, but because he didn't sell to kids, the law and the priests generally left him alone. Especially if Alkey made an appearance at the rectory on a regular basis and paid a friendly call on the sheriff's office every now and then when his latest batch of elderberry wine showed promise.

From time to time, some of the older kids who wanted to wet their whistle, would appropriate his canoe and row out to the island to steal some of his batch. Alkey really didn't mind as long as they didn't take too much beer or bust-up his equipment.

In summer, the kids especially liked to play pranks on old Alkey. They'd wait until he had taken his canoe and rowed out to the island, and once he was inside the shack, they'd swim out and untie his boat and let it float down river until it got hung-up on the Sheridan Dam. Then they'd swim back to shore and wait in the bushes until Alkey came out to go home. Manys the night, after a long evening of bottlin, cappin and sippin, Alkey would come out to make a bootleg run and find that he was stuck on the island until someone missed him and came lookin for him. When finally rescued, he'd threaten one and all with a good thrashin and that would be it, till the next time.

Alkey's downfall came in the spring of nineteen sixty-three. The old sheriff had finally succumbed to the flu that was makin its rounds in "Tha County" that year and a new and eager self-righteous little prick had been hired by the town manager to clean up the lawbreakers in Ashland, Sheridan, Masardis, Squapan and Garfield. Alkey was doing fine in his little business and had even managed to put somethin aside for a rainy day until he got too cocky and started selling booze out of the trunk of his car. He'd always sold it out of his car, but this time, he made a fatal mistake.

The Saturday night sermon that they usually attended at St. Matthew's in Sheridan had been cancelled because Father Drouin's housekeeper had taken ill, and he'd had to drive her to the hospital in Fort Kent. So, Gaetane, not wanting to miss mass, insisted that Alkey drive her up to St. Mark's in Ashland. Alkey loaded the trunk of his car with his latest batch and headed off to attend the service never once thinking about the newest lawman.

Alkey didn't really mind attendin mass with Gaetane, but he knew that Saturday night masses tended to run long. It was as though the priest, Father Michaud, who was rumored to be about ninety-five and unable to act like everyone else, stretched out the mass so that his parishioners would have even less time to drink and carouse and generally sink closer to the fires of Hell.

Alkey, hearin the ancient priest drone on and on about the evils of the flesh and the lure of sin, slid a little further down in his seat and laid his head against his wife's shoulder. Gaetane nudged him a little to get his attention, and then she smiled and let him be. Jist as he let out a little snore, Alkey felt a sharp jab in the back of his head. He jerked himself into a sittin position and turned around to give the person who had hit him a dirty look.

As he turned, he heard a familiar voice say, "Jaysus Alkey, could yah take a wee trip to the parkin lot with me? I need ta take a leak real bad." Recognizin the speaker, Wilfred Pelkey, and one of his best customers, Alkey nodded his head slightly, slid to the end of the nearly vacant pew and slipped quietly out the side door of the church.

Never havin to worry about the law before, Alkey didn't even give it a second thought. He strode over to where his jalopy was parked, opened the trunk and waited for his customer. After a couple of minutes had gone by and the customer still hadn't appeared, Alkey began to have a niggle of unease that ran from the back of his neck down along his spine. Only a slight niggle, but it was there all the same. Jist as he was about to slam the trunk shut, he felt a hand on his arm. Thinking that it was the customer, he lifted the trunk lid again, turned and said, "Jeesus Wilfred, I had about given up on you! What tha Christ took you so friggin long?"

A bright light was flashed into his eyes and the eyes he saw lookin back at him weren't the eyes of Wilfred after all. "Don't be lookin so surprised, Alkey, Wilfred won't be needin anything tonight, and you won't be sellin anything tonight either! Come with me!" Before Alkey could utter a word of protest, he felt himself propelled along the ground in the direction of the sheriff's vehicle. He was under arrest.

The next day, the Star Herald over to Presque Isle had a headline in big, black letters. It read: "Notorious Bootlegger Captured after Decades!" Alkey couldn't believe his eyes! The article went on to state that Alkey had been "wanted for bootleggin" by the local police for years, and they had finally been able to catch him red-handed, sellin booze from the back of his vehicle in the parkin lot of St. Mark's Church during Saturday night mass.

Alkey couldn't catch his breath! He read on and recognized nice words like "notorious" "infamous," "wanted rum-runner" "gangster element." Alkey was in deep ca-ca, no doubt about it. All he could think about was his "little" nest egg and how useful it was going to be. It's too bad that it was going to be used to pay for the services of a local lawyer, Mr. Seeley. Of course, Mr. Seeley would never admit to the judge, Alfred Turner, that he was a regular customer of Alkey's. Nor would Judge Turner ever admit that he'd also had occasion to use Alkey's services from time to time.

Gaetane, mortified at all the gossip and stress, wouldn't speak to him for the better part of two months and as the date for his trial drew nearer, Alkey was grateful that he'd had the sense to save what little money he had.

A week before the trial, Alkey received the best news of his tarnished, tawdry life. His lawyer phoned to say that the state's star witness against him had "disappeared" and it seems that the over-zealous cop had forgotten to confiscate the contents of his trunk on the night of his arrest. Thus, no witness and no evidence, equals no trial. Heavin a huge sigh of relief, Alkey sent the lawyer a money order for the remainder of his legal fees and headed for home, a poorer, but not necessarily a smarter, man.

MOTHER

Mother, most of all was a true survivor. There wasn't anything, if she put her mind to it, she couldn't do. She cooked, knit, wallpapered, painted, sawed, sanded and sewed. She tore old clothes apart and made new ones for us out of them. If there were any scraps leftover, she'd use the remnants to make us patchwork blankets. She never threw anything away.

Our old house didn't have running water or a bathroom as we know it today. We had to walk about five hundred feet down a trodden dirt path through an overgrown hay field to the Newell Smith barn to find the nearest pump. How many pails of water mother carried over the thirty-odd years that she lived there, only God knows. All of the water that she needed for our baths, dishes, cleaning and washings had to be carried from that well, be it spring, summer, fall or winter. The only reprieve that she ever got from that awful, thankless job was when it rained, and she was able to save some wash water in an old potato barrel.

The old farmhouse had five uninsulated rooms, and it was nothing more than a camp for day laborers and farm workers before we moved in. The first floor had a fairly large kitchen, a small living room and mother's bedroom. It had two large bedrooms upstairs with a walk-in attic that extended the length and width of the kitchen. There was a small hand-dug root cellar at the far end of the living room that mother used for winter vegetable storage and to hide Christmas presents in when she'd managed to set aside a little money.

Ever year, whether she could afford it or not, mother would wash and paint all the ceilings and woodwork and repaper the kitchen and living rooms. She was a demon about being clean, and she always boiled the water that she used to rinse our dishes. She and dad often had long "discussions" regarding the merits of using Lestoil as opposed to using jist hot water and soap. Dad absolutely hated the smell of Lestoil and bleach, and mother used these in abundance.

Mother could make anything grow too. She was a "naturalist" and she enjoyed a challenge. Every year she'd gather all the new seed catalogues and pour through them until she found the seeds that she felt would grow best in the short growing season of Aroostook County. It didn't matter that we didn't have running water, the standing joke in our family was, "Oh sure we've got running water, we jist have to run down the road to the pump to get it, that's all."

But lack of water didn't deter her. If the growing season was unusually dry, she'd make numerous trips back and forth from the pump to the garden to make sure the seedlings were watered. Or, if Uncle Hal's sprayer hole had any water left, she'd send us kids up there to get water for the garden. We weren't really religious, but as kids, we did an awful lot of praying for rain. She was determined that after having spent money, which we really couldn't afford, on seeds, she jist couldn't stand by and let the tiny plants wither and die from lack of water. When the garden had prospered, then began the back breaking work of digging, picking, cleaning, pickling and canning anything she could preserve to carry us through for the long, cold winter months ahead.

She was one of the first to grow a plant that she called a "Parlor Maple" in our neck of the woods. She would send us down to Aunt Cassie's for seasoned manure, and she'd mix this with dirt until she had the mixture jist right and then she'd tenderly pat the seeds into the dirt for her precious plants. Folks for miles around would come to see her Parlor Maples and buy or beg a slip or two from her.

She also loved geraniums and she'd have numerous plants growing in coffee tins all over the house, year round. She had white, red, pink and purple variegated geraniums on every available windowsill. Sometimes, dad would complain that they "stunk," but he could never pry them from her. She loved them and that was all there was to it. There wasn't anything that grew in nature that she didn't love.

Not only did mother know every edible berry that had ever grown in northern Maine, but she had also committed to memory exactly where each one grew too. It was a very common sight to see little, blonde and red headed Stevens' kids heading off through the tall field grasses, lard pails clutched in hand, to pick every berry for miles around. Blueberries, Strawberries, Raspberries and Blackberries, if they were berries, we picked them. We'd gather our bounty and hurry home with our treasures, and mother would immediately turn them into the most delectable, delicious deserts in the world.

Mother's wonderful cooking spoiled us for life. She was famous for her breads, jelly rolls, pies, date-filled cookies, and doughnuts. On each and every birthday, she made what she called a "Steven's Special" cake. It was a home-made double layer chocolate cake covered with a white seven minute frosting. After frosting the cake, she'd drizzle melted semi-sweet chocolate over the top of the white confection, and it was done. This was truly a dessert to die for. With eight kids and dad, she baked nine or ten cakes a year and hundreds over the ensuing years as we were growing up.

Mother was the total disciplinarian in our family because dad was always up and gone long before we awoke for the day, and he usually went to bed as soon as he'd eaten his supper, so that meant we did too. When we'd head up the stairs for the night, dad would usually allow us about half an hour of "fooling" around time, and then he'd come to the foot of the stairs and quietly say, "Settle down up there." That was all we needed to hear. Not another word was said. We would have died of shame if he'd had to raise his voice to us.

Mother, on the other hand, didn't care if she killed you! If we misbehaved, she'd grab whatever there was that was handy, an old hardwood chair rung, a broom handle or a switch. It really didn't make any difference to her. This was how she'd been brought up and this was the only way she knew of for maintaining control. Tears, yelling and promising didn't deter her. If your rear end needed a good "warmin" that's what you got, and she didn't wait till dad got home either! We all knew that when the deed was done, we were going to be punished, and that was that.

I remember the time Uncle Hal taught me how to throw a flat rock and make it skip across the water of the sprayer hole. I practiced all day until I had finally mastered it, and I rushed home to show my newly learned trick to mother.

It was a wonderful, sunny summer's afternoon, and she was

gathering her washing from the clothesline that was attached to the end of our shed. My then youngest sister, Shirley, was hanging on to her skirt and whining. "Look mother." I said to her. "Look what Uncle Hal showed me!" I picked up a small, flat stone and threw it under my leg jist like he'd taught me. The stone flew straight and true, but it didn't have any water to skim over like it was supposed to. It hit my little sister right between the eyes. Blood spurted and mother let out a yell. She quickly undid her apron, wrapped it around my sister's head, and then she took out after me. I'd have been dead for sure if my little legs hadn't taken on a life of their own.

I flew through the tall grass down the path to the pump with mother right behind me. Need-less-to-say, that was the end of my stone skipping career. To this day, I still feel guilty every time I look at my sister Shirley and see the tiny, silver scar that sits right there between her pretty blue eyes.

It was a hard life, growing up in Aroostook County. It was terrible, brutal work raising eight kids with so little money, no vehicle and no running water. Back then, we really didn't realize that we were poor because all our relatives and neighbors lived pretty much the same way we did. Mother was very conscious of the fact that we may have been poor, but we were clean! One of her favorite sayings was "Soap is cheap!" or "We may be poor, but we're clean!"

One time mother received a letter that made her so mad that she nearly had a stroke. We lived on the Goding Road which was a rural, country dirt road and the mail wasn't delivered down our road. If we had any mail, it went to Grampy Colbath's house, which was located across the swamp on the Masardis Road, and we always had to go there to pick it up.

The letter was from the Ashland Town Manager saying that because we had so many mouths to feed, we qualified for free food from the government. These government handouts consisted of canned pork, butter, peanut butter, cheese, powdered eggs and powdered milk, and we certainly could have used each and every one of them.

Mother read and reread the letter for a couple of days and she fumed and bitched about it. She was beside herself! If we'd had a phone, that town manager would certainly have heard an earful! After seething and swearing for the better part of a week, she finally sat down and wrote him a terse little note. It said, "Dear Mr. Hayward. Thank you very much for the offer of free food. To my knowledge, there ain't nothin free, and we ain't that poor!" But if she was offered any of these surplus goods that some of our other relatives had managed to obtain from the town office, she quickly accepted them. She knew we could easily use any of the food, but she jist didn't want the town or the town manager to know our business that's all.

Mother only went to school until the ninth grade, and she wanted us all to be well-educated. She didn't put up with any nonsense when it came to schooling either. If any of us got into trouble at school, no matter what the reason, we knew that it was going to be doubled when we got home. In mother's book, the teacher was always right!

I remember the time that Jake came home and told mother a dirty story. She gave him a look that would have withered a dandelion right down to its roots, and then she said, "Is that what I'm sending you to school for?" Jake's tanned and freckled face turned about three shades of red that easily matched his hair, and he mumbled something and took off out the kitchen door. Mother waited until he had rounded the corner of the porch before she collapsed laughing onto her rocker.

Of all the accomplishments that mother achieved, and there were many, she was to find defeat in only one thing that she ever attempted. She never learned to drive. They'd scrimped and saved for years until around nineteen fifty-five dad could finally afford to buy an old, green Ford pickup. It was the first vehicle that he'd ever owned, and it was his pride and joy.

At that time, dad was working for his relative, Newell Smith, and Raymond Davenport or one of his other work mates usually picked him up every day, so he didn't have to drive to work. He'd leave the old pickup parked in its special spot off to the right of the driveway on the grass in front of the porch.

Dad had an eagle eye, and he'd have known in an instant if any of us kids had touched that truck. And every night when he'd get home, even before saying hello to us kids or mother, as soon as he'd slammed the door to the pick-up that had brought him home; his blue eyes would immediately slide over to his old pick-up to check it out.

My older brothers, Walt and Jake, were known to steal it every now and then and take it for a wild, fast ride down our dirt road to the Hafford place and back. They only dared to do this if dad was working for the day up to the Masardis potato house and mother had gone to visit her parents for the day. This little theft was really more work than it was worth because our dirt road was then unpaved and the dark green pick-up would be covered, inside and out, with a heavy layer of dust. They would have to spend the remainder of the day, wiping the dust out of the inside and off the rest of the truck. Usually, if either Walt or Jake had any money, they'd bribe the rest of us kids to do the work for them.

It was on a fine spring morning when mother finally got the overwhelming urge to learn to drive. Seeing the sunlight dance off that little green truck sitting in her driveway day after day, must have been more than she could bear. She withdrew her wet, hands out of another dishpan full of dishes, slung her old faded apron over a kitchen chair and marched herself out to the pickup. She wrenched open the door and drew herself up into the tattered leather seat. She sat there a couple of minutes until her breathing returned to normal and then she reached down and turned the key. The old engine roared to life, struggled for a few seconds and then died. She pumped the gas pedal a couple of times jist like she'd seen dad do so many times and tried again. This time the engine roared and stayed running.

Blue, gas flooded smoke rolled out from under the truck and up around the hood.

Mother gripped the steering wheel until the fingers of her brown, work worn hands turned white. She pushed the clutch in with her left foot and with the other foot, gave it a little more gas. She smiled a tight little smile, and as she'd seen dad do so many times before, carefully thrust the gearshift into what she thought was first gear.

The pickup lurched backward across the sloping driveway with mother hanging onto the steering wheel for dear life. The truck rolled across the lawn and off the end of the culvert down into the ditch on the other side, leaving the front end, with the wheels still spinning, sticking up in the air.

Mother's mind shut down and she sat where she was for a couple of minutes. Then she finally gathered enough courage to turn the engine off and she ever so carefully opened the door and let herself fall to the ground. She scrambled up the bank and headed for the house as fast as her old legs could carry her.

The old pickup was still in the same spot when he got home that night. Dad, shocked by seeing his precious vehicle up-ended in the ditch, stood in the middle of the dirt road with his black lunch pail in one hand and his hat in the other. Walt and Jake came dancing off the porch, in a hurry to let dad know that for once, they were not the guilty party. Even before dad could ask, Jake sidled up to him and with a quick jerk of his head and a slid of his blue eyes towards the house, said. "You won't believe who did this dad, and it wasn't me or Walt neither!" Dad looked at his second oldest son and again Jake slid his eyes towards the house.

Dad shook his head in disbelief at the sight. After he, Raymond Davenport and the boys had finally pushed the old truck up out of the ditch and into the driveway; he headed for the house with the rest of us kids right behind him.

When he came through the door, a feast of the finest sort awaited him. There was a pile of three-inch high biscuits with golden tops on a plate in the center of the table. A huge bowl of fluffy mashed potatoes with a stream of yellow cow's butter running down the side was next to that. Fresh ears of sweet corn were on another plate. Mother was in the process of cooking deer steak that she had sautéed in crispy, fried onions. There was a large pot of steaming black tea and the piece-de-resistance was a huge strawberry shortcake for dessert. Dad didn't have to ask who'd been driving his truck. He later joked that he hoped mother would take up driving every day!

Mother never did learn to drive, and she left this earthly place on April 17, 1999. Her days of drudgery, toil and strife are over and done with, and I hope that she will look down on me from time to time and think that I didn't turn out half bad after all.

Postscript: Jist before mother passed away, she called me one day and after a rather convoluted, for her, talk, she finally got to the reason why she'd called. "I hear that you're writing a book," she queried. "Yes, I am mum," I answered. "What's it about?" she asked. "Well, it's about life in a small Maine town." "Is it about our family?" she asked. "Well yes, some of the stories are." I replied. "Are you worried about something, mother?" I asked. "Well," she said. "I was jist wantin to know if you'd ever read tha "Beans of Egypt Maine?" I laughed and then I knew what she was trying to ask. She was referring to a Maine writer who had written a book about incest. "Yes, I have read the "Beans of Egypt Maine and no mum, my book isn't at all like that." "That's good!" She said. "There's no need tah be spreadin stories all over tah hell and gone about our family, now is there?" "No mum, I guess there isn't," I laughed.

THA OUT OF STATERS

Even today, what with all the modern advances, you never know if the "newest" fly dope will work until you've spent a night in the woods of Aroostook County. The gatekeepers along the entrance to the northern Maine woods used to laugh to themselves when a vehicle full of "out-of-staters" stopped to pick up their out of state fishing and camping permits because they'd already spent the better part of their vacation, before driving on to "Tha County," shopping at "L.L. Beans" in Freeport. The visitors had already spent a fortune on all the latest fishing and camping equipment known to man. The gatekeepers could guess almost to the penny, upon seeing the non-Mainers strutting around in all their fishing gear glory, how much money they'd parted with at "L.L. Beans."

They were outfitted in the finest clothing that money could buy. Bean's chamois' shirts, the texture of soft cow's butter, adorned their well-fed bodies and their waterproof pants were made of one hundred percent Merino wool from Canada. Their high-topped "Bean's" leather boots guaranteed never to get their tootsies wet were de-rigueur for these fishermen. Their state of the art jackets were "Gore-Tex" and were guaranteed to keep them dry even in the strongest rainstorm, or even a small hurricane. Their lightweight goose down-filled sleeping bags were touted as "being the lightest, the warmest and the best that money could buy" and at two hundred dollars apiece, they probably were. Their matching vests served a three-fold purpose; not only did they serve as safety vests, but they were also waterproof and flame resistant. On their heads were identical hats that had a myriad of colorful flies for fly fishing hooked all around the khaki bands.

They didn't have jist one fishing pole apiece either; they usually had several custom-made poles that came from countries all over the world.

It wasn't uncommon to see one from Sweden, another from Portugal and even some hand-made ones from Maine. They'd come prepared for any contingency that they might encounter in the great northern Maine woods too.

They had a thirteen inch AC/DC color television, cell-phones, propane stoves, portable razors, butane warmers for their socks and sleeping bags, portable toilets and even toilet paper with built-in moisturizer. They were going to "rough-it" in the northern Maine woods all right!

Upon seeing all this extravagant fishing and camping gear, some of the old-time gatekeepers would snort in disgust and say, "We've gut some more of those sons-ah-whores sports from away, campin up tah tha Reality Road." The only thing the old-timers did admit was that most of these "sports" sure knew how to buy "good" liquor and they'd wait and hope that when the party checked out, they'd donate a few of their "left-over" bottles of expensive brew to the gatekeepers.

Their vehicles were "state-of-the-art" machines too. Usually, they were huge four-wheel drive suv's; jeeps or large pickups outfitted with pop-up tents and some of them even had global positioning systems in case they got lost. One sport arrived driving the newest copy of the military vehicle the Humvee. Sometimes, they'd drive up in an old turn of the century Ford pickup that had been rebuilt and was a bonafied antique or on a twenty thousand-dollar Harley Davidson motorcycle. You never could predict what in hell they'd bring for their stay in the Maine woods.

Strapped onto the top of their vehicles were the most perfect canoes that the gatekeepers had ever laid eyes on. The canoes, made at "Old Town Canoes," in Old Town, Maine had been lovingly handcrafted out of the best woods that money could buy. They had been shaped, sanded and shellacked until they could have hung in the finest museums in the world. They were truly works of art. Even the paddles were perfection, perfectly balanced, sanded smooth as glass and guaranteed not to raise a blister on the palms of even the most uninitiated sportsman.

When asked exactly what kind of fish they were looking to catch, the inexperienced men would look at each other covertly and reply, "Well, trout of course! Big Maine ones, I guess." The gatekeepers would eye their fishin gear and laugh to themselves that the salesmen at "L.L. Beans" had really outdone themselves this time because half of the equipment that they'd been sold was for deep-sea fishin!

After askin the group how long they planned to stay, the gatekeeper would read them the rules for fishing on private property and issue them a permit to enter the Great Northern territory. He'd then go inside and note the name of the party, the area they were supposed to be campin in and the day they were expected to return on the large calendar that was pinned to the back wall of the gatekeeper's station. Then, he'd call the local warden's office and tell him how many there were in the party and approximately what section of the northern Maine woods they were going to be fishin in. Then, he'd make a mental note and count the days until they returned.

Usually, the "first-timers" never spent the full time that they'd been allotted in the northern Maine woods. It wasn't uncommon to see them come flyin out of the woods like a bat-out-of-hell two or three days before they were due back. They'd pull-up to the gate and screech to a stop in a cloud of dust. The immaculate condition that they and their vehicles had been in when they'd arrived had completely disappeared over the course of a few days and nights in tha woods. They'd stumble out of their thirty thousand-dollar machines and shake the hand of the gatekeeper like he was a long lost friend.

Their faces usually had a drawn, haggard look and several days' growth of unshaven beard. Their blood-shot eyes told of sleepless nights, unrelenting insects and too much firewater. Their skin, the parts that you could see, was usually swollen and covered with red marks from all the insect bites and poison ivy blisters that they were still scratchin. They smelled to high heaven from not having bathed for several days too and the gatekeepers kept moving around in order to stay "up-wind" of them if at all possible. Their neat overloaded vehicles were not so neat any longer and half of their expensive fishing equipment had been abandoned in the woods where they'd been camping.

The "sports" sucked on large mugs of the gatekeepers fresh, hot coffee and related horror stories of insect attacks, thunder storms, wet wood that wouldn't burn, wood that emitted a terrible odor, humongous patches of poison ivy, poison oak, musty, foul smelling boots, cell phones that wouldn't work, swamped canoes, uneatable food, wild unidentifiable animals howling all night long and every other imaginable disaster that could only happen while camping in the deep woods of "Tha County."

The seemingly sympathetic gatekeepers would hastily refill the large mugs of coffee and wait until they'd wound down a bit and say, "So, I guess we can expect you back about the same time next year?" The fishing trip shocked, sleep-deprived, hung over men from the big city would look incredulously at tha person who'd been fool enough to ask such a stoopid question and spit out, "Bloomin Jaysus! If yah think that we're ever coming back to this friggin Christly place, you're crazier than we are!"

With that, they'd pile their stinking, bite covered bodies into their filthy, dust covered vehicle and hightail it down the Realty Road towards civilization and the bright city lights at a pretty fast clip, as thought the devil himself was after them, praying like hell that a huge moose or bear didn't step out into the dirt road in front of them.

GOIN HOME

Walt adjusted his sunglasses to block the early morning sun as it reflected off the edge of the Piscataqua Bay Bridge and directly into his eyes.   He leaned back and settled himself more comfortably into the soft, leather seat and let his mind wander a little, he was goin home. He looked up and saw his reflection in the side window of the bus, and then he lifted his hand and rubbed it across the day-old stubble on his face. The light brown beard was mixed here and there with jist a hint of gray and Walt didn't particularly like that thought at all.

He lifted his dark glasses and looked at his reflection in the window more closely this time. His eyes were still the muddy brown they'd always been, but the peripherals were dull and cloudy like the whites of a day-old egg.

Walt reached up and turned on the air over his head and immediately felt a shock as the brisk air rushed against his face. He inhaled deeply through his nose, and his nostrils rebelled at the unpleasant smell from the tidal pool and the marshy areas along the Maine coast. This was one smell that he had never grown to like, it reminded him of Nam, and that was one place he didn't want to be reminded of. No matter where his job had taken him around the world, he was and always would be a "County" boy.   The smell of the dirt in Aroostook County and the potatoes that he had picked when he was growing up were a part of his genes, and they would be with him till the day he died!

As his eyes surveyed the outskirts of the city of Portland, his mind wandered back to his childhood in "Tha County." He was the oldest boy of eight kids, and it had been a rough childhood by anyone's standards. His father had been a hard worker and a drinker to boot, but he'd seldom laid a hand on any of them, he had to give him that. His mother, on the other hand, would kill you without a moment's hesitation, and she had run a pretty tight ship too. With a husband and eight kids to care for, she didn't have time for gentleness, and she certainly didn't have time for foolishness either. Mother believed in that old adage,

"Spare the rod and spoil the child." "Mother never spared the rod, and she didn't have any spoiled children either," Walt chuckled to himself as he thought about all the numerous times that she'd tanned his ass for one good reason or another.

Both mother and dad were long gone now, and Walt thought of them often, especially when his mind wandered back home. He'd left Ashland right after graduation in June of 1959 and he'd never looked back. His mind slid back in time to the day he'd decided to join the Army.

It was an odd day in early May of 1959. It was odd because it was so warm, so early in the year in northern Maine and this fact itself was disconcerting. The early, warm weather would be a topic of conversation until winter hit again around the middle of September. The old-timers would gather around the glowing wood stove at Tibbett's' Garage on Main Street and predict that an early spring meant that they were in for one "hellava" winter, and usually they were right.

His father was ensconced in his usual place on an old car seat on the front porch, and he was sitting in his favorite position, hunched over with his elbows balanced on both knees, with an ever-present Chesterfield cigarette clutched between his nicotine-stained fingers of his left hand. Every now and then, he would inhale deeply on the cigarette, dragging the killing smoke deep inside and his worn-out lungs would rebel, sending dad into a paroxysm of uncontrollable coughing and hacking. Tears, brought on by the coughing spell, would roll down his cheeks, and he'd flick them away with his yellow-stained fingers. He'd curse a few times, wipe the tears out of his eyes with the corner of his sleeve and try to catch his breath. Seeing that he'd smoked his current cigarette down to a butt, he'd flick it away into the dirt driveway, and then he'd scrabble around in his pocket for his crumpled pack and another round.

Walt, standing in the doorway of the kitchen, watched his father go through this normal morning ritual for a few minutes, and then he ventured out onto the porch. Dad, hearing him approach, looked up, smiled and nodded hello. Walt shaded his eyes against the harsh morning light of the Eastern sun and looked out across the dirt road to the empty potato field. If this spell of weather held, it wouldn't be long before that field would be planted in long rows of Green Mountains or whatever the hell kind of potato they were going to plant again this year.

Dad was a "potato" man thru and thru. He'd been born into it and he was going to die because of it too. He'd worked in the woods at a loggin camp down around New Hampshire for a while when he was real young, but there wasn't enough work for him there and besides his heart really wasn't in it. And it wasn't too long before his feet were following his heart back to northern Maine.

When his great uncle, Newell Smith, offered him a job with Maine Seed Potato Growers, he'd jumped at it. He was a hard worker and well-liked by the men, and it wasn't long before he was foreman of a small crew of potato house workers.

In the summer, after the potatoes had reached a foot tall, dad had to begin spraying or the potato plants would be destroyed by every bug or blight imaginable. In the old days, dad sprayed from dawn to dusk with every chemical known to man. Some days he came home completely covered with a pale blue powder, and we knew that he's been engulfed in Blue Vitrol all day long.

On other days, if he arrived home covered in a fine yellow powder, we knew that he'd been spraying DDT and if it was a powdered sugar white, it was Malathion or some other equally deadly chemical. After twenty-five years of planting, hoeing, spraying, harvesting, packing and shipping potatoes, dad's drive was gone and so was his health. All the years of handling, breathing and ingesting all these chemicals combined with smoking too, dad was dying.

Now that the pomp and circumstance of graduation was over, Walt was itchin to go, and he heard the Army calling his name. Walt had tried to talk to his father about leaving, but he really didn't know what to say to him. So, Walt decided that he would jist tell him. "Dad, I know you ain't going to like this one bit, but I joined tha Army yesterday." Walt waited for his reaction but his father never changed position and never said a word. Walt inhaled and went on, "I'll be leaving on Monday." Not hearing any reply, Walt turned around and looked sideways at his father. Dad took a last hard drag on his cigarette and flicked it into the dirt at his feet. 'Well," he said softly, "A man's gotta do what a man's gotta do." With that, he pulled himself up and walked slowly back into the house. Walt breathed a sigh of relief; he couldn't believe that it had been so easy!

Come Monday, true to his word, Walt took the first bus leaving "Tha County" and he never looked back. And true to their word, the Army sent him down to Fort Dix, New Jersey for basic training and after a series of tests, designed to tell them jist what kind of kid they'd employed, they shipped him off to Officer's Candidate School in Virginia. It wasn't too long before Walt was on his way, career wise.

He'd heard all the stories about how the military used a guy up and spit him out when they'd gotten everything they'd wanted, but Walt thought, in a way, they'd saved him. They'd saved him from a life filled with potatoes, back breaking drudgery and long, cold snow-filled winters. He couldn't imagine a life like his father had and he knew that if he'd had to stay in "Tha County" and grow potatoes, well, he would have killed himself, and that was the truth!

The Army had sent him to all kinds of places and some he liked and some he didn't. He'd been assigned to the American Ambassador's residence in India and had liked the people, but hated the heat and the poverty and was glad when it was time to move on. His tour of duty in Germany and England had been interesting because he'd been assigned to the Intelligence Units, and he'd learned a lot about how the intelligence community works and about the world in general. Walt couldn't help thinking how naive the people of "Tha County" were when it came to world affairs.

After attending a particularly intense meeting where plans for future world involvement military-wise, were discussed and hearing jist how far some nations were willing to go to achieve their goal, this meeting shook Walt to his very core. He'd come out of that meeting with his head swimming and his heart pounding. He certainly was a long way from "Tha County" now, and maybe it wasn't such a good thing after all.

After a three-year stint that had taken him to England, Germany, India and last of all, to Vietnam, his tour was up, and he was a civilian once again. Like everyone the world over, you can leave your place of birth, but your place of birth will never leave you. You can "bad-mouth" your hometown every chance you get to one and all, but jist like a homin pigeon, Walt soon found himself on a Grayhound heading north.

Walt looked out the window as the bus pulled in to Houlton for a quick rest stop and to pick up passengers who were heading further north than he was. He unkinked his legs and slid out of the seat and stepped off the bus. He dug in his uniform pocket, fished out a Chesterfield and lit it. He laughed silently to himself as he realized that he may have been able to escape "Tha County" and the potatoes, but he'd been jist as hooked as dad by the tobacco companies.

As the large bus lumbered its way up the interstate towards Presque Isle, he found himself eyeing the scenery and being surprised at the beauty of the softly rolling green, farmlands all around him. "Guess it was good for me to be away for a while," he thought to himself. "I never really noticed how beautiful it is in this neck of tha woods." He settled back in his seat and watched as the never-ending potato fields flashed past his tinted window.

He'd already made arrangements at the rental place in Presque Isle to have a new, Thunderbird waiting for him. When the bus finally pulled into the station, he grabbed his duffel bag and walked the short distance down Main Street to the car rental office. He quickly signed all there was to sign, and he was out the door.

He threw his bag into the back, slid into the creamy leather bucket seat, adjusted the mirror and started the engine. He never ceased being thrilled by the sound of the powerful engine, and he revved it a couple of times jist for effect, before he shifted the car into drive and moved the Thunderbird out into traffic. He cruised slowly down the nearly empty street of Presque Isle and saw that nothing had really changed in the last three years he'd been gone. "No," he thought to himself, "I have to keep remembering, I'm the one who's different now, not them."

As the light changed, he shifted and turned left onto the Old Presque Isle Road towards home. He cruised through Mapleton and when the tiny village disappeared in his rear view mirror, and once he'd rounded Haystack, he gunned the powerful sports car and flew the rest of the way down the Presque Isle Road into Ashland.

His first impulse was to flash through town and give the hicks something to really talk about, but after looking at his watch and seeing that it was nearly five, he pulled a u-turn in the parking lot of St. Mark's Church and headed back through town and up the Masardis Road towards home.

He cursed as a truck turned onto the Masardis Road from the Goding Road, and the dust stirred up by the truck from the dirt road wafted over and into the car. "Some friggin things never change!" he thought as he quickly rolled the windows up and turned on the air conditioner. He'd have to find time to wash the car before he went visiting all his old high school buddies tomorrow night.

When he turned into the driveway at home, it was as though time had stood still. There dad sat in the same position on the old car seat jist as though three years hadn't passed at all. Dad, seeing the fancy car pull into his dirt drive, raised his hand to shield his eyes from the setting sun. He stood up and upon recognizing who was driving the car, a wide, slow smile spread across his tired, weather-beaten face. He waited for Walt to slide out of the car and then his father stepped forward with his left hand extended. Walt was home!

Walt spent the next few days getting reacquainted with all his old buddies and catching up on the local gossip about who'd married who and who was knocked up and who was leaving whom. He hadn't told mother and dad that he was out for good yet because he didn't know what he was going to do. He had thirty days to make that decision, so he put off telling them his plans because, the truth be told, he didn't really have any.

The days at home slid one into another and every night, he'd clean himself up, and jist as he was about to head out the door, he'd stop and wait. He'd grin to himself as he heard mother make her nightly, dire predictions about "drunks and fools" then he'd laugh out loud as he let the screen door slam behind him. He'd jump in the car and head down the Masardis Road headed to where ever his whim of the moment took him.

Sometimes, he'd head out to Portage Lake and Dean's Hotel, and he was always hoping that he'd run into one of his old girlfriends, but he never did. Sometimes, he'd head up to Eagle Lake or if the pickings, there were slim, on to Fort Kent to hoist a few. When he'd tired of those spots, he'd cruise over to Presque Isle and stop for a while at the Northeastland Hotel for a couple of rounds, but it wasn't too long before time began to lay heavy on his hands.

He and dad had talked themselves out and that was something for dad. He wasn't usually a talker, he was a listener. He'd listen as Walt related things he'd heard or seen in his travels around the world, and sometimes he'd even asked a few questions, but that was about all. Dad was still "babysitting" potatoes every day, getting up at four o'clock and going "to bed with the chickens" jist like he'd done all his life. Now that the potato seed was in the ground, dad's work would really begin. Walt knew the regimen by heart, jist as well as dad.

As the days of visiting slid by, one into another, Walt began to get that old familiar feeling in his head again. The feeling of panic about where he was going and what he was going to accomplish. He had to make a decision and make it soon. He had another week to go before he had to "re-up" in order to get the reenlistment bonus or get out of the Army for good. Strangely enough, it was his mother who finally made the decision for him.

It was Saturday night and Walt had gotten dressed up and headed for Ashland and Michaud's Restaurant to socialize with the local hangers-ons, the guys who jist had to drink a few before going on home to their wives and children.

By nine o'clock, Walt had hoisted quite a few, and as he got up to head for the men's room, he leaned a little too heavily on the back of one of the chairs as he passed a crowded table. Taking offense, the man that he'd leaned on, jumped up and grabbed Walt, and it was all over, but the shouting. Walt's military training had also included martial arts, and maybe he was drunk, but he was quick and very good. The other guy never knew what hit him.

After the quick skirmish, Walt took himself home and up the stairs to bed. Before he'd left for the evening, he'd asked mother to be sure and wake him bright and early the next morning because he'd made plans to drive to Caribou to see a girl that he'd gone to school with.

At exactly seven thirty the next morning, mother made her way up the long flight of stairs and knocked firmly on Walt's bedroom door. Getting no response, she rapped a little harder and called his name. Still no response. "That's funny," she thought to herself. "I know he's here because he woke me up when he came crawlin home last night." She turned the handle, and there he was in all his drunken glory. One arm flung over his eyes, mouth wide open and drunken snores coming at regular intervals. One long, white leg was half way off the bed, and a housefly was buzzing around his foot. His clothes were flung all over the place and the room smelled as though a Budweiser convention had been held there.

The sight of her first born son, looking and smelling like the town drunk she'd always feared he might be, was a little more than mother could handle. She hated drinking! She forgot that she was happy that her son was home. She forgot that it had been a long three anxiety-filled years without him. She forgot that she loved him as much as she did! She forgot all those sleepless nights she'd spent praying that he'd make it home safe from Viet Nam. She forgot everything! She pushed the bedroom door open with the flat of her hand and marched into the room like a general. It was the barroom smell of the bedroom that pushed her over the edge, and she grabbed Walt by the foot and gave it a good twist.

Walt, still half-drunk, felt the pain from his twisted ankle shoot up his leg and his military martial arts training took over. He flew out of the bed with his hands raised over his head in a "kill" mode. He never saw that it was mother. He never saw the shrunken old woman with a worn out red bandanna tied around her head, cowering in fear by the end of the bed! All he saw was a shadowy Asian figure with its arms raised, standing by the end of the mattress and his natural instincts told him to protect himself. A primal scream erupted out of Walt's mouth as he landed on his feet directly in front of mother. Mother gasped, grabbed her chest and staggered backwards and emitted a scream of her own. Dad came runnin and the rest is history. Walt re-upped the same afternoon and headed out for another tour of Southeast Asia.

When folks around town asked dad why Walt had reenlisted so suddenly, dad thought for a moment and said, "It was the best thing for him really. If he'd stayed around any longer, he might of killed his mother!" Folks didn't know jist what he meant by that, and they really didn't dare to ask him either....

THA TEETH

Old Perley Eastland had been planning this trip for a long time, a very long time, all of his life as a matter of fact. He'd waited, schemed and planned until the timing was perfect. His wife, Mazie, was going down to Smyrna Mills to visit her sister for a couple of days and he was going to sneak off to Madawaskee for a man's night out.

He'd been married to the same woman for fifty-odd years and it seemed like forever to him. There were times when he tried to remember when he'd last been single but his mind always played tricks on him when he got to rememberin. He'd known Mazie all his life and they'd been in school together too. In fact, his mother and father had been the ones who'd suggested that Mazie might make a man a good wife if, you know, he wasn't too choosy.

Times were hard all over and especially in northern Maine. The First World War was finally drawing to a close in Europe and the men who'd survived were straggling home more dead than alive. It wasn't uncommon to have a soldier show-up on your doorstep asking for food and a place to sleep. If they weren't dying from the mustard gas that was eating their lungs away then their mind was gone from the horrors they'd endured. They didn't stay in any place too long. One day you'd awake and they'd be gone, forever searching for the peace and a home that only existed somewhere else, in another place and time.

It was nineteen seventeen and Perley was sixteen. He'd quit school in the seventh grade and gone to work with his father in the woods up to Masardis. When he'd first started, he'd gotten all the friggin scutt jobs that could be found while workin in the woods. He cleared and burned the brush, carried water, filled pot holes, pulled out stumps, limbed trees, curried horses and cleaned the outhouses. If Perley dared to complain, his father jist looked at him and told him to "quit your bitchin!" He wasn't going to get any sympathy from him. A man had to work all his natural life and he was lucky to have a job at all, or so his father said.

As time passed, Perley slowly ascended the logger's ranks. He'd quickly learned what a "widow-maker" was and he could handle an ax and fell a tree as quick as tha next man. It had taken a while but he'd learned to handle the cross cut saw too. He'd quickly developed a new respect for the ax, especially after having seen a logger slice half his foot off in one bold stroke.

By the age of twenty, his body had finally filled out from all the hard physical labor and he'd grown into quite a good looking man. He had the wild, dark hair and beard of his French grandfather and the ready smile and clear, blue eyes of his Irish grandmother. He was often teased by the other men that he'd turned into quite a lady killer. He hadn't noticed any wimmin lining up, but he kept hopin.

At night, alone in his bunk, he'd lie awake hoping that some of the men would talk about the wimmen they'd known or loved. Perley was very interested in the "love" part. At his age, he hadn't known any wimmen and he figured that it was about time. Come spring, at the end of the logging season, they'd have a log drive down the Aroostook River to the big city of Bangor. Some of the men who'd been on the last drive told hair-raising and exciting stories about their visit to "the big city" and Perley questioned them about it over and over again.

The men, egged on by the young man's questions and his innocence, added to and embellished their stories jist to see his reaction. They told of how the wimmen, naked as blue jays, walked up and down the stairs of some of the finest hotels in "Sin City." And how they smelled of perfume that was sweeter than the sweetest rose. Of how they bathed every day and that their skin was as smooth and white as flour on a hot biscuit. On and on it went until Perley couldn't stand it any longer. He'd crawl out from under his heavy quilts and with the men's knowing laughter ringing in his ears, shoot out the back door to shake hands with himself behind the woodshed.

It was said that any man who returned to camp after the spring run, with a little jingle in his pocket, was a disgrace to all men. They didn't tell him about the diseases, the bed bugs, the fights and the whiskey that would eat your guts out. They figured he'd have time enough to find that out for himself later on when he became a "real" man.

But Perley, much to his regret, never made it down to the big city of Bangor. He'd met Mazie on the street in Masardis one Sunday after church and that was that. In the years that he'd been working in the woods Mazie had changed a lot. Her top teeth still stuck out in front jist a dite too much and one of her lovely blue eyes was jist a bit off center, but for all that, she was really quite a striking woman or so Perley thought. She'd finally shed her childhood braids and now wore her dark brown hair in an elegant roll at the nape of her neck. She was never going to be a looker by anyone's standards, but she'd do. It wasn't too long before their banns were read and the weddin was underway.

Perley had worked hard and saved his money and he wasn't about to part with any of it that he didn't have to. As the wedding day drew nearer, he and his father cleaned out the large chicken coop that was located at the back of his parent's house as a temporary first home. He'd bought large buckets of white wash and cleaned and white washed every inch of that coop.

Then he built a bunk across the wall at the far end of the chicken coop and made a bed for himself and Mazie. His father chiseled out a door in the front of a fifty-gallon oil drum and another hole for the top, shoved in a piece of stove pipe and they had themselves a wood burnin stove. Perley built a table and two chairs out of rough lumber and added a couple of shelves along the wall. Now the house was ready. The small building was only ten feet from the well and another fifteen feet in the opposite direction to the outhouse. Looking around at the snug little shack, Perley was proud of all his work. "Mazie should be happy with this," he thought to himself.

The weddin was a quick, simple affair. The priest mumbled a few words in his direction about taking this man and this woman, something about obayin and honorin, and it was over. Before he knew it Perley was forever a married man. After a simple supper at his parent's house, he walked Mazie up the hill past his father's place and down the path past the outhouse to the chicken coop. Perley pushed the makeshift door open with the toe of his good boots and turned to look at Mazie but Mazie wasn't looking at him. She pushed by him into the dim interior, took one look around and shot past him out the door and down the path towards her parent's home without a word.

That was Perley's weddin night. There was no lustin, no lovin and no discoverin. Mazie was gone! Perley, too proud to go to the house and have his parents know the details of the miserable event, lay curled up alone on the makeshift bed for the rest of the night. The next day, talk was all over town about the weddin that didn't take and the quick departure of the bride. His parents, shocked and ashamed of their son for the very first time in their life, didn't know quite what to make of it.

A bewildered Perley, ashamed and angry, fled back to the woods like a man being chased by a demon. He took his hurt and anger out on the trees as he sawed, limbed and cut with a vengeance. The other men, after hearing bits and pieces of his story, left him pretty much to himself. He'll come around in time, they said to one another. It wasn't the first time that a man had been made a fool of by a friggin woman and it damn sure wouldn't be the last.

Perley stayed in the woods and festered about the situation for the rest of that year and jist as the spring thaw and the rains began, making the woods work impossible, his father came with a message from Mazie. She was agreeable to restarting tha marriage if Perley was agreeable to live with her at her parents. She made it plain that livin in a in a chicken coop was jist too demeanin and that was that!

When this offer was put to him, Perley smarted and chafed for the better part of three weeks and then he capitulated. He slipped out of camp bright and early one Saturday morning and headed down the woods trail to Masardis. The twenty-five miles slid away and he was home before he knew it. After a wash and a shave, he made his way up Main Street in the direction of Mazie's house and the marriage was begun. What lovin there was and there wasn't much, didn't do much for Perley and he wondered why the hell he'd gotten married in the first place.

The years slid by one into another and life wasn't bad and it wasn't good either. Perley spent most of his time in the woods and that arrangement seemed to suit Mazie jist fine. If she didn't like it, she never said.

As the large trees became more and more scarce, the woods camp was continually being moved further and further back past Oxbow and beyond until it took three days of walking or riding jist to get to the outskirts of the small settlement which was Oxbow.

By now, it was nineteen forty-two and the Second World War was well underway in Europe. Perley was glad that he was too old to be drafted. By this time, he and Mazie had been married for twenty-five years and when his mother dropped hints that at the rate they were goin, she was never goin to be a granny; Perley'd jist mumble that he'd never spent enough time on top of "that woman" to ever have a kid and that was that.

The hardships and the long days of being a woodsman took its toll on Perley. His once perfect white teeth were long gone, replaced by a set of plastic sons-ah-whores that flipped and flapped in his mouth every time he tried to talk, so he only nodded his head or grunted if he was spoken to. And his head of curly, black hair was only a distant memory. Perley worked in the woods until his body jist plumb wore out. He kept goin until one day they found him pinned underneath a tree that he couldn't outrun. They pulled him out, patched him up and sent him home. Perley's days of working in the Maine woods were over.

After his father's death, Perley's mother up and went to live with her younger sister in Ashland and gave Perley the family home on Maine Street in Masardis. It didn't take long for Mazie to shift houses and they were alone for the first time in their marriage but this really didn't make any difference.

Perley, denied any real love and affection at home, became one of those frustrated old men who look, leer and lust after any female that comes into sight. He became the laughing stock around town because of the way he behaved. If he happened to be standin on a street corner shootin the breeze with a bunch of the old geezers and a person of the female gender walked by, old Perley would look at her so hard that his head would bob up and down in rhythm to her rising and falling bosom. Perley still loved wimmen, he jist didn't know what to do with them.

The men, seeing how their risqué talk wound Perley up, embellished and elaborated each and every story, until Perley was hungerin for the next chapter with his mouth hangin open and his loose fittin top dentures restin on his lower lip. One old geezer, a well-known philanderer around town, told of how he'd slipped off one night when his missus was ah-missin and drove all the way to Madawaskee. He told of how the place he'd visited was wilder than the old west. He said, with a wink and look in Perley's direction, that if a man wanted to have a "really good time," he should go to "Ma Maison" in Madawaska and ask for "Fifi." This information burned its way into Perley's brain until it was all he could think about. Someway, sometime, somehow, come hell or high water, he was going to go to Madawaskee!

Then the day finally came that made Perley think that he'd died and gone to heaven. Mazie announced out of a clear blue sky that she was going down to visit her sister in Smyrna Mills for a couple of days. Perley counted the days before she was due to leave with jangled nerves and baited breath.

The day before Mazie left, she called Perley into the parlor and laid down the law. She gave him a long list of jobs that needed doin and she expected him to have them all completed by the time she returned on Sunday night. Perley sat in his rocking chair by the kitchen stove and let her words slid past his brain and out the other side like water down the drain. He was already someplace else. He was thinkin of all the good times he was going to have in Madawaskee from Friday night till Sunday mornin.

Perley was up before the chickens the next mornin. He'd loaded Mazie's suitcase into his old clunker the night before and the only thing he needed to load now was Mazie. She slapped her traveling hat onto her head and thrust her hands into her good gloves and they were ready. Jist as she was about to go out the kitchen door, she turned and cast an eye in Perley's direction. "You do remember all the things you're supposed to do while I'm gone don't you?" She asked. Perley looked her right in the eye and his answer was jist as false as his teeth. "Of course I do dahlin," he said. "Don't you darlin me!" Mazie shrilled. "Jist make sure that you get those jobs done before I return!" With that final threat ringing in his ears, she turned and marched out the door to where the old truck sat waitin in the driveway.

Perley, anxious to be rid of his ball and chain, drove his ramshackle Ford at breakneck speed down the Masardis Road to Ashland. He skidded to a halt in front of the train station at the bottom of Station Hill and upon coming to an abrupt stop; he jumped out of the car with a new-found energy that belied his age. He ran around to the back of the car, took out Mazie's suitcase and puffing from the excitement of her finally leavin and the heaviness of the suitcase, he lugged it inside. He dropped the heavy bag on the floor next to where Mazie stood and with a wave of his hand and a dry peck on her wrinkled, powdered cheek, he was gone.

He threw the old wheezer into reverse and spun out of the parking lot and up Station Hill as fast as the old car could carry him. The last image he had of Mazie was lookin in the rear view mirror and seein her anxious face peerin out the railroad station window behind him.

He slowed down a dite as he hit the intersection of Main Street and then he flew up the State Road towards Presque Isle like a man on a mission. And on a mission he was! His head felt light, his breath was comin in short, quick gasps and he gripped the steerin wheel in hands that were wet with sweat. It was forty-five miles to Madawaska and the miles flew by. He never noticed the lovely blue sky of Aroostook County, the softly rolling green of the potato fields or the stands of majestic trees. All he heard was the little song that kept repeatin itself over and over again in his head. "I'm free, I'm free and I'm goin to Madawaskee!"

Perley drove into Main Street in Madawaska a little before noon and he coasted slowly through town until he could breathe a little easier. He finally pulled into the parking lot of Michaud's Grocery and went in. He scurried up and down the aisles until he found what he was looking for, a bottle of gin, some ginger ale and a package of Juicy Fruit gum. He carried his precious package out to his car and laid it carefully on the front seat. Then he made his way out into the slowly moving traffic. He drove until he came to Benoit's motel, stopped and went inside. He scrawled his name on the fly-speckled page of the motel registry book and took the room key. "Number twelve," he thought. "Yessirree, that's my lucky number!" His plastic teeth bobbed up and down in his mouth as he laughed to himself. He drove his car around back of the motel and parked in front of number twelve.

Perley slid out of the car and opened the door to his room. When his eyes adjusted to the dim interior, Perley looked around. An old, white chipped iron bed, covered with a stained patchwork quilt, occupied the center of the room. And along one wall stood a rickety dresser, the surface marred with cigarette burns and rings from numerous bottles. On the opposite wall hung a mirror that was so ancient that you could only see your reflection on one side of it. A faded, green shag rug covered the floor and the room had a strong smell of urine, vomit and beer.

Perley, tired from the long drive, lay down on the musty smelling bed for a little snooze and then woke with a start. It was half-past five and he was sleepin! He jumped off the bed and went to relieve himself in the filthy bathroom. He splashed some cold water on his face, dabbed a little Old Spice behind his ears and headed for the door. Jist before he turned the knob, he turned and glanced over his shoulder at his reflection in the shabby mirror.

The image of a little, wizzled, potbellied old man who would never see seventy again looked back at him. His hair had all but disappeared with the exception of a few greasy strands that stuck to the top of his head and his face had more lines than a road map. Heavy jowls hung down on both sides of his jaw and there was a huge flap of rubbery skin hanging jist under his chin.

He smiled at his reflection and the plastic gum of his false choppers was so pink that it looked like he had a rim of Pepto Bismal floating above his too perfect yellow teeth. His once proud chest had slid south and ended up sitting on his protruding belly. His clear white skin was now covered with liver spots and wrinkles. He was wearing his best shirt which was a dull green that had turned shiny in spots from all the ironin Mazie had put it through but Perley didn't see any of this. All he saw was a young man of eighteen, with a full head of curly black hair, clear skin, bright blue eyes and a smile that would knock your socks off. "Shitta-God-damn, good enough!" He said to himself as his eyes took in his reflection. He even gave himself a little wink as he turned and went out the door.

If skipping had been an acceptable practice for a man for that day and age, Perley would have skipped. He was so God-damned happy! He was finally in Madawaskee, the town he'd dreamed of his entire life! The town that he'd heard so much about. The loose wimmen and the bars. The hell raisin and the night life. The drinkin and the carousin. He had damn well earned it and he sure as hell was going to enjoy every last minute of it!

He strolled slowly down Main Street like a man about town until he finally saw the place he'd been hearin about for so long. The sign beside the door spelled "Ma Maison" in garish, flashing red and green lights.

Suddenly, his old body rebelled. His scrawny legs began to quiver and he thought he was going to topple over. His tired old heart was doing a tap dance in his chest and he had difficulty breathing. He leaned up against the old building until he began to feel a little better. "Jaysus," he thought to himself, "I've got a case of the friggin heebie-jeebies!" He forced himself to breathe deeply and slowly until his heart stopped dancin and his breathin had slowed down to a gasp.

This was going to be a day that he would remember all his life, he jist knew it! Perley gathered his courage and once his head had cleared and his heart had settled down a dite, he grabbed the door handle and pulled the heavy, battered oak door open and stumbled inside.

He stood jist inside the door and waited until his eyes adjusted to the dim interior and then he looked around. It was a large, square room that stank of booze, unwashed bodies and stale smoke. A long uncarpeted stairway took up one side of the room and a wooden bar, cluttered with dirty glasses and empty bottles, ran along the other side. Battered tables and chairs were scattered here and there and the wide boards of the pumpkin pine floor were littered with ground-in dirt and cigarette butts.

He glanced at his watch and it read six fifteen. "Where is everybody?" He thought to himself. Hearin a sound behind him, he turned and found himself staring into the eyes of one of the ugliest women he'd ever seen. She must have weighed three hundred pounds and her ample body was encased in a dress that had once been red velvet but now was jist a faded, reddish-orange rag. Her dyed black hair was piled on the top of her head in a twisted knot that resembled a rat's nest. She looked him over with blood-shot brown eyes rimmed with black paint. Her lips were plastered with a thick coat of orange lipstick and there was a heavy growth of black hair covering her top lip. The rest of her face was covered with a white powder that was embedded in the lines of her pock-marked skin.

She slowly looked him up and down in a way that was as old as time and her look made Perley feel all whoosey inside. She opened her mouth, slid her white coated tongue around her greasy lips and then she said, "What kin I do for you, my little man," The stench of her foul breath hit Perley full in the face and he closed his eyes. He tried to erase the sight of what he'd jist seen but it wouldn't go away!

He backed up until he felt the edge of the bar jab into his back. The woman leaned closer to him and she rubbed her beefy hand up and down his chest. Perley's old heart nearly exploded! She moved closer and leaned her ample chest into his. Then, she licked the edge of his ear with her crusty tongue and he felt her hot breath on his face. "What can Fifi do for my little bebe?" she growled in his ear. Perley couldn't move and he couldn't speak! He was like a dummy frozen in time. His brain was all jumbled-up and fragments of thoughts slid round and round in his head. He inhaled and smelled the odor of too much perfume on a body that had been unwashed for too long. He felt both revulsion and attraction at the same time.

Fifi, taking his inaction for acquiescence, took Perley's old work worn hand in her huge mitt and slowly led him up the shabby stairs. He stumbled along behind her like a small boat in the wake of a tug. She opened the first door on her left and pulled Perley inside.

The large, square room held a beat-up dresser, an unmade bed and a small chair loaded with dirty clothes occupied one corner. The faded yellow, wall paper hung in tattered strips along the walls. The single window was draped in a thin opaque material that was stained and torn. A single, fly speckled light hung from the center of the ceiling and the room had a smell that even Perley, who'd spent sixty years of his life in a back woods camp with unwashed men, couldn't identify.

Fifi gave Perley a playful shove that propelled him backwards onto the disheveled bed and then she threw herself down on top of him. Perley, smothered by her weight and affection, squeaked a mild protest and hearing this, Fifi drove her crusty tongue into his left ear. "Ah, my Cherie, at last you haf found your tongue," she crooned to him. She locked her large arms around Perley and crushed him against her in an ardent display of passion. Perley, unused to all this physical affection, lay where he was, thrust this way and that, like a rag doll. Fifi, picked-up Perley's hand, stuck one of his fingers in her mouth and sucked gently on it. Perley moaned from the sensation and the mere thought of what she was doing. Fifi, thinking that the seduction was well underway, slid off the little man and began a primitive sexual dance around the small room. She thrust her ample hips to and fro and slid her beefy hands up and down her muscular, hairy legs in a seductive manner. With fat fingers, strangled by rings, she grabbed the hem of her tattered dress. Perley, mesmerized, watched as the rag inched slowly upwards. His eyes were drawn to the dark area jist above her knees and Perley screamed as his mind registered what his eyes had jist seen. Fifi's private parts were parts that Perley had seen on himself all his life! Perley flew off the bed, out the door and down the stairs like a tom cat being chased by a dog. He never looked back and he didn't stop runnin until he reached the safety of his car.

With his breath coming in short, painful gasps, he tore open the package he'd bought at the grocery store, grabbed the bottle of gin and took a long pull. He gasped as the cold liquid burned its way down his throat to his belly. Every time he closed his eyes, the horrible image of Fifi slid before him and he took another gulp of gin. "Those sons ah whores in Ashland, I'm going to kill them me," Perley mumbled over and over to himself. Finally, drunk, he laid his tired old head back against the seat and slept.

The sound of a car driving past his parking space woke Perley and he sat-up and looked around. He was still in the motel's parking lot. His brain snapped and cracked like there was a lightening storm trapped inside his head. His eyes were filled with grit and swollen shut. He tried to swallow and his tongue drug and stuck to the roof of his cotton tasting mouth. He fumbled for his watch and saw that it read ten forty-five. "Good friggin Christ!" He thought to himself, "I've been out for four hours!" He fumbled for the key and after a couple of tries, the tired engine roared to life. He eased the car out onto the main drag and like a herd of turtles, headed south. Slowly and carefully he crawled down the deserted road out of Madawaskee.

A harvest moon was hanging low over the eastern sky and every time a bright shaft of moonlight hit his eyes, it felt like a laser burning holes in his retinas. He'd wipe the tears out of his eyes with the sleeve of his favorite green shirt and the horrible smell of Fifi's heavy perfume would waft up his nostrils. The fragrance would make his stomach flip right over and he'd grasp the steering wheel a little tighter, take a deep shuddering breath and drive on. Feeling a chill, he switched on the heater and a blast of hot air burned its way up his nose. He hitched himself forward on the seat and glued his foot to the accelerator.

The engine coughed a time or two and black smoke came creeping up through the rusted out floorboards. Perley gripped the steering wheel in a death grip and was surprised to look down and see the speedometer hoverin around seventy. "Jaysus!" he swore to himself, "All I need is a friggin big speedin ticket to have the perfect ending to this friggin day!"

The miles crawled by and after a while, the road signs began to look a little familiar and Perley realized that he'd finally reached the State Road. Another thirty miles and he'd be home. He gunned the old car and tore down the State Road towards Ashland and home. Suddenly, the cadence of his tires hitting the tar road, began to sing an all new song, "I'm sick, I'm sick, I think I'm gonna be sick!" was the song that rolled over and over in his addled brain. The exhaust fumes, combined with the heat from the heater and the alcohol downed on an empty stomach, were a lethal combination.

Perley lunged for the window and rolled it down. He gasped as the cold air hit him in the face. He opened his eyes and saw that he was jist starting down McHattan's Hill in Castel Hill and at the same instant his overburdened stomach rebelled! The contents of his stomach, along with his false teeth, shot out the window and hit the tarred road at seventy miles an hour. Perley heard a sharp click as his dentures separated and flew in opposite directions.

Overwhelmed by all that had happened, Perley slid his foot off the accelerator, slumped back in his seat and the car coasted to a stop at the bottom of the long hill. He lay back against the seat for quite a while and when his stomach had finally stopped its heavin, he wiped the sour spittle off his mouth with his sleeve, sat up and looked around him. He slid his fingers across his mouth and suddenly, his mouth felt awfully empty! "Oh my Gawd!" He groaned to himself. "My choppers, my choppers are gone!" He ran his hands all over the seat and they weren't there. Then he remembered. He wrenched the door open and staggered out into the road. He turned, squinted his eyes against the bright moonlight and looked up the long expanse of hill. He didn't see anything that resembled his teeth. "My Christly teeth must ta bounced off into the tall grass at the edge of the road!" he thought.

Perley staggered across the road, dropped down on all fours and began scrabbling in the roadside grass, looking for his teeth. He was moaning and swearing when he suddenly became aware of someone standing in front of him. "Is that you Perley?" A voice asked. "Yes and I wish ter Christ it wasn't," Perley answered. He looked up to see Hugh McHattan standing over him. "It's kinda late in the day to be looking for strawberries, ain't it?" Hughy joked. "Well," Perley lied, "I've been over ta Presque Isle to supper and the damn chicken musta been spoilt." He hiccupped and burped and a whiff of gin floated past Hughy's nostrils. "From the looks of you," Hughy laughed, "That must ah been one hell of a chicken en it looks like it got the best ah you." "Oh, it was Hughy, it was!" Perley whined. "So, are you lookin for the chicken?" Hughy joked. "Oh Christ no!" Perley moaned. "It's me choppers! When the chicken took off, it took my choppers right along with it!" "Well, where do you think you lost em?" Hughy asked. Old Perley looked up the long moonlit hill and said, "That chicken and me parted company about halfway down this jeezley hill!" Hughy turned and looked up the hill and at the vast expanse of crab grass at the side of the road. "Well, I'll give you a hand," Hughy told him.

The hours passed and the night wore on with no sign of the teeth. "Jesus Perley, Those teeth could be to hell and gone," Hughy said. "I doubt that you'll find them till spring!" "Spring!" Perley howled. "I can't wait till spring and besides, Mazie's comin home on Sunday and she's gonna friggin kill me!" Perley wiped slobber off his lower lip and then he said to Hughy, "You'd think them pink and white sons-ah-whores would be shinin like a pig's ass in the moonlight!"

There wasn't much left of the night by the time Perley finally made it home. And every time his blood shot eyes started to close, the image of Fifi's face would slide across his eyes and he'd come to with a start.

All the next day and night Perley's tired mind raced through one wild scenario after another trying to find an answer that Mazie might believe. Finally, he decided that he'd jist lie and tell Mazie that he'd sneezed while using the toilet and his teeth had fallen in and he'd flushed the toilet without thinking. He hated to give her so much ammunition to use against him but there was nothin else to do.

At four-thirty on Sunday afternoon, Perley, slid off the rumpled bed and made his way to the toilet. He showered and shaved then he made himself some strong coffee and drank it while he paced back and forth across the kitchen floor, rehearsin his story, until it was time to go pick-up Mazie.

Mazie was already pacing back and forth across the station platform when Perley pulled-up in a cloud of exhaust. He gave her a little half-hearted wave and without a word, threw her bag into the trunk. Mazie, like wimmen the world over, know when something isn't jist right with her mate and her bright blue eyes examined the length and breadth of him and it wasn't too long before she noticed the black circles under his beady eyes and his sunken cheeks. "Don't tell me that you were in such a hurry to come and get me that you forgot your teeth?" she asked. Perley flashed her a quick look and then turned his attention back to his driving. "Not exactly," he mumbled. "Not exactly what?' Mazie pressured. "Well," Perley whined. "I had a little accident while you was gone."

Mazie gave him another scorching look and then she asked. "What kind of accident, an accident with the car?" "Noooo, not with the car," Perley hedged. "Well, for good God's sake, do I have to be a detective or what!" Mazie exclaimed. "Jist tell me what happened to your teeth!"

"Well", Perley fumbled. Exasperated, Mazie swatted him on the arm with her pocketbook. "I sorta lost them down the turlet!" Perley answered and he slid a sideways look in her direction. A look of total disbelief slid across Mazie's face and she sat back against the seat with her mouth open. Then, her mind racin for an appropriate answer, she sat where she was, openin and closin her mouth without a word comin out. Perley knew that he was going to catch hell for a very long time to come.

From the moment that she'd learned about his missing teeth, Mazie never let up. She found one way or another to mention his teeth during every simple conversation. She told everyone they knew and some they didn't, how Perley had lost his teeth. Then she'd stand back with a smug, self-righteous "I told you so" look on her face while the neighbors laughed their asses off.

It had been a long, hellacious winter and finally, in the middle of January, a spring thaw came to the county. Mazie, seeing that the ice had melted off the State Road enough so that it was passable, called over to Dr. Rhodes in Presque Isle for an appointment for a new set of choppers for Perley.

It had snowed all night the night before they set out for Presque Isle and the landscape was covered with nearly two feet of fluffy new shit and the plowed back snow banks were nearly as high as the telephone wires. Mazie amused herself by singing along with the radio and watching the snow covered scenery as it slid by.

They were about halfway up McHattan's long hill, when something glinting on the top of a snow bank caught Perley's eye. He slowed down a dite to have a better look and what he saw made his old heart jump in his chest like a rabbit going across a potato field. Sitting on the top of the snow bank, like someone had placed them there, was the top part of his false teeth and they were sitting directly in Mazie's line of vision. Perley, hearing the sharp intake of Mazie's breath as she recognized what she had jist seen, gunned the old car and flew past the pink and white sons-ah-whores as fast as the old car could carry them....

JAKE

My brother Jake and I were born only sixteen months apart. At birth, he was given the Christian name of Arnold Louis, but our great Uncle Hal soon christened him "Jake" and this nickname was to stick with him throughout his life. He was a chubby little boy with carrot colored hair, and he had a dusting of light orange freckles scattered across his nose. His eyes were bright, blue and when he smiled in his lopsided way, huge dimples appeared in both cheeks. If you've ever seen one of Norman Rockwell's paintings of American children, then you've seen Jake.

When Jake was about three years old, he decided that he'd do a little exploring, and he picked a day when both mother and dad were busy in the garden that was located out behind our house. After having found nothing of interest on the two lower shelves, Jake climbed a little higher. He climbed up on the kitchen cupboard and stood up to see what goodies mother might have hidden in the top shelves of her cabinet.

First, he opened one cupboard door and lo and behold, what do we have here? He clasped his chubby hands around dad's half empty bottle of gin and after carefully turning around he settled his plump little bottom onto the edge of the counter with his feet dangling about three feet above the kitchen floor.

With his grubby little fingers, Jake tugged and pulled until he finally removed the cap, then he lifted the heavy bottle towards his mouth and the escaping fumes made his blue eyes sting and water, but that didn't deter him. Jake lifted the bottle until he had it aligned with his mouth and took a deep swallow. The undiluted gin seared its way down his throat, and he inhaled with a choking gasp. Tears ran unchecked down his fat, ruddy cheeks and his nose began to run. But being very inquisitive by nature, he wasn't about to give up so easily.

Jake wiped his nose on the back of his pudgy fist and decided to have another go. This time, he was a little more cautious and he succeeded in taking a smaller gulp. He continued this procedure quite a few times, and it was then that he noticed a burning feeling in his round little belly. Suddenly, it didn't seem quite so much fun anymore, this drinkin dad's gin! He leaned forward and tossed the nearly empty bottle of gin down onto the kitchen floor.

The sound of the falling bottle alerted my parents to the fact that something was amiss in the kitchen and they both came running. They arrived jist in time to see Jake hit the floor next to the open bottle of gin. But Jake didn't jist hit the floor and lay there, he bounced! And after he bounced a few more times, he proceeded to throw-up. Dad cleaned him up and put him in his and mother's bed.

The next morning when Jake finally woke up, he was an entirely different little boy. He didn't run around and shout like he normally did. He didn't move too much at first either and when he did move, it was very, very carefully. He jist lay there like a lost little soul in mother's large bed. His round face was so white that the scattering of red freckles across his nose looked like someone had painted them on. He'd open his eyelids to a small slit, gaze around the room until his blood shot eyes connected with the bright shaft of sunlight streaming through the bedroom window, then, he'd jerk his eyes shut, shudder a little and turn his little white face to the wall.

Mother went into her bedroom, had a good look at him and commented that "His eyes looked like two burnt holes in a blanket!" and she wanted to send for Dr. Varnum to come and have a look at him. But dad explained to her that Jake was jist fine, and that he must have one hell of a hangover. It wasn't too long and Jake had moved on to bigger and better things.

Living in way out in the "sticks" as mother liked to call it, we were allowed more freedom than most children can imagine. At that time, we didn't have any immediate neighbors with kids our age. We only had our brothers and sisters to play with and since there were eight of us, we always found something to do. We built tree houses by the score, played baseball in Mr. Beaulier's pasture, rode neighbor's horses, fished in the Aroostook River and hunted in the woods surrounding our house. We picked every berry that was known to grow in "Tha County." Blackberries, blueberries, raspberries and strawberries, if it was a berry, we picked it and there were also dandelions, fiddleheads and hazelnuts that we picked by the pail full.

The slow moving Aroostook River was located about a mile from our house, and it drew us to it like a magnet. On warm summer days, we'd walk the short distance down the hill to go swimming or fishing or whatever mischief that we had decided to do that day.

This particular summer's day was not only warm, but humid as well and when it's humid in "Tha County", it's humid! I was ten years old, Jake about eleven and Walt was thirteen. We hadn't had too much rain that spring so the level of the river was quite low, and we'd decided to go swimming. When we arrived at our favorite swimming spot the Chub Hole, the sandbar, which was about ten feet from shore, was sticking up out of the water for the first time that we could remember. We hurriedly waded out to the sandbar and discarded our unnecessary clothing.

Walt and Jake, both good swimmers, dove head first into the warm river water and shouted for me to hurry up and join them. I wasn't in a hurry to get wet and besides, I couldn't swim. Walt eyed me with a big grin and said, "Toots, don't be such a scardy cat. The water is very low here. Jist keep walking straight out." I looked at him and thought if my oldest brother was telling me this spot was safe, then surely I could trust him. After all, who can you trust if not your brother?

I took about four small steps, and suddenly the soft, sandy river bottom disappeared from beneath my feet. I found myself sinking into the warm water and in a panic, I thrashed around and my mouth filled up with the brackish water. Suddenly, I felt Walt grab me and pull me up out of the water and onto the warm sand.

Sitting up, I spat out a mouthful of stinking river water and howled with a mixture of fear and anger. Jake came running out of the water to see if I was all right. As I calmed down, I looked at my legs that were stretched out on the sand in front of me and somehow, my legs didn't look quite the same. There were little black things on my legs and on my arms, they were all over me! These little black things could move too! They were sliding and stretching, and some were getting bigger! I reached out and tried to flick one of them off with my finger, but it stayed right where it was!

At about this time, Jake became aware that he too was covered with these "things." He jumped up and down and began yelling to Walt, but Walt was busy with problems of his own. I looked down at my left leg and saw that one of these things had gotten considerably bigger and there was a small trickle of blood running down my leg where one creature was stuck. I let out a howl of fear, and this brought the two of them running back to my side. "Holy Jaysus Walt," Jake shouted. "This friggin place is crawling with bloodsuckers! Look at her, she's covered with them!" "No kidding Sherlock!" Walt snarled at him. "Have you had a good look at yourself lately?"

Walt grabbed one of my arms, and Jake grabbed the other, and they ran with me between them back across the shallow water to the riverbank. They hurriedly picked and scraped the leeches off me and off each other until they couldn't find anymore. It was a subdued threesome who finally straggled up the hill to our house that hot summer day. Need-less-to-say, it was many long weeks before we begged mother to let us go swimming again.

Dad was an expert hunting and fishing guide, and he had quite a collection of guns. He owned a twenty-two rifle, a thirty-thirty, a Colt 45 and a four-ten shotgun. On warm spring days, he and the boys, liked to take his guns out behind our house for target practice.

I'll never forget the day he finally "allowed" me to try my hand at target practice. My sisters and I were always went out to watch dad and our brothers target practice, but we'd never been invited to take part. But I wanted to know how to shoot a gun too; after all, I told dad, if Grammy Stevens can shoot a gun, why can't I? I knew that my argument had finally struck home when upon hearing this statement, he turned, looked at me, and with a little smile playing around his lips, he capitulated.

He handed me the four-ten shotgun along with a shell and showed me where to slide it into the chamber. The gun was quite heavy for me to hold so he inserted the shell and helped me close the barrel of the gun. Then he looked at me and said, "Are you sure you want to do this? It's got quite a kick, you know." I saw my brothers whisper something to each other and then they grinned. I wasn't going to back down now.

"Don't hold It too loose because it's got quite a kick and might hurt you," dad said. I had jist watched Jake shoot it, and he didn't seem to have any trouble.

I planted my feet squarely on the ground and dug the gun stock snugly into my shoulder, then I curled my finger around the trigger and with my other hand, I brought the gun barrel up into target range. I sighted along the barrel to get the target into focus like dad had instructed my brothers, and I heard dad tell me not to pull the trigger, but to squeeze it slowly. But I didn't listen. I took a deep breath and pulled the trigger. The gun erupted with a fantastic roar, and I felt the stock of the gun slam into my collar bone, then it glanced off my collar bone and hit me in the chin. The gun went flying in one direction and me in another.

The next thing I knew was dad bending over me asking if I was all right. I sat up carefully and nodded my head. My chest and chin hurt, they hurt like hell! My brothers were bent over with laughter. I heard Jake gasp something to Walt about girls being so friggin weak that they couldn't even fire a four-ten shotgun. Walt responded with the statement that it sure was funny to see me go "ass over teakettle" when I pulled the trigger. As I slunk off around the corner of the house to nurse my wounded pride and my burning chin, I couldn't find anything funny about it, at all.

Jake was a typical country boy. He loved to spend his time hunting, and if he wasn't hunting, he was fishing. If it was outdoors, he was doin it. When he was about thirteen years old, Jake decided that he was going to be a "fur trapper." He "borrowed" Uncle Hal's outhouse magazines, Field & Stream, Northern Hunting & Fishing Guide and The Maine Trapper and read every article in them pertaining to trapping wild animals. Then, he announced to dad that he was going to make a lot of money by trapping animals and selling their pelts. Dad jist looked at him for a few minutes and shook his head because dad knew that there wasn't any use trying to talk him out of this newest venture. When Jake set his mind on something, there was no dissuading him.

Jake took off up the road to tell his best friend Linwood Rushinal what he was going to do. That spring, between the two of them, they managed to scrape together enough rusty traps so that they could establish a trap line.

He and Linwood spent all summer planning what they were going to do with all the money they were going to earn. They spent hours trudging back and forth through the surrounding swamps trying to find the best places to put the traps once winter came.

The long awaited day finally arrived. It had snowed for nearly a day and a half and Jake was ecstatic! He rushed home from school, grabbed his rifle and took off down over the hill to the swamp to check his traps. He'd come home from time to time with a rabbit or a squirrel, but usually the larger fur-bearing animals eluded him. The traps were empty and the bait was always gone.

Since Jake and I were so close in age, he sometimes "allowed" me to accompany him on his trap line tours. On this particular day, Jake informed me that he would "let" me go with him, and he would even "let" me take the four-ten shotgun. I was overjoyed! I grabbed my jacket and ran out to where he was impatiently waiting for me. Then, he told me that I had to walk in front of him if I was going to have a gun. After we'd walked about two miles, I turned around and asked him when he was going to give me a bullet for my gun. Jake stopped dead in his tracks and looked at me. "Are yah crazy Toots? I don't want to git shot!" I was outraged! Not only wouldn't he give me a bullet, but he made me walk in front of him so that I wouldn't shoot him with my empty shotgun!

We continued on our way and suddenly Jake ran off past me into the thicket. I hurried to catch up with him, and I was jist in time to see him come to a dead halt on the trail in front of me. I peered over his shoulder and saw what he was staring at. Off to the side of the trail was a huge skunk with one of its legs caught in Jake's trap. It wasn't moving, so Jake nudged me with his elbow and muttered, "Toots, you go ahead and take it out of tha trap." Surprised, I looked at him, and he dropped his blue eyes and mumbled, "I git to do this all tha time so, I'll let you have tha chance if you want to." I looked at the big black and white skunk and wondered how I'd been selected for this dubious honor. I looked at Jake again, and he muttered, "Well, you wanted to come didn't you? Anyway, what are you scared of, it's probably dead!" I knew then and there that if I ever wanted to go trapping with him again, then I had better remove the skunk from the trap.

I leaned the empty four ten against a tree and walked toward the skunk. I turned around to look at Jake, and it seemed to me that he had retreated jist a little. "Are you sure it's dead Jake?" I asked him. "Sure! Sure!" Jake answered. Suddenly, the "dead" skunk came to life! It swung swiftly around and lifted its tail straight up and the air was filled with a strong, nauseating odor. The full brunt of the skunk's spray missed me, but Jake wasn't quite so lucky. The skunk sprayed him full in the face! Jake was gasping and yelling and rubbing his face and eyes with his hands. "Oh God! Oh Jaysus!" Jake yelled as tears ran down his red face. He kept moaning and hopping from one foot to the other. I stumbled against a tree and slid slowly down to the ground. The searing in my lungs hadn't abated yet, and I was having difficulty getting my breath back.

Jake tore his jacket off and tried to wipe himself. He collapsed to the ground and sat there for the longest time. Then he looked at me. "Jaysus Toots, what are we goin to do?" I shook my head dumbly. "Mother's going to kill us and the kids at school…," Jake's voice trailed off. We jist looked at each other mute, envisioning all the horror and humiliation that lay ahead of us in the coming days.

Finally, Jake stood, picked up his rifle and shot the skunk and removed it from his trap. Turning to me, he said, "We might as well git it over with," and he started down the trail towards home. I picked up my shotgun and raced off after him. I grabbed him by the arm, and he stopped and looked at me. "Don't you want tha skunk?" I asked. He looked at me for the longest second and a light moved through his blue eyes, and I knew that, that was the dumbest question I'd ever asked. As we trudged on in the direction of home, our thoughts were palpable in the air regarding the reception we were going to get when we finally got there.

Our arrival home was announced in advance by our old dog Tippy. With a long, low growl, she came running off the porch with her hair raised on the back of her neck. Jake knelt, held out his hand and called her. Tippy stopped growling, but she still whined even though she had recognized his voice, and she wouldn't come near us. Finally, Jake was able to get a little closer to her, and she sniffed his hand and then backed off with a low growl in her throat.

By this time, everyone had come outside to see what was ailing the dog. Dad looked us over and then a huge grin spread across his face. He told us to go in the shed and wait there for mother. She gave us several baths with homemade lye soap, and then we were finally allowed into the house. Dad asked us what happened and after Jake had explained, he paused and looked at dad and said, "There's one good thing about getting pissed on by a skunk!" "Oh," Dad replied with a smile on his face, "What's that?" "Well," Jake answered, "We weren't bothered by midges, black flies or mosquitoes all tha way home!"

When the bus rolled around again on Monday, the smell had worn off a little, but I can still recall seeing the kids sniff the air after we had gotten on the bus and hearing them say, "Somebody must have run over a skunk around your house!" Jake and I didn't answer; we jist looked at each other with "I told you so's" and sank a little lower in our seat.

The skunk incident didn't cure Jake of his hunting and fishing fever though. He still enjoyed these activities immensely, and I heard mother mutter to dad one evening, "I'll sure be glad when he discovers girls!" Dad jist looked at her, laughed and said, "You don't know what you're saying, mum."

Jake wasn't interested in school the way Walt was, and it took mother a little by surprise when he announced that he was going to the library after school the next day. Sure enough, he came home loaded with library books. He carried the armload of books into the house and dumped them on the kitchen table. Dad picked one up and looked at it. The title read, "How to be a Taxidermist in Your Spare Time." Another title was, "Taxidermy Made Easy." Another, "Stuffing Animals for Fun and Profit." Dad looked at Jake and saw the gleam in his blue eyes. It was going to be quite a long haul till he discovered girls!

Jake was off again! He read night after night. He asked incessant questions until everyone got sick and tired of hearing about dead animals. We generally avoided him like the plague because his hands were usually grubby and stinky from trying to scrape the flesh off dead animal hides. And he smelled! Usually he'd bully or bribe one of us younger kids into being his helper, and I could often be found holding a piece of dead animal skin so that he could scrape it easier. He didn't have enough money to buy all the chemicals he needed to cure the pelts so, we'd walk for miles along the Masardis and Goding Roads to gather bottles and cans and anything that was saleable so that he could buy the rest of what he needed.

Finally, after about two months, he was ready. He had all the necessary chemicals, and he selected the pelt of a red fox as his first try. He did everything according to the instructions and finally, when he thought he'd done everything right, he hung the pelt inside the shed door to finish curing. Every day, after hopping off the school bus, he'd run into the shed to check on it.

Finally, the pelt was ready. It was cured! He brushed the red fur until it shone, then he slid it around his neck, and wrapped it around his head. Then he announced that he would keep this one jist for himself. He promptly took it upstairs and placed it lovingly on the floor nearest his bed. In no time at all, the shed was adorned with pelts of all kinds, and he loved it! He'd drag his friends home to see his collection and God help you if you touched one of those friggin things! When my brothers went to bed at night, there was always much discussion regarding how much money they were going to make from the sale of those pelts and what they were going to do with the money.

Because we were eight children and there was so much for mother to do, she didn't concern herself too much about the bedrooms on the second floor. It was our responsibility to keep the beds changed and the rooms reasonably clean. She rarely came up stairs, unless she needed some of the canned goods that she kept in the attic which was located jist off the boy's bedroom.

Jake had been in the taxidermy business about three months when mother began noticing a faint and elusive odor coming from somewhere inside our house. Our mother was clean! One of her favorite sayings was, "We may be poor, but soap and water are cheap!" When mother persisted about the odor that permeated the stairwell, dad explained it away by saying that perhaps a rat had crawled into the walls of the old house and died there.

As time passed and the smell became stronger, mother was determined to find out where the smell was emanating from. Since it seemed to be coming from upstairs, she marched up the steps to have a good look around. When she reached the head of the stairs, she stepped into the boy's bedroom and came to a dead stop. She got a pinched look around her mouth and without a word; she marched over to Jake's bed. Then she looked down at her feet and on the floor next to his bed lay Jake's precious red fox pelt. Mother reached down and lifted the edge of the pelt with her hand, and a horrified expression came over her face. She dropped the pelt with the look of someone who had jist burned her fingers, and she turned and ran down the stairs like she was on fire.

A few minutes later Jake shot past me and flew up the stairs to his room. The rest of us kids ran up the stairs after Jake to see what was going on. He was on his hands and knees on the floor by the side of his most cherished possession. We gathered around and watched as he gingerly lifted the pelt off the floor, and then we too, saw what had horrified mother. On the floor under the rug were hundreds of little white worms! "Oh No!" Jake cried. "Oh No!" and he dropped the pelt back on the floor. With a stunned look on his face, he got up and walked over to his bookshelf. He took out one of his taxidermy books and flipped through it until he found what he was looking for. A small footnote at the bottom of one page read, "Maggots may develop if the pelt has not been properly cured." Jake dropped the book onto his bed with a groan, "maggots!" He said out loud. "It's loaded with friggin maggots!"

Suddenly, there was a lot of commotion on the stairs behind us, and it was mother, charging up the stairs with every kind of cleaning paraphernalia imaginable. She marched into the bedroom and plunked everything down on the floor. Then she looked at Jake, and he got up off the bed and walked over to where she stood. She handed him the mop and pail and said three short words, "Clean it up!" And then she pointed at his precious red fox pelt and said, "And you know what to do with that!" Then she turned around and marched back down the stairs.

It took Jake the better part of the day to clean the room to mother's specifications, and then he took his beloved red pelt out behind the shed and buried it. We thought that this would be the end of his wanting to be a taxidermist, but boy, were we wrong!

About a month later, one of our neighbors, Mrs. McVey, committed suicide, and we were all shocked because we all knew and liked her and she was a wonderful artist. The suicide was a much discussed topic at our house and I can remember lying in bed one night and listening to Jake and Walt, who were in their bedroom next door, discussing the tragedy in minute detail. Evidently, Jake was still very much enthralled with the idea of being a taxidermist because I heard him say to Walt, "Wouldn't it really be something to stuff old Mrs. McVey!" Walt groaned and told him to jist shut up!

Every once in a while, dad would get a hankering for some home-made beer, and he'd convince mother to setup her old wash tub behind the kitchen stove and he'd commence to make his brew. I remember the smell as the hops, yeast and sugar reacted to the rest of the ingredients and the pungent smell of the yeast as the fermentation process began.

When the homebrew was nearing maturity, Walt and Jake used to sneak downstairs after mother, and dad had gone to bed to sample the mixture. Dad didn't mind if they drank a little of it, but it was an entirely different story with mother. She considered you to be an alcoholic, even if you only drank one sip of beer. Sometimes the boys got a little carried away with the beer sampling, and they'd pay for it in the next day.

Mother always yelled up the stairs every morning to wake us up and one morning, we could hear low moans and groans coming from the boy's bedroom, and they were the last to come straggling down the stairs. Mother took one look at them, and you knew that it was going to be a very long time before dad got to make home brew again.

Since we lived in the country, we all used to pitch in to help the local farmers harvest their crops. Walt and Jake always earned extra spending money by helping Uncle Hal bale his hay and put it up for the winter. This was hot, dirty work and on that fateful day, Jake and his best friend Linwood, were taking a break as they waited for the next load of hay to arrive. Lying behind a pile of hay, they watched intently as one of the hired workers carried his six pack of cold beer into the barn and placed it carefully behind a bale of hay. Jake nudged Linwood and they waited until the man had left, and then they jumped down out of the hay mow. They ran over to where the beer was hidden, took the beer and snuck around the corner of the barn and proceeded to drink it. The first cold beer went down in a flash, the second one was equally as wonderful and Jake couldn't even remember drinking the third.

The boys knew that if the worker came back and found them with his beer, then all hell would break loose so he and Linwood staggered over to where Linwood had left his bicycle. Linwood managed to climb onto the bike, and Jake scrambled onto the crossbars. They took off down the circular driveway out into the Goding Road.

Neither one of them was used to drinking that much and now, in the hot noonday sun, they felt the full effect of their stolen beer. Linwood's knees became wobbly and he was having difficulty steering. Jake, afraid that they'd end up in the ditch, pushed Linwood's hands off the handle bars and announced that he would do the steering. It was a case of the pot calling the kettle black! Jake couldn't steer or see any better than Linwood and when Linwood complained, Jake told him to shut up and keep pedaling!

They started up the steep hill for home, and Linwood was peddling for all he was worth. At about the halfway point of the hill, there was a very deep ditch that ran along the right side of the road. As they neared this section of the road, Jake turned and burped into Linwood's face, and then he mumbled that he was going to be sick. Jist as Linwood applied the brakes, Jake turned around, and as he did so, he turned the handlebars with him. He heard Linwood give a healthy scream, and it was all over, but the hurtin as the two boys and the bicycle sailed over the edge. They landed in the deep drainage ditch with the bicycle on top of them.

It wasn't too long before Uncle Hal came by and found the two boys and the bicycle lying in the ditch. He picked them up and he told dad later that he figured that something was the matter with Jake because when he propped him up against the bank, Jake jist lay there, grinning foolishly. Uncle Hal piled the two of them, along with Linwood's mangled bicycle into the back of his pickup and brought them to our house.

Mother helped carry Jake up the stairs to bed. Uncle Hal, knowing how mother felt about drinking, didn't dare to tell her that Jake was drunk. In her concern to take care of the two boys, she never noticed the smell of beer that surrounded them. She rushed to and fro declaring that Jake had better learn not to ride his bicycle so fast, he was lucky he hadn't been killed!

When Dad got home that night, after checking on Jake, he didn't have to be told what had happened. Dad never did tell mother the "real" story because he knew that if she ever found out that Jake was drunk, Jake would have another accident right there in his own bed!

Jake recovered and finally discovered girls. He proceeded to marry and produce five children in rapid succession. By this time, the war was raging in Vietnam and Walt, and Bub went off to serve, but Jake like dad, had too many children and a heart murmur, and he wasn't accepted.

Mother and dad were never quite the same when on July second, nineteen seventy-nine, Jake died of a massive heart attack at the age of thirty-five. He left behind a wife and five grieving children. Mother and dad never could get over the fact that two of her sons went off to fight a war in a far off land and might not come back alive, and the one who should have been safe at home, was the one who died.

I miss you and love you Jake, but I know that we'll meet again in another place, another time....

THA SUIT

Dad said that the first time he'd ever laid eyes on "tha suit" his Uncle Jimmy was wearin it, not well, but wearin it jist the same. Dad was nineteen years-old by then and it was nineteen thirty-nine. The First World War was jist a bad memory in most people's minds and Grammy Stevens kept sayin "Thank You God!" because none of her family had been called up to lay their lives on the line for that shitty war!

Dad looked out from under his eyebrows at his uncle and seein the spectacle he was makin of himself, wondered why any fool would go and buy an ugly thing like that! Tha suit seemed to take on a life of its own as old Jim flashed himself here and there around the crowded kitchen.

The old farm house on the Garfield Road still didn't have electricity and the dull light from several kerosene lamps only served to illustrate the fact that tha suit was a hideous mustard brown. The roughly woven material had a somewhat "nubby" weave and if one ventured closer, you could see a thin, shimmery metallic thread runnin through it at irregular intervals.

Old Jim was as proud as a peacock to think that he was the only one at the wake who was wearin a suit. In his mind's eye, as he flashed himself here and there, he thought that when he approached a knot of people and folks stopped talkin and stared at him with their mouths open, they were jist takin note of how good he looked. "They're jist envious," he told himself, but in reality, everyone was commenting to each other about how friggin horrible tha suit really was.

Nobody was payin any attention to the grieving widow or to the elderly man lying in the coffin. Every time Jim swept past, all conversation stopped and folks laughed into their sleeves about jist how stoopid he looked, but Jim was oblivious to it all. But as the hour got

81

later and the liquor got stronger, folks began makin outright comments regarding his clothing. "Say Jim, where in hell didja say yah found this thing?" they'd ask as they gingerly lifted the edge of the heavy lapel. Unhappy at havin someone touch the precious material, he'd quickly reach up, smooth the collar back into place and reply in a huffy voice, "Got it down tah Bangor at one of tha finer men's stores. Yah'd never be able to find anything like this in any of the stores in this part of "Tha County!" Folks would snort and chuckle at his remarks and quickly agree amongst themselves that they hoped tah hell they'd never find anything like it ever in their lifetime.

And with that, he'd move on to someone else who, after havin consumed several bottles of rotgut liquor, mustered the courage to ask another question about his precious suit. "So Jim, how much didja have to part with to git this friggin thing?" Old Jim would simply back away from the probing fingers, and the stale whisky breath, smile proudly that his suit was gittin so much attention, slide his hand into the poorly lined pockets, throw his scrawny shoulders back and reply, "Oh, it didn't cost all that much. I got a real good buy cause tha feller that ordered it, dropped dead en it didn't fit anybody else." And he'd move on.

Hearin this explanation, folks would nudge each other, wink and laugh figuring that the real truth was that when the buyer laid eyes on tha suit for the first time, that seein something so ugly, up close, well, it musta been tha shock that had probably killed him!

As the years wore on, Old Jim and his precious suit made the rounds in Aroostook County from weddings, to funerals, to barn raisins, to open houses, to graduations, to baby showers and Christenings. If it was a social occasion, Old Jim was there. He was really a social animal and if there was any kind of shindig goin on within a radius of fifty miles of his old house, he'd be there come hell or high water! By now, he and the brown suit were famous. He, for bein a genuinely nice guy and tha suit, for bein so friggin ugly.

Folks said that the older tha suit got, the rattier it became because the small, shiny thread that ran through tha material became very brittle over the years and began breaking apart and stuck out all over the place. People laughed their asses off at Old Jim as he came struttin down the street, looking jist like a friggin big, brown, prickly porcupine.

Old Jim's suit was the butt of town folks jokes all tha time as they said things to each other like, "Say Bernie, wasn't that your youngest kid who cried all through his Christenin tha other Sunday?" "Yah, Jaysus it was!" "Well, was tha kid sick or somethin?" "Nope, he wasn't. It's jist that he looked up en saw Old Jim in that Christly brown suit en it scared him half to death, en we jist couldn't shet him up!"

Or... "Swear tah God! I was passin Old Jim's place tha other day en I saw him splittin his wood." "Well, what's wrong with that?" "Nothin, nothin atall, but it sure seemed funny to see his coat tails flappin every time he swung tha ax!" "Yah mean he was wearin tha suit tah chop his wood?" "Jaysus! Yah certainly are slow! That's what I've been tryin to tell yah!"

Sometimes, folks jist have to bow to their meaner sides and they'd begin placin bets as to when Old Jim might wear tha suit next. It might be ninety degrees in tha shade and he'd still appear all done up in his mustard brown or shit-brindle brown suit as some better educated folks had taken to callin it. Rivers of sweat would be runnin down his freshly shaved cheeks and he'd simply reach up with a thick work-worn finger and flick the offending stream of sweat off his face or neck and carry on as if he was the coolest dude in "Tha County." It wouldn't be too long before flies, mosquitoes and mingies, attracted by his smell and heat, began following him around in swarms.

Folks, upon seein how hot Old Jim was, tried time after time to pry the tawdry suit jacket off his scrawny body, but he jist wouldn't part with any part of it. He never let the temperature, be it ninety degrees in tha shade or thirty clapboards below zero, deter him from his social obligations. He and tha suit were always there. Folks said that Old Jim and his ratty suit could clear a party quicker than any pickup full of cops.

At the years drug on, Old Jim aged and shrunk and tha cuffs on the jacket hung down over his fists and the hems of his pants drug below the heels of his shoes in the dirt. Some of the church guild sewing ladies, upon seeing how seedy Old Jim looked, talked about offering to alter tha suit a dite for him, but somehow, they couldn't bring themselves to make the offer. It was jist too ugly and they valued their reputation as being fine sewers too much to ever attempt the alterations. There wasn't anything one could do that would have improved that suit!

83

The day finally came when Old Jim died and upon hearin the sad news, folks were beside themselves with curiosity. "Would his long-sufferin wife bury Old Jim in his precious suit?" This was the question that was on everybody's lips. Folks all agreed that this funeral would be one of the best attended in Ashland's history.

Folks couldn't wait to see that friggin ugly material buried six feet under the fertile soil of Aroostook County. Some folks even kidded quietly to one another that it was a good thing that the material was going into the graveyard because sure as hell nothin would ever grow where that material had been buried! "Probably wouldn't burn either," they speculated.

Mother said that a couple of days before the funeral, dad received a call from Mr. Seeley, Old Jim's lawyer, that he needed to see him in regard to his Uncle Jim's final bequest. Dad, upon hearin this surprising piece of news, hurried off to the lawyer's office. Mother said it wasn't too long before dad came back and he had a large bundle gingerly tucked under his arm and he didn't look too happy about it.

Dad came into the kitchen where mother sat shellin peas and heaved the heavy package onto the kitchen table. Mother said she looked at him and jist as the questions came onto her tongue, dad stalked over to tha fridge and grabbed one of his cold, home brews. After he'd sucked down half the bottle, he slid into his regular place at the head of the table and finally told her what had happened at Mr. Seeley's office.

Dad said he was shocked beyond words when his Uncle Jim's final wishes were made known. Old Jim's final words were specifically for dad, his favorite nephew. He stated that of all the folks who had loved his dearest treasure, it was dad, who had commented most often about it every time Old Jim was wearin it. So, it stood to reason that dad should inherit it over everyone else in town. Since it was dad who'd loved it almost as much as Old Jim, he was leavin his precious brown suit to dad!

Dad said that upon hearin this unwelcome piece of news, he'd sat back in his chair and refused to touch it and when Mr. Seeley had handed the paper wrapped package to him, dad had held it like it was burnin hot! Folks around town, when finally hearin the story, laughed their asses off. Poor dad got an awful lot of good natured kidding by everyone who'd heard the story. Folks even asked him if he intended on wearin tha suit to the funeral. Dad jist smiled and changed the subject.

The day of the funeral dawned bright and clear and folks came from miles around to see Old Jim put in the fertile ground of "Tha County" and they all agreed that seeing Old Jim layin in his casket gave them all a good start. "What do you mean by that?" they were asked. "He was an old man and yah can't expect to live forever!" "Well," they replied. "It was jist somewhat disconsertin to see him layin there in a different suit that's all."

When they'd finally gotten home after the ceremony, mother looked around tha kitchen and finally asked dad where he'd put tha suit. Dad, pourin himself a tall shot of Gin, gave her a long look and before he answered, took a quick swig of the drink. Mother said dad's blue eyes danced a little like he was enjoyin the situation for the first time and then he said, "Well mum, there's moren one way tah skin a cat." Mother, her curiosity peaked by this cryptic remark, waited for him to explain.

"You know that my last batch of homebrew was an especially good batch this time?" Mother nodded her head. "Well," dad went on. "And you know that old Mr. Stimpson has an unusual fondness for strong spirits?" Again mother nodded her head. "Well," Dad explained, "All I had to do was offer tha undertaker a couple of bottles of my new brew en he would have done anything I wanted." Mother, finally saw the light and then she asked, "Okay, I understand all that, but where is tha suit?' Dad looked at her, grinned his widest grin and said," It's finally restin exactly where it should have been all these years. It's down tha Sheridan Road in tha Ashland Cemetery, six feet under Uncle Jim! I figured it'd make a nice sort of cushion for Old Jim on his final journey because none of tha creatures that live in tha dirt in tha cemetery are ever going to eat that thing anyway!"

Martha Stevens-David

PROTOCOL OF POTATO PICKING

Growing up in Aroostook County, Maine, we knew a lot about potatoes, not because we were particularly interested in them, but because they were always all around us and dad worked with that specie all of his natural life.

In nineteen fifty-nine, I had jist turned fifteen and mother had finally agreed that I could wear a light colored lipstick but no other makeup. I still wasn't allowed to go to high school dances unless my older brothers, Walt or Jake would be there too. Walt, a senior, had discovered the fairer sex eons ago but Jake was a slow-learner when it came to girls. As far as he was concerned, they were last on his list of priorities.

Jake, still only seventeen, was running all over to hell and gone trying to trap any and all animals so that he could practice the art of taxidermy. Now, if there had been a female in "Tha County" who had fur down to her ankles or could climb trees like a porcupine, he'd have been mightily interested, but at that point, he still hadn't found a girl who looked like that.

So, in the summer of fifty-nine, I'd taken a babysitting job for a French-speaking family in Ashland and their home was about five miles from our house on the Goding Road. I'd stay with the Morins all week and only return home on Sunday for a few hours visit and then go back to stay the rest of the week in town. I soon discovered that it was pretty difficult for mother to hear what I was doing that summer in regards to makeup or boys because she only came to town on Saturday night to do her shopping and we still didn't have a telephone at home.

That summer, I learned how to lighten my hair with house-hold bleach, tweeze my eyebrows to a fine line and apply blush and mascara. I'd put all this stuff on my face very early in the morning and only wash it off before I went to bed at night. I used to take the two small children I was babysitting for a walk around town everyday but I never really got to meet very many boys because most of them had summer jobs too. But when I went home for a short visit on Sundays, I always had to remember to wash everything off so that mother wouldn't have a conniption fit when she saw my pale face slathered with makeup.

Dad, after fathering five daughters, was pretty much unfazed by all us girls and left us for mother to manage. I guess he figured that we were mother's domain and she could run her mouth very well when she wanted to. The only thing I remember dad saying, after one of his daughters had snuck his razor to shave our legs with, was, "Looks like these blades don't stay as sharp as they used to." And he'd look all around the kitchen at his guilty harem with a little smile on his face. And Grandfather Colbath used to put in his two cents worth too, upon seeing one of us with a lot of extra makeup on our faces, "Power and paint, sure makes a woman what she ain't."

The summer of fifty-nine was a turning point for me. It had been a warm summer for "Tha County" and the state of Maine as well. Dad, ever the potato babysitter, came home day after day, red-faced and sun burned to a crisp, swearing that if the crop didn't git some water pretty soon, the whole damn county was going to dry up and blow away into Canada!

Because he always slapped a hat on his old bald head jist as soon as his feet hit the floor in the morning, it was always surprising to see jist how white his scalp was and how the skin on his head glowed when he removed his sweat-stained hat at night. His poor ears would be peeling and sore, but there was always a light in his bright-blue eyes and a grin on his face when he came through the door each night.

Finally, the heavens answered all the farmer's prayers and rain descended upon us and it was as though Mother Nature couldn't send enough "wet stuff" our way. The poor, dried-out soil sucked up the first downpours, but after a couple of days of incessant rain, the ground was totally saturated and water began running in torrents down the potato rows, washing out the half-grown plants and the small, pale, sickly lookin spuds lay rotting in the fields.

Now, dad came home every night still complaining about the weather, but this time it was complaints about too much rain! Water ran everywhere and not only was dad unhappy about the rain, he was upset because the rain-swollen Aroostook River had flooded and he couldn't get to his favorite fishin hole on the Garfield side of the river. He was one unhappy man.

It was September and school started and as always, it closed almost immediately for three weeks so that the farmers, with the help of local families, could get their crops harvested and off to market. Picking potatoes back then isn't like it is now. We didn't have all the "modern" machines to do the work for us. Mother used to get us up at four am and we'd hurry to eat and get dressed for the long, grueling, dirty day ahead. We always picked for our Great Uncle Hal each year and when his work was done, if any of the other farmers in our area still weren't finished digging, we'd go to work for them too until it was time for us to go back to school.

That fall, after a horrible summer that was too hot and dry and then, too wet and cold, it turned out to be pretty nice. I guess Mother Nature, after trying our patience for so long, decided to give us a better ending for the season. Anyway, from the first day of picking, the sun slid over the eastern horizon right on cue and it was nice and warm by the time Grampy Colbath dropped us off in the potato fields every morning.

Uncle Hal had planted over two hundred acres that spring and he had smoked Camels until his own skin had turned yellow, worrying that he's never get all the spuds out of the ground before the first snow flew into Aroostook County around the middle of September. At the beginning of harvest, he'd asked all of us to stay overtime every day while the weather was still holding. So, we were in the fields from sunup till nearly sundown. It made for a very long day.

That year, I'd grown an inch taller and I was nearly filled-out if you know what I mean. My best friend, Dorothy Rushinal and I constantly compared notes about our development and she still lagged somewhat behind me in the chest department. I had nothing to brag about either, but I wasn't as skinny or underdeveloped as she was. But Dorothy was much savvier in the boy department because she had several older sisters and she'd learned things from them that I'd never even heard of.

Having been picking potatoes since the age of two, when mother first took me to the fields with her, I knew everything there was to know and a lot I didn't want to know about picking potatoes. It was excruciating, dirty, backbreaking work. The farmer, sitting on his tractor, would go down the rows pulling the potato digger along behind him. The digger, back then, was designed to cover two rows and when it was lowered, the front part of the machine, dug into the dirt beneath the grown potatoes. The metal racks would roll back over the rollers and carry the uprooted potato plants along with it, filling the ground with freshly dug potatoes, rocks, potato vines, dirt and bugs. The farmer would continue in this mode until the field was dug, it was lunchtime or the digger broke down.

Back then, most people paced off a piece of the field that they felt they could keep picked and either dropped down on their knees to pick the spuds or put their basket between their legs and bent over and filled their baskets that way. No matter which way you chose, it was terrible, hard work and it took an awful lot of those spuds to fill a potato barrel. In 1959, we were being paid the scant sum of 15 cents per barrel. By the time you got home that night, your nails were but a distant memory, your nice, white legs would be black and blue from kneeling on rocks all day and dirt would be imbedded in any and all parts of your body.

That fall, we, younger girls, "got lucky" if you want to call it that. Uncle Hal normally hired old, worn-out men, who were usually our cousins or neighbors, to help him drive and load the potato trucks, but that fall, the older men, having been lured away by another desperate farmer who'd offered a better pay for the season, Uncle Hal had no choice than to hire a couple of French boys who were visiting from Canada and staying with relatives jist down the road from our house.

When my cousins and I heard who were going to be working for Uncle Hal, we were beside ourselves with excitement. Not only were these guys handsome and our own age, but they couldn't speak very much English either. It was going to be a very interesting harvest to say the least. Dad, after hearing all our talk about the new guys, cocked his eye at mother and said, "Guess I'll have to oil my shotgun ah-gin."

Thus the quest to be noticed began as the female population of Aroostook County prepared for potato harvest. Dorothy and I decided that if we were going to be "noticed" at all, we'd have to do something spectacular and we set about trying to decide what to do.

We bought and read every glamour magazine we could find at Chasse's Drugstore so that we could still look beautiful as we drug ourselves through the mud and the dirt while picking potatoes. We devoured every up-to-date article about makeup, hair styles and lipsticks we could find.

We dyed our faded jeans so that they would appear brand new and secretly altered them until they fit jist right. We stole some of our brother shirts and practiced tying them around our waists to make them fit better and we slathered egg whites on our wan faces because mother had told us that fresh-beaten egg whites, made your facial skin softer and even whiter than the store bought beauty stuff. We stole some of Dorothy's sister's perfume and sprayed ourselves with "Tweed" until it left us gasping and coughing. But we sure smelled good or so we thought.

To get ready for the potato field, we took long baths, washed our hair, shaved every place on our bodies where an offending hair might sprout, plucked our eyebrows until they were nearly nonexistent, cut and painted our finger and toe nails, applied several body lotions, deodorant and anything else that we thought might help us stay young and beautiful. We wanted to be the best looking, best smelling girls in that entire potato field!

Then, we ventured down over the hill and begged my great Aunt Cassie to give us a home perm. Hearin our request, she looked at us for a long moment and then she said. "Tooter, both you and Dorothy have hair that is fine and wispy. I wouldn't dare tah give you girls a perm even if I had tha time. That lotion is purty strong and it jist might burn all your hair to a crisp. Why don't you do what we used to do when we were young?" Anxious to hear her beauty secrets, we plied her with question after question and then we rushed home to give them a try.

That night, before going to bed, we washed our wispy, blond hair and then we tried what Aunt Cassie had told us to do. We laughed and giggled as we soaked our locks in her secret beauty agent, rolled our hair in stiff, pink plastic rollers, tied a scarf around them and snuck up the stairs to bed.

We didn't get much sleep that night because every time we laid our heads on the pillows, the teeth on the rollers bit into our scalps and those tiny plastic teeth caused a never-ending pain in our heads. I remember looking across at Dorothy and was shocked to see that she'd found a way to sleep jist the same. She was lying there with her head hanging over the side of the bed, snoring long and loud. Envious of her ability to sleep, I slid down on the end of the bed, hung my head over the edge like she had and finally, finding relief, soon, I too, was sound asleep.

The next morning, mother yelled up the stairs for us to get up and we straggled down the stairs to the kitchen, holding our sore necks and aching heads. Mother, took one look at us and burst out laughing. "What in God's name were you thinking?" she asked. "You're not going to a beauty pageant you know." We glumly nodded our heads and took another bite of her homemade doughnuts and prayed that our heads would stop aching sometime before noon.

Finally, it was time to take the rollers out of our hair. Dorothy started to unroll hers first and as I struggled into my potato picking clothes, I heard her let out a scream. I turned and looked at my friend. After all that time and struggle, she had only managed to get one roller out of her hair! Her hair was curled all right; it was curled in a frozen position with the roller still inside the curl.

It seems that Aunt Cassie's hair curling potion had worked too well and the rollers wouldn't come out without pulling half of your hair out too. Dorothy looked at me and I began trying to unroll my curlers with the same result as Dorothy. Our hair was stuck together and to the rollers too. With a loud wail, we looked at each other and rushed down the stairs to complain to mother.

Mother, hearing what Aunt Cassie had advised us to do, couldn't stop laughing. She was laughing so hard that she had to sit down. Finally, she wiped her eyes on the edge of her apron and said, "I don't know, but if it was me, I'd soak my head in water and then take tha rollers out." "But mother," I cried. "We don't have time to do that and dry and curl our hair again before we have to leave. " Mother laughed some more and said, "I wondered what happened to tha rest of that can of Carnation milk that was in tha fridge."

Dorothy and I decided that we'd jist have to leave our hair in the rollers and wrap a scarf around our head like a lot of the older, married women did and pretend that we were jist trying to keep the dirt out of our hair.

We carefully applied our makeup which meant foundation, rouge, lipstick, eye shadow, mascara and penciled in our skimpy brows and then went outside to wait for Grampy to come and get us. We'd jist have to make it through the day and then we could wash our hair when we got home that night.

That was the longest day of our young lives. When we'd gotten to the potato field at six am, it had been foggy and damp but by ten o'clock, the sun had come out and it had turned hot and humid. Hurrying from the freshly dug row to the potato barrels with our heavy baskets caused us to sweat and the sun beating down on our bound-up heads soon caused Aunt Cassie's secret hair-setting solution to start running down our necks, our faces and into our eyes.

It wasn't too long before, all kinds of nasty insects, drawn by our putrid smell, began buzzing, biting, diving and flying all around our heads. Dorothy and I, with jaws tight and painted lips curled into a thin, red line, commenced to picking with a fury, hoping and praying that Uncle Hal or Cousin Arthur wouldn't drive up to where we were picking our section with those two handsome French boys on the back of the truck.

When six o'clock finally rolled around that night, we didn't wait for Grampy to come and get us. We shot out of that field and walked home as fast as our tired legs could carry us. We couldn't wait to get that sour, stinky milk out of our hair.

Aunt Cassie later told mother that she'd watched out of the corner of her kitchen window as we'd slunk by and that she'd yelled out to us that if we ever needed any other of her "beauty secrets," to jist come and see her any old time. We didn't even respond, we tucked our smelly, insect laden heads down and headed up the long hill for home.

That weekend, Uncle Hal dropped by our house on his way to town and had a chat with dad and the story of our potato field disgrace came up. He said that everyone in the potato field that day could look up and tell where we were jist by the huge swarm of mosquitoes, moose flies, wasps and bumblebees that were buzzing all around our heads. Uncle Hal allowed that he didn't think that dad had any worries about us getting carried away with those two handsome Canadian boys because the boys thought Dorothy and I were the strangest girls they'd ever seen. They told him that they had never seen any French girls in Canada that had attracted bugs like the two of us.

THA LOON

Jake laid his fishin gear down in the bottom of dad's old, green Old Town canoe and slid the canoe quietly into the slowly moving water of the Aroostook River. The canoe rocked slightly as he settled himself into the dilapidated seat and picked up the paddle.

He paddled silently in the river as he slowly made his way downstream to where the water divided and then he cut across the current in the middle and paddled until he reached the opposite side. He lay the dripping paddle across his knees, lit a cigarette and let the canoe, pulled by the current, glide along the edge of the riverbank.

Although he'd been cruisin this river ever since he was old enough to use a canoe and paddle, he never got over the feeling he had when he saw the river again and he knew every crook and bend and where every sand bar was as well. It was jist as much a part of him as the blood that coursed through his veins.

Jist as the canoe started to go around a bend in the river he reached up and grabbed a low-hanging branch of a river birch and pulled hard to the left. He guided the canoe into the mouth of the fast-flowing Trout Brook that emptied into the Aroostook from the Garfield side. He stood, and still holding the branches, pulled the canoe up along the edge of the brook until he reached his favorite fishing spot and then he quickly anchored the canoe.

He'd begun fishin here when he was five, over fifty years ago, when his father had first introduced him to this quiet place and he'd considered it to be his private fishin hole ever since. Dad was long gone now, but Jake, somehow, always felt closer to him, in this spot.

Jake reached down and dug through his fishin gear until he found his rusty can that held his angle worms. Withdrawing one, he swiftly threaded the twisting, pink worm onto his hook and dropped it over the

93

side of the canoe into the clear, cold water. Then, he shook a Chesterfield cigarette out of a crumpled package, stuck it in his mouth, lit it and let his mind slide back to another place, another time. A time when he was jist a little red-headed, freckled-faced boy and both he and his father were sittin right here in this very same spot all those many years ago.

His father had been the one to teach him all the fishin tricks he now used. "It's good to have rituals and customs," he thought to himself. "It keeps a man on an even keel."

He snapped out of his reverie when he felt his fishing pole being pulled downwards and he leaned forward and looked intently at the spot where his line met the water.

Ever widening circles in the water moved away from his line and he watched until he saw what had pulled on his hook. It was the biggest, most beautiful rainbow trout that he'd ever seen! Seeing the lovely creature swimming jist a few feet away made Jake's heart jump and he felt a thin film of sweat break out on his sunburned forehead.

He didn't know what to do first! He scrambled to shift his pole over to where the large fish was lazily swimming around in circles and the canoe rocked back and forth.

"Calm down, man! Calm down!" He commanded himself as he loosened his grip on the pole and took an extra long pull on his cigarette. He let the smoke curl up out of his mouth, past his nose as he tried to regain some of his composure. When he was nearly calm again, he set about tryin to catch the fish.

He reeled in the sickly looking white, waterlogged worm and stripped it off his hook. Quickly looping a fresh, worm on the hook, he slipped it quietly back into the water. Then he jiggled the hook gently up and down a couple of times jist to catch the trout's attention. Jake watched as the large fish floated over to his hook, nudged it a little with the side of his nose, slid past and kept right on goin. "Son-of-ah-bitch!" Jake swore to himself. He wanted that fish in the worst way!

Jake sat where he was for the better part of the mornin, watchin that fish go through every kind of teasing motion that was possible. It would come floating up to the top of the water, turn on its side and slip past Jake in a silent salute and then it would slide silently away again into the swirling, blue water.

Seein the fish, glide, slide, float and jump jist out of reach reminded Jake of a finely choreographed dance routine. The fish would come up to the top of the water, turn on its speckled side and in a flash of sliver, slide past the canoe where Jake sat, with one fin up in the air, in a silent salute as if to say, "Catch me if you can, sucker!"

The large fish slid by and rolled over, jist out of reach; in front of him so many times that Jake was able to memorize every colorful detail of that fish! Seein the fish, so close yet so far, made Jake's blood boil. "Teases yah jist like a friggin woman!" Jake thought to himself for the hundredth time.

This frustrating routine was repeated over and over again and at one point, as the sun rose higher and as Jake grew hotter, he lost control. He jumped up, grabbed his fishin net and began thrashin the water every which way, to no avail. The trout was still free, swimmin out there in the peaceful Aroostook River, somewhere jist beyond his reach.

Finally, Jake caved. His stomach was growling so much that he couldn't tell if it was his stomach or thunder rumblin off in the distance towards Garfield and his bladder was way beyond screamin.

Normally, he would have stood and relieved himself over the side of the canoe but after seein that fish swimmin there all day, he jist couldn't urinate where that fish swam. He jist couldn't!

He untied the canoe and with a last, longing look at the magnificent fish, grabbed his paddle and headed upstream for home. Jist as he rounded the corner, he turned, looked back at the mouth of the brook and yelled. "I'll be back Mr. Trout! You can bet your ass on that!" He wiped the sweat out of his eyes and bore down on the paddle. "Maybe next year I'll cave in and buy myself a trolling motor." He said to himself. "Maybe next year!"

Preoccupied and jist a little pissed off with the day's disappointing events, he ate his supper in silence, replaying in his mind the happenings of the day. His wife tried to make simple conversation, but he only grunted an answer here and there and after a while she gave up tryin to talk to him.

He spent the entire evenin in his den readin everything ever written about rainbow trout and their habits. He planned, he schemed and he prayed that jist one piece of all the information that he'd read would be the one thing he needed to catch that fish.

95

Finally, along about midnight, he lay aside all the fishin magazines, slathered some of his wife's moisturizer on his pickled face and neck and slid into bed alongside his long-sleeping wife.

He fell into a fitful sleep and he thrashed and turned so much that his wife, tired of him pullin the sheets off her and gettin kicked every couple of minutes, slapped him on the arm. He mumbled incoherently and fell back into his dream of catchin the fish.

Along towards mornin, when the moon was jist a sliver in the western sky, he began talkin. "Oh baby," he moaned. "Come to papa, that's it honey!" He turned and threw a heavy arm across his wife's chest.

Surprised and still half-asleep, she turned to her husband, wonderin what had put him in such a romantic mood so early in the mornin.

Jist as she was about to put her arms around him, Jake sat up in bed and yelled, "I'm gonna get you, you friggin fish, if its tha last thing I do!" Hearin this, his wife cuffed him across the back of the head and this really woke Jake up.

He rubbed his head and looked at her in the dim light. "What's tha matter with you anyway?" he asked. His wife gave him one of her "if looks could kill" looks and snapped. "I might ah known that it was a friggin fish you was talkin to!" And she moved over to the far side of the bed. Not only was Jake gettin the cold shoulder from the fish, now he was gettin it from his wife too!

Jake watched the clock all day at work at Pinkham's Mill and as soon as the five o'clock whistle blew, he was out tha door and down the Portage Road in a cloud of dust. He'd packed all his fishin gear the night before and he flew past his house and down over the Sutherland's flats to the Aroostook River.

He slid his canoe out of the reeds and into the water and he didn't bother trying to be quiet either. He paddled like a man in a rowing competition; he could have crewed for Yale!

He paddled across the current until he reached the Garfield side and then he floated down river until he reached the mouth of Trout Brook and it was only then that he finally breathed. "Oh please let him still be here." He prayed for the hundredth time. He slid up into the mouth of the brook until he was in the same position as he'd been in the day before and quickly tied up to the same branch of the river birch.

He sat where he was for a long moment and jist looked at the brook where it joined the river as it flowed past. The water from the brook was so pristine and clear that he could see the green river grasses as they flowed and shifted in the bottom current.

He watched as water bugs skated across the glassy surface and then he smiled as once again, he saw the huge fish, rise, open its mouth and feed on one of the insects that waited there on the top of the water.

Seein the fish, Jake's old heart jumped and danced in his chest and he had difficulty catchin his breath. He couldn't believe his luck! The trout was still here! He'd worried all night that it would be long gone by the time he got back. But there it was! "Well, I'll show him who's tha boss this time!" Jake said to himself as he hurriedly cast his hook into the swirling water.

It was a repeat of the day before. The fish, as though sensing Jake's desperation, began the old teasin routine again and it had it down to perfection too.

He'd slide up through the murky river water and the settin sun would reflect off its silver belly into Jake's eyes. It would roll completely over and then it would slip away, as silently as it had come.

This appearin and disappearin act set Jake's teeth right on edge and he commenced to prayen with the fervor of a convert. He mumbled prayers to every deity he could think of and even a few he made up, like the "Fishin God of the Universe." "Yah never know, it might jist help!" He thought to himself.

This little game of bate and switch was really takin a toll on Jake's nervous system, his heart, his stomach and his bladder. He was fallin apart and he wondered how much longer he could keep this up. He tried every lure and fly in his tackle box and every fishin trick he could think of and nothin enticed that fish!

When Jake finally looked up, he noticed that the settin sun was hovering jist above the horizon and he slid his cuff back and looked at his watch. It read eight fifteen and he knew that he should be makin plans to head for home in another half-hour or so.

Suddenly, he became aware of a pair of loons that had paddled into his line of vision. He watched as they floated together along the top of the water and every now and then, one of them would dip down into the water and come back up with a good-sized fish wriggling in its mouth.

"Friggin loons!" Jake moaned to himself. " Now I've really got competition!" He watched them for a couple of minutes longer and then turned back to the task at hand, prayin all the while that the loons stayed where they were.

He reeled in and removed the fly that had been driftin along the top of the water and reached for his fishin tackle box. He poked around until he found the sandwich bag that he'd put in the night before.

He took out a piece of half-cooked elbow macaroni and a piece of hard cheese and he slid these on the end of the hook. Smilin to himself at the ridiculous bait combination, he sang a little song as he carefully cast the bait into the water. "Fishy, fishy in the brook, come and bite my great big hook!"

Resigned to the fact that it was probably a losin proposition, he was shocked when he felt a slight nudge travel up the line and down the pole to his hands. His fishin reflexes kicked in and he gave a sharp tug on the line. The next thing he knew, he was hanging on to the pole for all his might! He'd caught somthin, by gorry, he had! What it was, he really couldn't tell, but he knew that it was big and that was all that interested him.

He stood and braced his feet in the canoe and again gave a hard check on the line. Suddenly, he saw what he'd caught! It was a loon! He nearly fell out of the canoe in his shock and then he saw that he was wrong. He'd caught a fish and a loon! "How could that be?" He asked himself.

He pulled on the line again and reeled in the some of the slack and the large bird, feelin the tug on the fish in its mouth, squawked, flapped its wings and dug its feet into the water. It was a standoff! Jake wanted the fish and the loon wanted the fish! Somthin had to give!

Jake, seeing that the western settin sun was makin a fast descent, knew that he had to do somthin soon and he began jumpin up and down in the canoe, hopin against hope that he could scare off the loon. To no avail.

Jake began screamin and shoutin at the big bird, but the loon still wouldn't let go of the trout. "That's my trout you stoopid ol bird! I caught it before you did!" Jake screamed until he couldn't scream anymore, but it did no good. The loon jist sat there in the water, lookin back at him with the precious trout held firmly in its mouth.

Desperate to win, Jake's brain and his common sense shutdown. He slid his fishin pole between his knees and he grabbed his paddle. He picked it up, turned it around in his hand and brought it back behind his head. Steadying himself, he threw the paddle, like a javelin, at the loon with all his might! The paddle flew through the air and hit the water with a loud smack jist to the right of the stubborn bird. Startled by the sound of the paddle hitting the water, the loon dropped the trout and took off across the river.

Jake, beside himself that his ploy had finally worked, quickly sat down and began reelin in his prize. As the fish came slidin up to the canoe, he reached over the side and grabbed it by its gill. He hauled it in and sat lookin at it.

The loon may have been startled into releasing the trout but it had left its mark anyway. The once beautiful trout was all mangled and the skin was missin in several places. Jake sat where he was for the longest time and then he thought, "Might jist as well give it back to tha friggin loons," he thought to himself, "I don't want to take it home lookin like that." He carefully removed his hook from the trout's mouth and slid it back into the river. As soon as the fish felt the cool water on its skin, it was gone with a slap of its beautiful tail, back to deeper, water.

It was then that Jake realized that he was in a huge predicament. He had thrown his only paddle at the loon and had no way to get back upstream to where he'd parked his truck. Jake spent a long cold night huddled in the bottom of his canoe and when he didn't return home that night; his wife called the warden's service to look for him.

When Jake's story was told around town the next day, everybody laughed at him, but nobody really believed his story about the loon stealing his trout.

Thereafter, whenever he saw a Bangor Daily Newspaper article about changin the lobster on the state of Maine license plates to a loon, he fired off a lengthy, angry letter of protest to the Maine State Legislature.

Martha Stevens-David

SUMMER CAMP

In our small town, there were eight churches of many different denominations. We had the Roman Catholic, the Seventh Day Adventist, the Pentecostal, the Protestant, the Episcopalian, the Baptist, the Congregational and the Jehovah Witness. Because there were so many churches in such a small area, competition between the ministers and the priests, over lost souls, was fierce to say the least.

Dad professed not to have any particular religious leanings and he didn't encourage us to become involved in religion either. He felt that when we were old enough we should make that decision for ourselves and besides, he always said that "more wars were fought because of religious differences," than for any other reasons.

Mother, on the other hand, was of a different persuasion. School was over for the summer and she could see the writin on the wall. Two and a half months with one husband, five children and another due in the fall, well, to her way of thinkin, it was goin to be an extremely long summer.

Nineteen fifty-two was nearly the ruin of Jake and me. I was eight and Jake was nine. Summer had come to the county early that year and already it promised to be a hot and humid one. The temperature, during the early weeks of June, hovered around eighty degrees and to us in "Tha County," anything over seventy was a heat wave.

It was hot and sticky and we'd been quarrelling all day over one thing or another. We'd been in and out of the house time after time, pestering mother with complaint after complaint and she was fed up with the lot of us. We knew that we were right on the edge between living and dying when Jake, after having yelled "Mother" several times, heard her yell thru the kitchen window screen, "Why don't you call your ass mother next time and see if you get an answer!" She was worn out and her nerves were frazzled and we knew we were going to die if we bothered her one more time! Finally Jake sidled up to the kitchen screen door and mumbled to her that we'd like to go swimmin down to the Chub Hole. Mother threw up her hands in relief and off we flew. She was glad to be rid of us.

Every now and then, an over-zealous minister or priest, lookin for converts, would come cruisin down the Goding Road leaving a trail of dust in the hot afternoon air. He'd come to a screechin halt at our house and after peeling his black, sweat soaked clothes away from his hot body, he'd stroll up to the house with his trusty bible in hand. He'd come prepared to convince mother that she really should be concerned about her children's lack of religious education.

Mother, who was only slightly religious, wasn't overly concerned that all of her kids were going straight to hell. Some days, when she'd been up at the crack of dawn, lugged seventeen pails of water, washed six loads of clothes by hand and kept an eye on five mischievous kids, well, hell sounded pretty good to her!

If it was a "minister sniffin day," it wasn't his religious bent that swayed her; the thing that motivated her most was if she'd had a particularly bad day with all us kids. Then, she'd sign us up for "Summer Bible Camp" without a second thought. It didn't matter to her which denomination it was either. As long as it took some of us kids away for a few weeks and didn't cost her any money, that's all that really counted.

When mother broke the news to Jake and me that we were goin to "Summer Camp," we didn't know what to think. She told us that there was going to be lots of fun things to do and we would learn a whole bunch of new stuff. Hearin this and the vagueness of it all, Jake asked her if there was goin to be any swimmin, boatin and fishin. Mother only hesitated for a second, she looked up from her cooking and with a very straight face, she lied. "Of course there'll be boatin, fishin and swimmin! I'm sure they'll have all kinds of excitin things for tha two of you to do." Then, she turned back to the stove and her cookin and her shoulders seemed to shake a little. Jake and I looked at each other and he nudged me out the screen door. "Mum must really be goin to miss us if she's cryin already," he said.

On the appointed date, the minister and his wife arrived to pick us up. As mother packed me and Jake and our meager belongings into the large, black dust-covered sedan, she reminded us and Jake in particular, not to swear while we were there and to be sure and change our underwear. And off we went to swim, boat, fish and eat free food for three weeks in paradise.

The Pentecostal Campgrounds were located on the Houlton Road a few miles jist outside of Presque Isle and the thirty-five mile drive from our house to the camp was the beginning of three weeks of pure misery for Jake and me. I'm sure we were considered "heathens" by the minister and his wife because we didn't go to church and we were continually questioned, examined and grilled about the bible on the long, hot ride to hell!

We were only about half a mile from home when the "games" began. The minister cast his beady eyes on us in the rear-view mirror and then he yelled a biblical question at us over his shoulder. "What happened to Lot's wife?" With fingers drumming on the steering wheel to mark time, he waited for an answer. Jake, not knowin what to say, shot me a confused look and slid a little further down in his seat. I didn't know any of the answers, so I didn't say anything either. After a couple of long, miserable minutes, the minister and his wife shouted out the correct answer in unison and the next biblical interrogation round would begin.

After the lengthy bible question and non-answer session on our part concluded, the hymn singing began. The minister was a large, heavy-set man with a deep, baritone voice and he sang with gusto and majesty, all the old hymns that we had heard at some point in our life, but we really didn't know them well enough to sing along with him. His wife, on the other hand, really shouldn't have sung anything, ever! Her voice was high and nasally and when she attempted to hit the high notes, they turned on her. Her horrible singing slid inside our ears and tormented our brain until our eyes watered. When they'd finished with one song, she'd turn around in her seat and give us a smug little smile that said, "We're going to heaven and who's not!" With that nice bit of encouragement, she'd turn back around and off they'd go into another hymn. Jake shot me the most miserable look that I've ever seen on his round little face that said. "I'm already friggin dead, jist bury me!"

By the time we got to the campgrounds, Jake's eyes had glazed over and he was leaning his little red-haired head on tha edge of the door.

The minister ground the car to a halt and with great enjoyment, jumped out, wrenched the car door open and Jake tumbled out onto the dusty ground. The minister stepped back and with a dramatic sweep of his hand, bellowed, "Here we are!" "Welcome to God's Kingdom!" We looked wearily around and saw "God's Kingdom" in all its glory.

In the middle of an overgrown, dried out field of weeds, stood a small, sagging building that was in desperate need of paint and repair. The only reason you knew it was a "church" was because it had a huge, black cross nailed directly over the front door. The cross was so big that it looked like it was crucifying the church. Off to the right were several small dilapidated buildings that were to be our "home" as we looked for the "Lord" for the next three weeks.

At the far end of the campground was a slightly larger structure that served as the dining hall and meeting place. A hand pump had been installed on a wooden platform at the side of the building and there were narrow little paths through the grass that led from the front of each building around to the back where the outhouses were located. The circular dirt drive wound around the front of the small cabins and the dining hall back out to the Presque Isle Road on the other side.

Jake was taken in one direction and me in the other. The next thing we knew, we'd been deposited along with our meager belongings, in one of the small, musty smelling cabins and instructed that one of the older "angels" would be along shortly to help us. The interior of the cabin wasn't any better than the exterior. There were rudimentary bunks built into the walls on each side of the room and a crude, hand-made desk and chair stood under the small window at the opposite end. Several rusty nails, to hang our clothes on, were pounded at different heights into the wall by the door. Fly strips, completely filled with dead flies, were hanging from the ceiling and they turned round and round in the slight breeze. No frills here, we were here to do the "Lord's" work.

My "angel" finally arrived in the shape of the Pillsbury dough girl. She was about sixteen and had short, curly hair the color of over-done carrots. Her otherwise peaches and cream complexion was marred only by a scattering of brown freckles across her turned-up nose. She and Jake would have been taken for brother and sister had they stood side by side.

She bounded into the small room and the old, wooden floor boards creaked and groaned under the extra weight. When her eyes had finally adjusted to the darkness, she spied me slunk against the rough, woolen blankets of the lower bunk. "Oh, what a cute little thing you are!" she sang in a chirpy voice. She threw herself down on the opposite bunk and began to talk to no one in particular. She talked and talked and never stopped. She talked until she finally fell asleep still talking. Suddenly, I had never felt so tired, my head was tired, my ears were tired, my eyes were tired, I was tired all over. I lay down on the moth eaten blanket on the musty bed and fell asleep too.

It didn't take too long for Jake and me to realize that mother had lied. There wasn't going to be any fun things to do like boatin, fishin or swimmin at all, because the camp was located right in the middle of a dried-up potato field and we certainly knew a potato field when we saw one!.

The daily bible camp routine went like this. Up at five am every morning, rain or shine and kneel by your bunk for a short "Good Morning Jesus" prayer. A fast cold water wash at the old pump and a "Thank You Jesus for the Water" prayer. Then off to a breakfast of lumpy oatmeal or a runny egg, preceded by a "Thank You Jesus for This Food" prayer. Then off to bible study, interspersed with more prayers for various and sundry reasons.

Lunch, was a baloney sandwich and a glass of watery Kool-Aid and another "Thank You for This Food" prayer. More bible study, hymns and prayers all tha long, tedious afternoon. Supper consisted of a stiff pork chop, some lumpy potatoes, wimpy peas, runny Jell-O, and another "Thank You for the Food" prayer and then it was evening congregation time, with more prayers, songs and testimonials. Then a quick wash and tooth brush at the old pump and a trip to the outdoor toilet. This was the only time we didn't have to say a prayer. I guess that nobody had bothered to think up a "Thank You Jesus for the Bowel Movement Prayer." Then finally to bed, with a "Good Night Jesus" prayer.

There were about sixty kids, who had been "abandoned" by their mothers for the summer, at the camp and we were divided into groups according to age and gender. The first day we were there, we were all herded into the small church to hear a welcoming sermon from the minister, Mr. Jacob Snow. He was dressed in a long, flowing black robe and with his black hair and dark eyes, he was an imposing sight. He stood in the middle of the ramshackle stage in front of the tiny pulpit and slowly looked us over and then he threw back his large head and roared, "Jesus!" "Jesus!" "Jesus!" Each time he yelled the word "Jesus," he'd hit the podium with his huge, beefy red fist.

I jumped at the shock of hearing that word yelled so long and so loud and looked around for Jake. I finally spied him and he was sittin straight up on a high-backed wooden bench with his bright, blue eyes locked on the minister. Finally, sensin that someone was starin at him, he turned his head and our eyes met and I saw a big smile on his face. Mother had warned us not to swear and here was the minister yelling all those swear words! Jake was in heaven! This was his kind of language! He'd finally found somethin that he could personally identify with. He settled back in his seat and waited for the next round of swear words to roll over him and the minister didn't let him down either. "Damnation!" "Hell!" "Jesus Christ Almighty!" came rolling over our heads in the stifling air and Jake was enthralled! He was beginnin to like this religion thing!

I didn't get to spend too much time with Jake what with all this kneelin and prayin, but every now and then we'd meet each other comin or goin on the path to the outhouses and he'd slide me a look that said it all. "When tha hell are we goin home?" By then, we'd lost all track of time and we didn't know one day from another. The only way we knew that a real church-going day had arrived was when we were told to wash up extra good and to put on our "nice" clothes. Then we knew it was Sunday.

One day, we actually got to sit next to each other in bible study and after a long drawn-out lecture about all the good things Jesus had done for us, we were instructed to draw a picture of a loving and peaceful Jesus. I didn't know what Jesus was supposed to look like, but Jake grabbed a black crayon in his left hand and began to draw without any hesitation. I watched as his drawin took shape. When he was finally done, satisfied, he gave a large sigh and sat back in his seat. I looked at his artwork and there was somethin vaguely familiar about the drawing. He'd drawn a tall, thin man in green work clothes and the man had blue eyes and there was a slight smile on his sun-burned face. This man had a fringe of white hair on his otherwise bald head and he was holdin a cigarette in his left hand. Suddenly it dawned on me who the man was. It was a drawing of dad!

Finally, with our ears flattened, our butts sore and our brains dead, our long ordeal was over. We were goin home! The ride home was a repeat of the ride over. But some of what we'd learned had sunk in and we were able to join in the biblical "games" and sing all the hymns clear through too. The ride home seemed to take forever because Jake and I had never been very far from home before and we were nearly home before familiar landmarks began to catch our attention.

As soon as we pulled up in the yard, Jake and I shot out of that car, into the house and up the stairs to the attic. We didn't even take time to say hello to mother or the other kids. We were home and that's all that mattered to us. Mother called a couple of times for us to come down and say goodbye to the minister and his wife, but we hid in the attic until they left. It was only after the dust from their departin vehicle had settled back on the dirt road that we dared to venture down stairs to where mother waited. Remembering her lies to us and with a hint of a smile on her face, she told us of the lovely supper she was going to cook for us to welcome us home.

That night after dad had gotten home and we'd eaten our fill of mashed potatoes, fried chicken, pickled beets, hot rolls and a "Stevens' Special" cake, dad slid his tea cup back and asked, "So, how'd it go?" Jake shot mother a long look and then he replied, "They didn't have any boatin or swimmin or fishin or nothin fun like that and we had to pray all tha jeezley time. It wasn't too bad, but they sweared more than we do!"

DAD—THA BEGINNING

Dad was a typical Mainer, in that, he believed in the old adage, "an honest day's work for an honest day's pay," and he was honest to a fault. He always gave more than an honest day's work in any job in which he was ever employed. Dad was a man of few words, and he was especially well-liked around our small town of Ashland, mostly because he minded his own business.

In the early years, before he met my mother, he'd migrated down to Berlin, New Hampshire where he worked for a while as a lumberjack in the woods and when he returned to Ashland a couple of years later, he went to work for his great uncle, Newell Smith, who owned Maine Seed Potato Growers. Newell Smith was said to be among the earliest people to plant the potato tubers in the rich soil of Aroostook County, Maine.

Mother said that the first time she'd ever laid eyes on father was when Grammy Colbath sent her with two of her sisters to town to buy some canning jar rubbers. She said that when they passed one of the potato houses, a tall, handsome blond-haired man was leaning against the door of the potato house, smoking a cigarette. Their eyes met and she turned to her siblings and said, "That's tha man I'm goin to marry!" and marry, they did.

Dad built their first house on a small plot of land about a quarter of a mile down the Masardis road from grandfather Colbath's house. In nineteen forty-five, when I was about five months old, dad was burning brush around the house as was the custom back then. It had been a wet spring, but the wind that swung around from the south drove the small fire towards the kerosene tank, and that was all it took to burn the small house to the ground.

It was then that Newell Smith, offered dad the use of a vacant "migrant worker's house" that he owned on the Goding Road. We lived in that house rent free for some thirty-odd years, and if it hadn't been for the fact that we didn't have to pay rent, dad never could have made it on his small wages. He worked twelve and fourteen hour days, six days a week and was lucky if he brought home fifty-four dollars a week.

Most mornings, dad's inner clock rang long before the yellowed by age clock on his old bureau went off each morning at four am. He'd shove aside the heavy homemade quilts and slide to an upright position on the edge of the bed where he'd inhale carefully and his next moments of wakefulness were consumed with jist trying to breathe normally. His cough began somewhere around the bottom of his lungs and slowly made its way up through his congested airways until it erupted in a great, gurgling, choking cough that didn't end until he was flushed and white and out of breath.

He'd reach out and grab the nearly empty pack of Chesterfields that lay where he'd left them on his night stand the night before and with trembling hands, shake one free and stick it in the corner of his mouth. With a quick flick of his wrist, he'd flip the top of his old Ronson lighter open with an expertness that told of a lifetime habit and light the first cigarette of the day. He'd drag the life-killing smoke deep into his tortured chest until his lungs rebelled again. Another paroxysm of coughs, combined with the sound of rolling mucus, filled the bedroom along with the yellow-tinged smoke of his cigarette.

Wiping tears from his eyes with the back of his hand, he'd cough another long, tortuous cough, and spit the heavy, yellow mucus that had come roiling up out of his lungs into a red cotton handkerchief that had been washed so many times that he could see right through it. Then he'd smoke the cigarette down to the very end and drop the butt into the old, chipped shaving mug that had been his fathers. The still glowing butt hissed as it hit the half-filled mug of water and died.

Dad, finally stood, adjusted his long johns and headed out the bedroom door. He continued on through the kitchen and out the door to the outhouse located at the end of the shed. A soft snore emanated from mother's side of the bed, but she wasn't really asleep, and so their day began….

THA BEAR

Old Piney Woodsman had a really bad habit and this habit drove everyone who knew him jist a little bit crazy. He had the habit of stretching the truth jist a little and some folks thought that he stretched the truth more than jist a little, if the truth be told.

But in a small town where everybody knows everybody else, folks, upon spying old Piney shuffling towards them down the street, did either one of two things. They immediately headed in a different direction to avoid direct interaction with him or stayed where they were and put up with him and all his tall tales.

On Saturdays, most of the male population of Ashland usually headed for Philbert's Barber Shop which was the only barber shop for miles around. Old Philbert opened his doors promptly at seven am and if you were one minute late, you had to wait and this was the time that the men liked the most. It wasn't the waitin that they particularly liked, it was the telling of tall tales while they waited, that they enjoyed.

In Aroostook County, which is the largest county in the state of Maine and the largest county east of the Mississippi, there are plenty of things to do especially if you are the hunting, fishing and outdoors kind of person. "Tha County" is home to so many different kinds of wild animals to hunt, trap, fish and stalk that there are always an endless variety of stories or tall tales being told about these creatures and each person always tries to best his neighbor.

Piney had been born in the small settlement of Squapan around the turn of the century, to a large French family that had migrated across the vast border that separated the state of Maine and Canada. His mother often told the neighbors that no sooner was the crib vacated by one kid learnin to walk when another little "Christer" arrived to take its place. Piney had been christened Pinotte Arthur Woodsman, but his name soon got shortened to "Piney" and he liked it that way.

Even as a little boy, he was always runnin around with one tall tale after another. If an older brother told of how, on his way home from school, he'd seen a large, bull moose crossing the road, Piney would sit and listen carefully to the story and after digesting the information for a couple of minutes, he'd jump up and begin telling of the huge moose that he'd jist seen down by the river on the same day. No matter what anyone else professed to havin seen, Piney could and did, always go them one better.

As the years went by, Piney acquired the reputation around town and the better part of Aroostook County as being a pest, a bore, ah pain in tha ass, a liar, a fool and every other derogatory epithet that anyone could think of. Town folks, upon being accosted by people from away, soon got into the habit of sicing them on Piney. Then they'd slip into Philbert's Barber Shop or Chasse's Department Store, peek out the window and laugh their asses off as they watched Piney fill the vacationer's heads full of lies and tall tales.

Now, local folks being who they are, couldn't come right out and call old Piney an outright liar, but most folks agreed amongst themselves that he was. And like all small towns everywhere, folks recognize that everyone has a differing view of things and pretty much accept people as they are, especially if they've known you all their lives and they jist might be related to you in one obscure way or another. So, when Piney started with one of his long, tall tales, local folk's jist rolled their eyes, nudged each other in tha ribs and slid off to finish their shopping or find someone else who had a more credible story.

By the time Piney had reached his middle sixties, he had told uncountable stories over the years about every conceivable creature that was known to exist in Aroostook County and several that didn't. If his wife saw a mouse in the kitchen, it immediately got changed to a rat when Piney retold it around town later on that day. He jist seemed to have to embellish, enlarge and fabricate each and every story he told.

However, the story to end all stories never got told by old Piney. It was his final story so to speak and it was all about him. Years afterwards, when folks sat around their stoves in the dead of winter and the temperature outside hovered around thirty clapboards below zero, Piney's story was the one that folks often remembered first and it usually put a clutch of fear in their hearts as they retold it.

It was fall and the leaves were in varying degrees of changing color. Frost had slid into "Tha County" overnight and some trees were totally bare while others were hanging on to their leaves for their last harrah. Others were every color that Mother Nature could make. The area of Aroostook County where Piney lived was on the 45th parallel and the seasons changed swiftly there, sometimes over night.

Like most Saturdays, Piney's wife was on a roll. She'd nudged his ample union suit clad body out of bed at the crack of dawn and before he knew it, she'd swiftly remade the bed before he could even think of slidin back into its warm interior. She'd been naggin him for the better part of the month of October that he needed to put up the storm windows and do the bankin around the house before tha first snow flew, but after forty years of marriage, Piney had perfected the art of turnin a deaf ear to her many wants and needs. It's not that he wanted to ignore her or anything like that, but he had other priorities and those priorities jist weren't the same as hers.

On this particular day, Olene had had about all she could take of her lazy, lying husband and she chased him out the kitchen door as soon as she could. She had things to do and didn't need him at home to git in her way. Piney was still tucking his shirttail into his shabby, wool pants when the kitchen door reopened and she heaved a heavy sack of trash out onto the frost-covered grass behind him. He turned in the path and seeing Olene looking at him out the kitchen window, he gave her his middle "fickle finger of fate" salute, grabbed the heavy bag of trash, turned and headed for the shed.

Saturday had a ritual all its own at the Woodsman's house. If it was Saturday, Olene expected him to take the trash that had been accumulatin all week in the bed of his pickup, to the town dump and after having disposed of the trash, he was to pick up the groceries that she'd written on a list and then come straight home.

Piney heaved the heavy sack of trash onto the top of the pile in the bed of his old truck, opened the door and pulled himself up into the sagging front seat. He slid his knarled, right hand down into the back of the seat cushion beside him and felt for the cold bottle of Narragansett beer that he had stashed there. He smiled to himself as he thought about drinkin the cool brew at the dump and how refreshin it always felt as it slid down his parched throat.

He slid his dirt encrusted work boots along the floor until he found the starter and he stomped on it. The old engine rolled over a couple of times, coughed, spit out a cloud of heavy, black smoke and died. Piney swore out loud, pressed the accelerator to the floor and stomped on the starter again. The smell of gas permeated the cab and Piney coughed as the fumes crawled into his nose and down his throat. Finally, the engine caught and settled into a rough idle. Piney backed carefully out of the garage, slammed the gear into first and the old pickup crawled past his dilapidated house and out into the gravel road in a cloud of blue exhaust. He turned the heavy steering wheel a sharp left and headed down the Masardis Road towards town with the bags rolling around in the bed of his truck and loose bits of trash and paper flying out into the road behind him.

He slowed to a crawl as he neared Jimmo's Market and continued on up Main Street towards the next intersection. He slid his old, blood-shot eyes towards Sealey's Diner as his protruding stomach grumbled beneath his worn out leather belt. Olene used to make him wonderful breakfasts when they'd first gotten married, but as the years passed, she'd somehow forgotten that a man still needed to eat. "I'll stop there and git myself a good, big breakfast on my way back," he promised himself as he drove on by the empty diner.

When he reached the intersection of Main and School Streets, he paused for a couple of seconds, looked right and left and then he drove through the empty intersection down over the hill towards the dump that was located outside of Sheridan jist before the Catholic Cemetery.

Upon nearin the dump, he wrenched the steering wheel a hard left and turned the truck onto the dirt road that led to the dump and it wasn't too long before he was starin at a huge pile of trash. He followed the pot hole filled road around to the back of the pile and jerked to a stop. He looked around him and all he saw was ripped, plastic bags of trash, broken furniture and other people's junk. He always parked in the same spot every time he came because the huge trash pile shielded him from view when he wanted to drink his beer and smoke a cigarette.

Piney shoved his stubby fingers down into the back of the seat cushion, grabbed the neck of the beer bottle, pulled it out and got out of the truck. He walked slowly around to the back of the pickup, wrenched open the tailgate and pulled it down. Then he hefted himself up onto the rusting, green metal and sat down. He pried the cap off the bottle, took a long pull of the cold beer and set it down next to him on the tailgate. Feelin warm, he unbuttoned his red and black wool jacket and fished around inside until he'd located his crumpled pack of Camel cigarettes in his shirt pocket. He shook one out, stuck it in his mouth and lit it. He sucked the strong, yellow smoke deep into his lungs until they protested and he coughed as the smoke curled out of his mouth and up past his nose. His eyes watered and he wiped his scratchy, woolen cuff across them. "Jist like coffee," he thought to himself. "Tha first cigarette of the day is always tha best!"

He sat there in the wintery sunshine nursin his beer and smokin for the longest while. He usually spent his Saturdays this way because he didn't have any place else to go and Olene sure as hell didn't want him at home. He'd sit on his tailgate and watch the wispy clouds as they drifted silently across the clear blue northern sky or he'd count the crows as they flew from branch to branch on the many trees that ringed the dump. Sometimes, he'd see small creatures as they scuttled from one mound of trash to another, lookin for food or a place to hide.

He lifted the beer bottle, drained the last bit of amber liquid into his mouth, took the empty bottle and heaved it towards the vast pile of trash. Then he stubbed out his cigarette butt on the tailgate and slid off the end of the truck. He turned, reached into the bed of the truck and grabbed the first bag of trash and grunting, heaved it towards the large mound in front of him. His bag hit about halfway up the side of the pile and slid down until it rested on the ground. He drug out the remaining bags from the bed of his pickup and heaved them in the same general direction until his truck bed was empty. He picked up his cigarette stub, dropped it to the ground and jist to be sure it was out, ground it into the dirt with the heel of his boot. Then he turned and started past the rear fender and headed for the cab.

Suddenly, he heard the clinking of bottles in the pile of trash and the sound of the mound of debris being moved in the pile behind him. The hair on the nape of his neck stood up and he turned jist in time to see the large mountain of trash slide in his direction. He couldn't believe his eyes! Something was underneath the pile of trash and it was movin slowly towards him!

He stumbled towards the cab and scrabbled for the rusted door handle. The door screeched open and jist as he was about to lift his foot onto the running board, he saw something appear behind him in the small side view mirror. When the large black image that he'd jist seen reflected in the mirror slid onto his brain, the wind was sucked out of his congested lungs. "That couldn't be what I think I saw," he said to himself as he looked into the mirror again. But there it was! Standing on its two hind feet was the biggest, blackest bear that he'd ever seen. It stood where it was, surrounded by trash, not movin, jist sniffin the air to get his scent and direction.

Piney didn't move an inch as he slid his watery brown eyes to the small mirror again and took another look. His old heart did all kinds of things that it had never done before and he was breathin in short, quick gasps. His addled mind was tryin to grasp the situation. The bear was only about ten feet away and Piney knew that it could cover that distance to him in a very quick manner. The seconds ticked away and Piney ran through his mind all the terrible things that could happen to him. He couldn't outrun a bear and there wasn't another living soul around to hear him, even if he yelled for help.

"I'll jist slide into the truck, slam the door and take tha hell off!" he thought to himself. He slowly lifted his right boot up onto the running board and jist as he started to pull his heavy bulk up into the cab, he heard the bear movin quickly through the debris behind him.

He gasped and tried to pull himself up into the seat, but his body wouldn't cooperate. His legs had turned to jelly and his foot fell back to the ground and he began to tremble. He shot a look at the side view mirror again and what he saw caused him to lose control of his bowels. Hot, sticky matter slid out of his underwear, down his legs into his boots. The bear was moving towards him and it was nearly at the end of the tailgate. Suddenly, Piney remembered the old gun that was tucked out of sight behind the front seat. He couldn't remember when he'd last used it and he couldn't even remember if it was loaded.

The bear stopped about four feet away from Piney and again lifted itself up on its hind legs and stood there casting a long, dark shadow over him. Piney slowly turned and saw that the creature was lookin at him with eyes the same color as his. Somehow this thought caused him to laugh and the dry, hacking sound filled the air as Piney tried to gain control of himself. Sweat ran down his face and the bear turned its head back and forth as it smelled his fear and what had happened in his pants.

Piney slowly slid his right hand behind the seat until he felt the stock of the gun fill his hand. He carefully pulled the gun out, cocked it and turned around. At the sound of the click, the bear turned its head and looked directly at him. Piney quickly brought the gun up to chest level; he didn't bother to aim because he knew that he couldn't miss at such close range. He didn't think that he could kill it, but maybe he could wound it jist enough to give him time to get into the truck and get away.

The bear, sensing the danger, dropped down and started towards him. Piney pulled the trigger and he saw the path of the bullet as it split the skin on the top of the bear's skull. The bear screamed in pain, shook its massive head as though it had been stung by a bee, growled low in its throat and hurled itself across the short distance that separated it from Piney.

Piney held the empty gun out in front of him for protection and gasped as he felt the long, claws tear into his legs and suddenly he smelled the bear's putrid breath as it reared up on its hind legs directly in front of him. The bear cuffed the useless gun out of Piney's hands like it was a toy and knocked him to the ground. It drew back it's large paw and hit Piney on the side of his head. Piney felt the burning pain as the yellow claws dug into his head and the skin on the side of his head was ripped from his skull!

The bear grabbed the back of Piney's wrinkled, scrawny neck in it huge jaws and sank its long, yellow carnivore teeth into him. He screamed as the bear raked it claws down through the back of his woolen jacket and into the skin on his back. His last living memory was of searing pain as the bear swiftly disemboweled him.

The bear stayed a long time beside Piney's lifeless form, sniffing him, giving him a slap every now and then and nudging him with its head. When the bear was convinced that its enemy was no longer a threat, it wiped a bloody paw across its eyes jist the way that Piney had done earlier in the day.

As the sun began its slow descent into the tree line on the Garfield side of the western horizon, the bear gave Piney a last, long sniff, reared up on its hind legs, looked all around, dropped back down on all four feet and ambled slowly off towards the trees, the Aroostook River and the coming darkness.

As night began to fall, Olene, agitated, pissed off and angry because Piney hadn't returned with her groceries, finally called around town to see if she could find him. It wasn't until later the next morning, when someone else taking their trash to the dump, that Piney was found, half buried under a mound of trash. The finder, screamed when he saw the terrible sight, scuttled out of the dump and went running up the Sheridan Road towards Ashland as though the devil himself was after him.

What was left of poor old Piney was gathered up, given a Christian ceremony and buried in the Catholic Cemetery next to the dump. Folks thought it was an ironic ending that after bragging and lying about all the huge bears that he's seen, shot at, or professed to having killed in his life time, he never got to tell the story of his real encounter with the biggest bear he'd ever seen. "Sometimes," folks said, "life's like that...."

THA POACHER

Sonny Campbell was a game warden and his father and grandfather before him had been wardens. It was often thought by folks around town that there wasn't any way that Sonny could have been anything else. After all, hadn't his great, great grandfather been one of those Campbell's who'd come from the area over around New Brunswick and his grandfather looked exactly like the pictures of the Indians in all the history books. There isn't a better game warden than a man with a little Injin blood now is there and everyone knew that if you came from over that way, you had to have some Micmac or Maliseet Indian blood in you.

Sonny still lived in the house where he was born, that his grandfather had built at the turn of the century. The old Campbell place was located on the Garfield Road in Garfield Plantation and it was built in a very strategic spot high up on a bluff that overlooked the rolling Aroostook County country side for miles around.

All Sonny had to do was stand out on his crumbling front porch and look down across the open fields and he could see the Aroostook River where it lay like leaden silver in the late afternoon sun. Hearing gunshots, he'd cock his head, listen intently and after a couple of minutes he could pretty much tell you where the gunshots came from, the caliber of gun and most probably who had done the shooting too.

Sonny wasn't really a large man. He stood about five feet ten in his stocking feet, but he hadn't an ounce of fat on him. He had a shock of thick, black hair that strayed out from under his warden's hat no matter how he combed or cut it. His pupils were deep brown and the whites of his eyes had a bluish tinge to them and it didn't matter if it was summer or winter; his skin had a mahogany cast to it that never changed with the seasons. His most prominent feature was his nose though. It was the

117

thing that one noticed first about his features. Folks often said that if you turned Sonny sideways and looked at his profile, it looked exactly like the Indian on the old Indian head nickel.

His only companions in the decrepit old house were a mangy Maine Coon cat and a Blue Tick hound named Percy that someone had left to die up in the woods on the old Realty Road. Sonny had brought the dog home and nursed it back to health and there were times when he deeply regretted keeping Percy. On nights jist before the full moon, the hound would sit out on the front porch and bay until it nearly drove him and the neighbors crazy.

After the neighbors had complained for the umpteenth time about the dog keeping them up all night, Sonny would keep a close eye on the moon. When it was due to be full, he'd herd Percy into the warden's truck and take him for a long drive up into the Great Northern woods where there wasn't another living soul around to disturb. Sometimes though, he'd run into folks who were camping and after a night in the woods, the campers would come back to town and laugh about the crazy game warden and the howling dog. They said he spent the night driving up and down the deserted timber roads while his dog lolled his head out the window of his truck and bayed at the moon.

Sometimes, he'd pitch a tent and spend the night. Once, Sonny made a mistake and the moon wasn't full until the next night, but the hound didn't care. He slept straight through the first night without a single howl and began howling right on cue with the full moon, the next. There jist wasn't any fooling that dog. Percy's howl began deep in his throat at a very low pitch and gradually climbed into the higher range until it ended on a note that set your last teeth right on edge. The sound could make someone who wasn't used to it or had never heard a hound dog howl before, very nervous and jumpy especially, when you've left your nice snug home in suburbia and driven five hundred miles into the northern Maine woods with nary a sign of civilization anywhere.

A lot of campers checked out of their camp sites earlier than they intended the day after the full moon when they'd heard Percy's howling all night. It was usually the out-of-staters that the howling affected the most. The gatekeepers knew that the morning after a full moon, they were going to be asked a lot of questions about what kind of animal might have caused that howling. Mostly, the gatekeepers blamed the howling on a wolf or coyote.

One gatekeeper told of how he'd overheard one camper talking to another as they were getting ready to leave. "I really don't know what the hell it was or what it wasn't, but you can be God-damned sure, I ain't never coming back! When I heard that sound, I was so scared, my testicles crawled up inside my belly and I may never see them again!"

Sonny was well-known and respected by all those who knew him because he had the reputation of being fair and that carried a lot of weight in our neck of the woods. A game warden actually has more power under the law than a policeman, but Sonny didn't abuse it. He worked twenty-four hours a day, seven days a week. He loved his job and didn't really consider it work.

Sonny was also known for his even-tempered disposition. It took a lot to get him riled and most folks couldn't recall the last time they'd ever seen him angry. There was one thing that made Sonny angry though, and that was a poacher.

Sonny might look the other way if he caught a hunter hunting out of season, especially if that hunter was simply trying to feed his family. He was even known to look the other way when he caught a bunch of kids fishing without a license, but there was one thing that he wouldn't overlook and that was poaching. He hated poachers who killed jist for the sake of killing and left the animal there to rot. He would go to any means to catch them.

The notorious Keen family was the one that took up most of Sonny's official time as a game warden. He was always chasin one or another of them for various infractions of the law. Personally, he would have liked to gather them all up and put them on a slow boat to China, he was so sick of dealin with them.

The Keens all congregated in the same little area called Squa Pan which was located about halfway between Ashland and Masardis. Their homes consisted of several shacks and many rusty trailers, which were in a continual state of disrepair. It wasn't uncommon to see kids, dogs, chickens and pigs all erupting from someone's doorway. There were so many kids that most of the mothers only clearly remembered the names of their first-born and who their father's were. It didn't really matter anyway because the kids ate and slept wherever they were when it was time to eat or go to bed.

They didn't have running water, but they sometimes had electricity which was usually around the first of the month after their AFDC, Unemployment, Disability or Social Security checks arrived. The first things they bought were whiskey, cigarettes and beer. Whatever money left over was squandered on whatever whim they had that week.

The local cops used to dread the beginning of the month. They knew that sooner or later there was going to be a call from a pissed-off citizen that there was a problem at the Keens. The Keen trip was usually designated to the newest rookie in the area. He'd turn on his lights and siren and come tearing down the Masardis Road around eighty miles an hour and pull to a screeching halt in front of the rundown dwellings. He'd hop out of his vehicle, stride to the nearest shack, trailer or shanty and demand to know what tha hell was going on. Keens of all shapes and sizes would come pouring out of the shacks and trailers. When they saw it was the law, they'd usually throw whatever was handy at the poor cop. Overwhelmed and outnumbered, the rookie would high tail it back down the Masardis Road at the same clip he had jist driven up it, hoping like hell that he'd never have to return again, at least for a while.

Even though none of the Keens worked at a regular job, they wanted for nothing. If you happened to drive by their place on any given day, you'd find their yards filled with all kinds of expensive recreational equipment. They all drove new pick-ups with long antennas for the latest CB's and they had new snowmobiles strewn around everywhere. There were color television antennas sticking up on poles all around the shacks.

Out behind the settlement were several banged up skidders and bulldozers jist rustin away. They had the latest in hunting rifles and there were a couple of expensive Old Town canoes rotting away in the knee-high grass along the road. Several newer ATV's, in various states of disrepair, lay on the grease stained, beer bottle littered ground in front of the trailers.

Roger Keen usually stayed with his elderly father when he was home. From time to time, he'd shacked-up with several women in the area, but he didn't want to have to pay child support so, he never stayed with anyone too long. It was no secret that our town poacher was Roger Keen and he made no bones about it either. Each and every time he broke the law and got away with it, he'd drive like a bat-out-of hell, down the bumpy Masardis Road to Ashland to boast and brag about what he'd jist done.

Roger hadn't attended any school long enough to really say that he'd gone to school. He came from a long line of non-attendees. Folks used to say that the Keen kid's aversion to school was something hereditary and there was no use bothering with them. The whole Keen clan didn't do anything like "normal" people did. They didn't work, they didn't clean, they didn't go to church, and they didn't marry. But there were a lot of things that they did do. They smoked, they drank, they stole, they lied and they cheated. There were so many kids by so many different women that one couldn't tell one kid from another. If the law had to call on the Keens because one of them had broken the law, usually the cops jist gave up. The kids were so close in age and some even had the same first names or nicknames that one really couldn't be certain jist which Keen they were looking for.

Sonny and Roger had been adversaries for a long time. It irked the hell out of Sonny to have to drive through town and hear all the stories from the old codgers about how the poacher had bagged another one. Everyone, including Sonny, knew who the poacher was, but knowing it and proving it was another thing. Try as he might, Sonny hadn't been able to pin anything on Roger. He'd even pulled a surprise search on old man Keen's house and nothing had turned up. He'd taken to stopping Roger every time he'd had a chance and a good excuse and still couldn't find where he was hiding the poached goods. Sonny was beside himself, there had to be something he'd overlooked.

Sonny was a damned-good game warden. What with his Indian blood and all the knowledge from his years in the north Maine woods, he couldn't understand why he couldn't catch his man. Every time Sonny heard another poaching story involving Roger, his guts burned and shriveled up inside him until he couldn't stand it. He'd lie awake night after night and try to put himself inside Roger's head to think like him, but nothin helped.

Roger still went his merry way and every time the two of them passed on the road, they would slow down and glare at each other. Roger, with a big smirk on his face, would give Sonny the old middle finger salute, laugh right in his face and drive on by.

Sonny finally caved in and asked his boss if he had any ideas about how to catch that friggin poacher. After hearing the entire story, the Superintendant of Wardens laughed, shook his head and said, "What makes you think you're so special? I tried to catch his father, old man Keen, for many years and I was outsmarted for a long time too. I did finally catch him, but I've never told anyone where I finally found tha poached bundles of meat and fish." Sonny looked at him and waited. His boss looked out the window for a couple of minutes and then he said, "Old man Keen's mother was sick abed and when he saw me coming, he took everything out of the freezer, went in and lifted her up and hid everything under her legs." "Well," Sonny asked, "How'd you know it was hidden there?" "Well, it was a Christly hot day and that room must have been a hundred and ten and the old lady kept complainin that she was friggin cold! It took me a good while to figure it out. Jist remember one thing, when you're dealin with that kind of mind, expect tha unexpected!"

What used to be a desire to catch the poacher now became an obsession. Sonny's plots and schemes and plans took up all his time and energy. He was like a general preparing for battle. He drew maps and diagrams of the surrounding areas that Roger was known to frequent. He bought all kinds of military equipment from the Army Surplus Store over to Presque Isle. He sent away for a night vision scope for his rifle. He tore the engine out of his warden's pick-up and replaced it with a suped-up engine from Fenton's Junkyard in Presque Isle. He changed the suspension on the warden's truck until the truck was jacked-up off the ground by about two feet. He scouted around until he found four oversized all terrain tires and mounted them on his truck. Then he drove over to Loring Air Force Base and purchased a beacon runway light that he attached to a portable generator in the back of his pickup. When he flicked it on, the illuminated area lit-up like a light from hell. Then, he drove to Fort Kent and wrangled a winch out of another warden and they welded it to the undercarriage of the vehicle. The green, state of Maine warden's truck now looked like a modified military Humvee.

Now he was ready! Sonny loaded old Percy into the truck, slapped his warden's hat on his head and turned the key. The engine shuddered and caught with an ear deafening roar as black smoke poured out of the two chrome pipes running up the back of the cab. When Sonny downshifted into low range the huge engine purred like a contented cat from the jungle.

Sonny tore out of his driveway and down the Garfield Road so fast that the power of the engine caused old Percy to fall backwards in the seat. Percy, not used to being treated this way, shot Sonny a look of pure venom, and then he crawled off the seat and lay on the floor with his head between his paws. Every time Sonny tore around a sharp corner, Percy emitted a loud howl and dug himself deeper into the floor mat.

Sonny crossed the bridge into Ashland at an illegal rate of speed, then he floored the truck as he came up over Station Hill. As he approached the Inland Fisheries and Wildlife offices, he slowed down a dite, made a sharp right and ground to a stop in front of the building. Upon hearing all the noise, the other wardens came flying out to see what the hell was going on.

Sonny strode past them into his office. "Jaysus Sonny, what the hell have yah done to your truck?" One of the wardens asked him. "That's for me tah know and for you tah find out," was the curt reply. Sonny stuffed his ten-cell flashlight and some extra clothes into his knapsack and went back out to his truck. He wheeled out of the driveway and straight up over tha hill to Main Street. He drove slowly down the Main Street of Ashland and folks, hearin tha sound of his truck; rushed out of tha stores to see what tha hell kind of vehicle was makin all that noise.

When Sonny reached the intersection of the Presque Isle Road and the Masardis Road, he kicked the truck into high and for the first time in his life, left black marks on the tar behind him. He flew down the Masardis Road with the speedometer hovering around seventy. He slowed to a crawl as he came upon the Keen settlement and when he reached old Mr. Keen's house he stopped and gunned the engine a couple of times. Black smoke roiled out of the chrome pipes and drifted upwards in the clear, blue sky.

Heads popped out of every door and window to see what was making that sound. He gunned the massive motor a couple of times more jist for good effect. "That ought tah do it!" he grinned to himself. "It shouldn't take too long before tha friggin news gets around. I'm the warden and I mean business! Tha shit is really goin to fly this time!" He patted old Percy on the head to stop his trembling and headed home to Garfield.

Sonny stuck pretty close to home for the next couple of days hopin to hear something and when he couldn't stand it any longer, he headed for town to see what the latest news was. He stepped off the porch and snapped his fingers at Percy, who was lying at the far end. Percy lifted his mangy, old head and looked at him. "Come on old feller, want ta go for a ride?" Sonny asked the dog. The hound dropped his head onto his paws and didn't move a muscle. No matter what Sonny did, Percy couldn't be persuaded.

Sonny hitched up his pants, climbed up into his super-charged truck and turned on the ignition. The engine caught with a mighty roar and a cloud of black smoke permeated the air behind him. Percy, still lying on the porch commenced to howling like he never had before. His howls blended with the whine of Sonny's engine and he looked at the dog in amazement. As Sonny pulled the truck out onto the Garfield Road he looked in his rearview mirror and all he could see was Percy slinking off into the woods at the side of the house.

Sonny glanced up and caught his reflection in the mirror and he was shocked at what he saw. His black hair was sticking out of his hat in every direction and his brown eyes shone like two bits of coal in the moonlight. Sonny decided that it was jist about time to get his ears lifted and he headed down the road for town.

He rolled down the Main Street in Ashland and came to a stop in front of Philbert's Barber Shop. The sight of his suped-up truck caused all of Philbert's reluctant patrons to come rushing outside. Sonny elbowed his way into the shop and sat down in the empty barber's chair.

Old Philbert turned his watery blue eyes on Sonny and asked, "What'll it be sonny?" Not waiting for an answer, he rambled on, "Say, are yah new in town?" Sonny knew it was hopeless to try and explain anything to Philbert and he said, "Cut it the same way you always do, Philbert, only, I'd like two sideburns this time instead of one."

Hearing the muffled snickers and snorts from the other customers at

Sonny's reply and feeling that somehow he'd been insulted, old Philbert commenced to cutting with a vengeance. He zoomed up one side of Sonny's head and down the other with his electric razor. Sunny felt a tightening in his belly as thick black hair flew in every direction and he began sweating jist a little. When he finally dared to look at his reflection in the mirror, he couldn't believe his eyes! For the very first time in his life he had a Mohawk! Sonny ripped the barber's apron from around his neck and threw it on the floor. "For good Christ's sake! Philbert, you've really done it this time!" Sonny bellowed. "Look at me!" Old Philbert shuffled as close as he dared and ran his watery eyes over Sonny's head. "Don't see nothin wrong with your hair. If you ask me, it coulda been a little shorter! And besides, you moved!" old Philbert shot back defiantly.

Hearing the commotion inside the shop, all the hanger-ons crowded through the door to get a whiff of what had jist happened. There was dead silence as they looked at Sonny's head. The nostrils in Sonny's large nose flared and the anger he felt inside came through as two red patches warmed themselves up on his high cheekbones.

He didn't wait to hear any comments. He pushed past the gaping onlookers and stalked over to his vehicle. He hitched himself up into his truck and the last thing he heard as he drove away was, "Jaysus, Philbert, you've turned tha game warden into a friggin Comanche!"

Now that his truck was ready, Sonny commenced to set a trap to catch the poacher. He didn't eat and he didn't sleep. He spent night after night sitting at his kitchen table. He tried to coax old Percy into the house to eat, but the old hound came as far as the screen door of the kitchen and after one look at Sonny's hair, let out a blood curdling howl, turned around and high tailed it back into the woods.

Sonny slowly began baiting his trap. He let it be known around town that there had been some poaching up along the Canadian border and he'd be staying up to Churchill Lake for a while. He figured that this ought to trickle down to Roger and sooner or later, he'd let his guard down and Sonny would finally have his man.

Sonny examined every map he could find of the areas that Roger was known to hunt. He tried to put himself in the poacher's shoes to try and determine jist what spot he might choose next. Sonny circled some spots on his map and decided that he'd give these areas a try. He knew that poachers liked to strike jist at dusk, or in the wee hours of the morning. If he was going to catch Roger, he had to start thinking like him. He decided that first he'd have a little look at the area behind the Keen settlement to see if Roger was still hanging out there.

Around four o'clock that afternoon, Sonny doused himself with the tried and true fly dope, "The Woodsman's Friend," pulled on his old army fatigues and drove down to Rafford flats, which were located about a mile behind the Keen's settlement. He locked his truck, picked up his heavy knapsack and started off through the woods. He moved carefully as the trailers and shacks came into view and he slipped his gear off his back and hid it in some bushes. Then, he dropped and began crawling on his belly through the waist high grass towards the shacks.

As he crawled closer, Sonny noticed that off to his right behind old man Keen's shack was a newer looking outhouse. It wasn't the run-of-the-mill-outhouse either. Looking at it from the rear, Sonny noticed that a great deal of attention had been spent on the small building. Not only did it have a cinder block foundation, it also had electricity! "Leave it to tha Keens tah think of that," thought Sonny. "They're probably the only people in the whole state of Maine who have an outhouse with electricity!" He maneuvered himself around the other outhouses until he had what he thought was the optimal view. Then, he settled down to wait.

The long night slid into a day and a half and Sonny, bleary eyed, bug bitten and hungry, roused himself so that he could watch the comings and goings of the Keens. Sonny had been on many stake outs during his career in the warden's service, but this had to be one of the most miserable of all. It was now the middle of June and every conceivable insect that the northern woods are infamous for, was now feasting on his tired, dirty body.

He'd hidden in the tall grass not daring to move for the better part of two days and he'd lain awake for the past two nights and nothing had happened to arouse his suspicions. The only thing he'd noticed was that Roger or his elderly father made frequent hurried trips to the newer outhouse behind his father's shack. "Must be having a touch of tha runs," Sonny chuckled to himself. "Maybe some of that poached meat was jist a little rancid when he finally cooked it." It made Sonny feel a little better to think that his prey wasn't faring any better than he was.

He was sun burned, wind burned and so bitten by insects that he could barely see out of his eyes. The fly dope he'd slathered all over himself jist plain didn't work and the smell, a mixture between tar and kerosene, was making him sick. He had bug bites all over his body and his skin twitched as he stifled an intense urge to scratch. His ears rang from all the noise the kids made as they played around their shacks. His heart had leapt into his throat a couple of times, when some of the kids began playing hide and seek in the tall grass around the rusted vehicles and he knew it wouldn't be too long before they made their way in his direction. Sonny decided he'd give it another twenty-four hours and if something didn't happen pretty soon, he'd slink off home to recover for a few days.

As the sun sank out of sight and the mosquitoes and no-see-ems began their nightly onslaught, Sonny crawled a little closer to the outhouse to get a better look at the building. "Funny," he thought to himself, "There's no smell and no flies either." As the moon came up over the ridge behind him, the door at the rear of the shack opened and Roger came out and headed towards him, down the path to the outhouse. Sonny flattened his tired body against the ground and tried not to breathe as Roger passed by within a few feet from where he lay.

The poacher opened the door of the outhouse, turned the light on and stepped inside. He left the door ajar and Sonny heard what sounded like another door being opened and closed. Then Roger turned off the light, stepped outside and closed the door. It was then that Sonny noticed the heavy bundle that swung to and fro in Roger's hand as he made his way back up the path to the shack. "Now ain't that odd." He thought to himself. "That's got to be tha first time that I've seen a man go to take a crap and come out of tha outhouse carrying a bundle."

It took a few minutes for all this to sink in and then, Sonny realized what he'd jist seen and it wasn't too long before the tantalizing smell of poached deer meat, cooking in a bed of fried onions, wafted across the tall grass to where Sonny lay. His mouth began to water and his stomach constricted as the aroma reminded him jist how long it had been, since he'd last eaten.

Along about midnight, all the lights in the settlement finally went out and when he was certain that everyone was asleep, he slowly crawled over to the small building. He stood and quietly turned the door handle and the door opened. He didn't need to turn on a light to know that this wasn't really an outhouse. As his eyes grew accustomed to the dark, he saw that there wasn't any toilet seat either. In its place was a large, shiny, upright freezer.

He stepped inside and opened the freezer door and Sonny smiled for the first time in two days as his tired, bloodshot eyes slid over the neat packages of poached fish and meat lying on the shelves. He carefully closed the freezer door and stepped out into the warm summer night. Suddenly, the bone tiredness he'd felt jist a few minutes before, slid away like dust in the moonlight. All his aches, pains and itches were gone! He felt fine! He felt wonderful! He'd finally caught his man!

As he loped off through the tall grass towards his truck and home, all he could think about was how he'd been out smarted by an outhouse. He could jist imagine the flack he was going to catch when all the other game wardens and old cronies around town finally got wind of the shithouse that wasn't....

THA FISHING POLE

Our great Uncle Hal had a fishing pole that he treasured beyond anything else. He'd saved his money for a long time and finally, when he had enough, he'd sent all the way down to "L. L. Beans" in Freeport to get it.

Two weeks later, when it finally arrived, we all gathered around to see this wonder of wonders. Uncle Hal was jist as excited as we were and we crowded closer as he withdrew it section by section from its case.

He slowly and lovingly began assembling his precious fishing pole. Finally, he had it all together and he made a few tentative casts around the room. The fishing line whistled and snickered as it snaked through the air and dropped to the kitchen floor exactly where he wanted. As he quickly rewound the line, Uncle Hal's face shone with joy as he imagined himself casting his line into the rapidly moving water of the Aroostook River.

It was still two weeks away from the official opening of fishing season in "Tha County" and Uncle Hal was chafing at the bit. He was ready! He knew that this was going to be the year! He was going to catch the biggest, most beautiful trout that had ever been caught in the Aroostook River.

The long awaited day finally arrived and Uncle Hal jumped out of bed at the crack of the crack, pulled his pants on over his union suit and padded swiftly down the stairs. His head was heady with the thought that he was finally going to try out his new fishing pole.

He hurried down the stairs, through the parlor and into the kitchen. He walked over to the kitchen windows and pulled aside the curtain and stared in the direction of the island. The eastern sun was jist coming up and it glinted off the flood-covered land. "That friggin water ought to have dropped enough for me to get down to the island okay," he thought to himself as he dropped the curtain back into place and hurried to make some breakfast.

With trembling hands, he lit his first Camel cigarette of the day and impatiently blew on his steaming cup of coffee to cool it. He again ran his fishing list that he'd made the night before, through his mind. He wanted to be certain that he wasn't forgetting anything.

He dug his old watch out of his pocket and glanced at it. It read five ten a.m. "Time's ah-wastin!" He thought to himself as he dumped his coffee cup into the sink. He slapped his faded, sweat-stained Ford hat on the back of his baldhead and grabbed his fishing gear. The house shook as he slammed the door and headed down the back stairs with his fishing stuff out to his truck.

He carefully placed his new fishing pole on the front seat beside him and dumped the rest of his gear into the back of the pickup. He switched on the ignition and the engine of the old truck coughed once or twice and died. He pumped the gas pedal impatiently several times and swore his usual blue streak of swear words out into the cool morning air, this was one thing he hadn't thought of.

After several more tries the engine finally roared to life and blue-black smoke rolled out of the exhaust and filled the air around Uncle Hal. He revved the engine a few more times jist for good measure and then he slammed the truck into gear. With a screech of tires, the old Ford lurched forward and he roared off down the circular gravel driveway around the back of the barn till he hit the dirt road.

Uncle Hal was notorious for his poor driving and his driving was often the topic of discussion around town. People would say things to each other like, "I saw old Sutherland go by on tha way to town tha other day." "Oh yah, well, which side of the road was he driving on?" The older he got, the worse his driving became and today was no exception!

On this particular morning, he didn't even see the road. He didn't see anything, but the huge trout he was going to catch. He flew at breakneck speed across the Bangor and Aroostook railroad tracks and down the muddy road to the flats, through the hub high water towards the bridge. When he finally reached his destination, he slammed on the brakes and the truck slid to a stop in the muddy water jist short of the makeshift bridge. He hopped down out of the truck with the lightness that belied his sixty-odd years and headed toward his favorite fishing spot.

Uncle Hal was very good to us kids. He gave us spending money, he gave us jobs. He picked us up and took us to town whenever we wanted to go. He brought us home from basketball games and dances and he taught us to say all of his favorite swear words at a very early age. There wasn't too much Uncle Hal wouldn't or didn't do for us. But, there was one thing that we knew we shouldn't mess with and that was his fishin gear.

The bridge that crossed the Aroostook River was a temporary affair. Uncle Hal had built the bridge so that he could cultivate his potatoes on the island that the Aroostook River ran around. The bridge was made out of a couple of railroad ties and long planks that were jist wide enough to hold the wheels of the tractor and sprayer. This makeshift bridge usually washed out every spring when the river flooded over his island and Uncle Hal would have to rebuild it all over again.

He settled himself carefully on his favorite perch on the end of a railroad tie and began threading a pale angle worm on his hook. He sat there hour after hour, smoking one endless Camel cigarette after another, cursing and swatting at numerous insects. He'd pick at the small black sore on his lower lip, that kept growing larger each year, and curse loudly at the never-ending onslaught of mosquitoes, midges and no-see-ems that kept finding a way up his sleeve or down his wrinkled neck. But, he never got tired of fishing. He jist knew that he was going to catch a big one and it was going to happen this year because of his wonderful new "L. L. Bean" fishing pole.

He'd smoke one cigarette after another and when one pack was empty, he'd heave the package into the swirling water, then he'd fish around in his pockets until he'd found another. Every now and then, he'd cuss like hell when he'd see a large fish come up and check out the cigarette butt that he'd jist flicked into the fast moving current. The fish would come up next to the butt, look it over, roll its beautiful white belly into the sunlight and with a flick of its majestic sliver tail, it'd be gone, leaving Uncle Hal all the more determined that he was going to catch that friggin fish!

When he felt the call of nature, he'd slip the end of his precious rod under the railroad tie, weigh it down with a good sized rock, scramble up off his perch and head for the nearest bushes. He always prayed that he didn't have to do anything too serious while his tuther end was so exposed and vulnerable because he hated to give all those insects such an unprotected target.

Sometimes, in his haste to get his clothes pulled back up, a couple of mosquitoes or no-see-ems would get trapped inside his underwear. And it wasn't too long before he'd be doing a little dance all around the river bank while the imprisoned insects played hell with his scrawny, white bottom.

Uncle Hal would resolutely sit on his perch about ten feet above the swiftly moving river until he had no choice, but to go home. When the sun had slid below the horizon and he couldn't see to fish any longer, he'd carefully and lovingly disassemble his precious fishing pole and put it into its case. Then, he'd slide the case into a small crevice he'd scooped out under the railroad ties.

Uncle Hal had thought long and hard about how he was going to hide his new fishing pole from other fishermen and us kids, in particular. "I'll be back in tha morning right after I make a flying trip to Presque Isle to get some parts for my tractor," he told himself as he pushed the fishing case under the railroad ties. Then he wearily made his way up the flats towards home.

We could easily see the island from our front porch windows and we waited impatiently over the next few days for the rest of the flood water to recede. It was a rule in our house that we weren't allowed to go fishing till the water had gone down off Uncle Hal's flats. On this particular morning, the sun was a red fire ball in the eastern sky and school was out. Tired of our harassment and cajoling, mother simply opened the kitchen door, pointed towards the dirt road and said, "Git!" We and we were off. We arrived at the bridge in a fever of excitement. The four of us looked at the rushing, swirling black water and babbled excitedly to each other about all the fish we were going to catch.

Our fishing equipment was rudimentary to say the least. Jake had a "real" pole with a crooked reel, hook, line and sinker. I had a pole with no reel, but I did have a line and sinker. Bub had a stick tied to a line with a hook and a bobber. Helen, who was deathly afraid of all kinds of insects, including worms, got to hold a rusty tobacco can full of them.

Time passed slowly and we didn't get one bite. Not one! Jake scuttled over the railroad ties and settled himself into Uncle Hal's favorite spot right on the very edge of the railroad tie. He dropped his line into the turbulent Aroostook River water and waited. He sat there for quite a while without a bite and he complained loudly and often that dad's predictions that the fish weren't biting because the water was still too high and too cold must be true.

Suddenly, something in the high, black current caught his eye and he leaned over the edge of the railroad tie to have a closer look at the swirling water. As he leaned forward, he saw the end of Uncle Hal's fishing pole case stored carefully under the makeshift bridge. Jake let out a whoop and chucked his old pole onto the green grass at the edge of the bridge. He snaked his left hand down under the railroad ties and withdrew Uncle Hal's new pole from its hiding spot. He quickly reassembled the pole and cautiously threaded a fresh worm onto the hook. He wiped his dirty, sweating hands on his jeans and in one swift motion, swung the pole back over his head and snapped the line forward as hard as he could. The fishing line sang as it spun out of the shiny new reel and down, down until it disappeared into the swirling river current.

Satisfied with his first cast with Uncle Hal's pole, Jake happily settled himself on the railroad tie to await his first bite. Every now and then, he'd give the line a little jerk and the red and white bobber would dip and bob in the fast-moving water, but no fish came to his bait.

We weren't too scared that Uncle Hal might come home unexpectedly and catch us using his pole because we could readily look up and see his house and anything that was going on clear up the road to our house. Any vehicle coming down the Goding Road left a tell tale sign of dust that quickly alerted us to the fact that someone was coming. We'd know immediately if he drove out of his driveway to come fishing.

Time moved slowly and we didn't talk because Jake believed that the fish could hear us and besides, he'd swat us if we talked too much. The sun grew hotter as it moved up slowly into the clear blue sky of "Tha County." Jake, sitting in the same place for so long in the warm sun, began to doze and he started to fall forward. Suddenly, he let out a yell and nearly fell off the railroad tie. To keep from falling into the river, he let go of the fishing pole and grabbed hold of the railroad tie with both hands. The glorious pole seemed to take on a life of its own and it went sailing down into the fast moving current of the river. Jake stared after the swiftly disappearing pole with a look of horror on his face. His blue eyes bulged out of his head and the mass of brown freckles stood out on his white face like spots on a Leopard's back.

"Oh Jaysus!" "Oh God!" Jake yelled and he stood up and began tearing off his clothes. Oblivious to the fact that it was still early spring and the rushing, swollen water was going to be horribly cold, he kicked off his sneakers and flung himself head long into the cold dark water. He swam frantically along in the swift current trying to locate Uncle Hal's pole, but it was long gone!

Cold and exhausted, he finally swam over to the river bank and pulled himself up out of the icy water. He collapsed onto the green grass of the river bank and lay there shivering in the bright sunlight. We all stood around kicking our feet and trying to come up with an idea that would somehow redeem the situation. Jake lay where he'd landed, shivering uncontrollably, so I went and gathered his clothes and draped them over him.

We finally decided that there was only one thing for us to do and that was to lie. After much arguing, we decided that on our return home, we'd walk along the riverbank until we were out of range of Uncle Hal's house. Then, we'd cut through the Alder swamp jist below Mr. Beaulier's home and follow the Bangor and Aroostook railroad tracks until jist below our house. If mother happened to see us coming up the back way and ask us how our fishing had gone, well, we'd jist tell her that we'd gone down to Beaulier's flats instead of Uncle Hal's. Our huge lie agreed to, we gathered our fishing gear and headed for home as fast as our legs could carry us.

By now it was around ten o'clock in the morning and we knew that Uncle Hal would be coming home soon from his trip to Presque Isle for his tractor parts. Sure enough, it wasn't too long before he came tearing down our dirt road in a cloud of dust. Seeing all of us kids standing on our porch, he tooted and waved as he flew past. We all looked glumly at each other because we knew that it wouldn't be too long before the fishin pole shit hit the fan.

From down below the hill, we could hear the clanking of metal upon metal and the cacophony of swear words that accompanied the work as

Uncle Hal pounded the new part onto his old Farmall tractor. We waited until those sounds ended and time hung long and heavy in the morning air. It wasn't too long before we heard him rev up his old tractor and we watched in horror as the faded red Farmall rounded the driveway and headed towards the bridge. Uncle Hal, oblivious to the fact that he was pulling a fully loaded potato sprayer behind him, went flying down the dirt road towards the island, hell bent for fishin.

Jake ran around to the back of our house and climbed up on the roof. His sneaker clad feet made scrabbling sounds as he scrambled over the rough shingles to the desired spot next to the chimney. He was jist in time to see the tractor and sprayer come to a halt near the bridge. "What's he doing now Jake? We asked. "Don't know," Jake mumbled. "What's he doing Jake?" We screamed. Jake craned his head forward and then he turned and ran down the roof and jumped off. He threw himself down in the long grass behind the house and stared up into the bright blue sky. "He knows it's gone." He said in a hollow voice. Visions of no more candy, no more ice cream, no more rides to basketball games, dances or fairs, no more visitin tha farm and petting tha animals, slipped through our minds again and again.

We hung close to home all that day and still Uncle Hal never approached our house. Mother kept looking at us like she knew that we'd done something, but she didn't have a clue what it was. Finally, when we couldn't stand it any longer, Jake announced that he'd better head down over the hill to Uncle Hal's house to see what was going on. He heaved himself up out of the crab grass, adjusted his pants, and crawled around the corner of the house like a condemned man destined for his execution.

It wasn't too long before Jake was back with good news. His whole demeanor had changed, his blue eyes were shining and he had a huge grin on his face. Aunt Cassie had told him that Uncle Hal was livid. It seemed that Uncle Hal thought some lousy thieving bastard in a canoe had stopped down at the bridge to fish and made off with his new fishing pole. We all looked at each other in disbelief. All of our feverish prayers to tha fishin Gods of the universe had been answered. We weren't even suspects!

Once again, Uncle Hal bought himself another fishing pole from

"L.L. Beans," but it didn't seem to have the same "magic" for him that the other one had. There wasn't a day that passed during fishing season that he didn't mention the theft of that other pole and Aunt Cassie said that he was getting to be a nuisance because he took to stopping every person he came upon, who was fishing around the island, to see if their fishing pole was the one that had been stolen from him.

Spring slid into summer and finally fishing season was over. We all heaved a sigh of relief at the close of summer and once again school occupied most of our spare time. We only thought about the fishing pole a couple of times that winter when we went skating on the very same river that it had fallen into. Jake used to lie down on the frozen river's surface from time to time to see if he could see the pole down in the water, but he never could.

Spring rolled around again, but Uncle Hal didn't seem as keen to go try his luck as he had the previous year. He'd lost all interest in fishing when his precious pole was "stolen." He still left his "new" fishing pole in the same place as the other one, but it remained where it was, we didn't dare touch it. It jist wasn't as tempting as the other one had been.

Then one day, I decided to go fishing by myself. I was sitting on the bridge, in Uncle Hal's favorite spot on the end of the railroad tie, in the bright sunshine when I felt a tug on my line. Excited that I finally had a serious bite, I scrambled back onto the bridge and stood up. I held the pole in one hand and swiftly reeled the line in to see what I'd caught. As I reeled and tugged, I became aware that there was quite a lot of resistance and that I must have caught a rather large fish! As the fish broke the water, I saw that it was the largest trout I'd ever seen! It came up to the top, flashed and roiled in the clear blue water and disappeared again. I tugged harder and it finally came free of the swirling current. The beautiful fish wriggled and jerked trying to free himself as I proceeded to reel him in.

I flipped the large trout over my head onto the grassy bank behind me. Then, I dropped my pole and ran to pick the fish up and began to remove my hook from his mouth. And then I saw it! There was another hook protruding from the fish's mouth and the second hook was all rusty and scar tissue had formed all around it on the fish's lip. I stared at the second hook for the longest moment and then I realized that there was a fishing line still attached to the old hook.

I tossed the wriggling, slippery fish further up the bank and then I started pulling the second line out of the water. It was then that I realized that the line was also attached to something. I pulled and pulled and finally I saw the tip of a fishing pole come up out of the water. I pulled the slimy pole out and wiped it on the grass. It was Uncle Hal's precious fishing pole! It was almost too much to comprehend!

I laid the slippery pole down on the bridge and tried to think what I was going to do. If I took the pole up and gave it to Uncle Hal, then he'd know for sure that we'd been the ones who had taken it. It was then that I decided to throw it back. I stood up and quickly tossed the fishing pole back into the water. Then I scooped up my beautiful trout and headed for home.

As I made my way past Uncle Hal's house, Aunt Cassie spotted me scurrying past with my treasure and she yelled at me out the kitchen window to come and show her my fish. I ran across the lawn and as I got closer, she exclaimed about what a beautiful fish I had. She hefted it in her hand and looked at me with a sly look on her face. "You know Tooter," she said, her crafty brown eyes shifting from me to the fish. "Uncle Hal sure would love to catch one like this and he'd sure love to eat one like this too!" She looked at me keenly and then she said, "Tell you what; I'll give you a dollar a pound for that fish right now! Uncle Hal will love to have this for his supper tonight, especially since you caught it." With that final compliment ringing in my ears and the guilt hanging heavy in my heart, I capitulated.

As I slowly walked up the hill towards home with the money jingling in my pocket, I began to feel a whole lot better. I figured that everything had turned out all right in the end after all. Uncle Hal had the beautiful trout that he'd coveted for so long, I had some spending money and only God and me knew what had really happened to the first "L. L. Bean" fishing pole....

137

PHILBERT

The residents of Aroostook County, Maine generally consider themselves to be conservative by nature, and it usually takes quite a while for new styles and fads to catch on. When the news finally reached Ashland in the early nineteen sixtys that longer hairstyles were "in" for men, the news was greeted with wholehearted enthusiasm. The entire male population heaved a sigh that was equal to a condemned man's relief, when he hears that his death sentence has been rescinded.

The only barber shop in town was located on Main Street in Ashland and it was sandwiched in between Michaud's Restaurant and Bushey's Clothing Store. The barber's name was Philbert and he was nearly seventy years old. At the mere mention of Philbert's name, most of the male population quivered in their boots and headed for their liquor cabinet, the Maine State Liquor Store or the nearest bar.

In his younger days, Philbert was a pretty competent barber, but with advancing age and declining eyesight, he became known as the local menace. Any man, who needed to get a haircut, would usually stop off at Michaud's Restaurant first to fortify his courage with a few bottles of beer or a large shot of whisky before venturing on to the barbershop.

The conversation in the bar tended to run a little like this. "Jaysus Jake, ain't it time you gut your ears lowered?" "Yup, I know. I've been puttin it off as long as I could, but this mornin my old lady told me not tah come home until I gut a haircut." "In that case Jake, let me buy you another beer, you're really gonna need it."

Philbert was a good old guy, but he jist wouldn't admit that he was gettin old and his eyesight wasn't what it used to be. He'd squint at the next customer who was sidling into the crappy old barber's chair and ask his standard question, "What'll it be sonny?" And he never waited for an answer. He'd whip out his electric razor and with a touch that was akin to Braille, zoom up the back of the head two or three times, take a feel of what was left of the left sideburn and grunt as though being satisfied at his latest work. He wouldn't touch the right sideburn at all. He'd then drop his electric razor; grab his rusty scissors and he'd lift some of the hair on the top of the head, snip or as some folks said, pull out most of it by hand, and you were done. He'd whip off the hair encrusted cape, peer intently at the next victim and say, "What'll it be sonny?"

Sometimes, he'd take a long look at the person sitting in the chair and say, "Say, you must be a newcomer around here. I don't think I've seen you in here before." "Jaysus Philbert," the angry customer would reply, "I've lived here all friggin my life. Why don't you git some new glasses?"

Sometimes, Philbert would grab a warped mirror and shove it into the victim's hands to show them what a good job he'd done. If the customer happened to be stupid enough to point out to Philbert that he'd forgotten to cut off a few long hairs here and there, the old barber would simply grasp the offending strands between his thumb and forefinger and rip them right out! After experiencing that traumatic event, most people never bothered to point out anything he might have missed. They'd wait till they got home and let their wives finish the job.

Most of the town's kids used to whine and plead with their parents not to force them to go to Philbert's for a haircut and over the years, Sears & Roebuck and Montgomery Wards catalogs did a brisk business in and around the Ashland area in the "do-it-yourself" home haircutting kits. All the kids would rather risk having their mothers make them look like fools rather than take a chance on Philbert.

London had nothing on Ashland in regard to the "latest" hair fashions either. We had the punk rock haircut in our small town long before it became popular in England. The standard comment in the fifty's and sixty's at Ashland Community High School upon seeing someone with a really strange hair cut was: "I see you went to flub-up Philbert's again."

The other oft-told story told around town was: "A man went into Philbert's for a haircut tha other day. Old Philbert peered at him and said, "How do yah want it sonny?" The customer, with jist a hint of sarcasm in his voice replied, "I want you tah shave off tha left sideburn right up to my temple, but leave tha right sideburn alone. Then I want you to cut all my hair off in tha back right down to tha bare skin. On tha top, jist take one swipe down tha middle, but leave a long fringe on my forehead hangin right down over my eyebrows." Hearing this odd request, Philbert would blink a couple of times, squint his watery eyes and gape at the man. "Jaysus sonny, why in hell would you want your hair cut like that?" "Well," replied the customer. "That's tha way you cut it tha last time!"

Philbert may have been old, but he had the mind of an eighteen year-old! If anyone was foolish enough to insult him or his haircutting ability, he remembered it till the day he died, and he always paid that person back, in one way or another. If he even heard that a "regular" customer had slid away to another barber's establishment in the neighboring towns of Squa Pan, Masardis, Sheridan, Portage, Mapleton or Presque Isle, he'd lie in wait like a clever, old fox and he was very, very patient.

Every now and then, he'd toss the missing patron's name out in a general conversation and wait to see the reaction of the man's friends. Upon hearin their friend's name, the other customers would slide their eyes sideways and lie their asses off. "Did you say Roger Dion?" They'd ask innocently. "Why, I believe he's workin up along tha Canadian border for tha Great Northern." Or "Henry Sirois?" "Oh, I jist heard yestiday that he'd taken a job for a farmer down tah Mars Hill." They'd lie all the while knowin that both Roger and Henry were slinkin off to another barbershop somewhere close by.

But old Philbert was a patient, patient man. He's long career of dealin with the public had taught him a couple of things, one, a man's hair never quit growin and two, an emergency like a funeral or a surprise weddin, always brought those little rats crawlin back to his shop. Sooner or later, they'd be standin in his door wantin a quick trim. The barber would eye them up and down real good and then he'd flip his hair-encrusted cape sideways with a snap like a bullfighter and in a tone, heavily laden with sarcasm, say, "Please ta meet yah, stranger. Now what kin I do for you today?" The offending customer would sidle into the barber's chair, hopin against hope that the old man wouldn't have noticed that he'd not entered his shop for a period of several months.

But the old barber wasn't fooled, not one bit! He'd grab his trusty,

rusty old clippers; flip the switch to on and with a sound that a B52 makes as it begins its final landing approach over to Loring, he'd commence to trimmin. He trimmed so much and so close that the customer would slide way down in the ancient barber's chair, trying not to give Philbert so much head to cut on.

As old Philbert made his last cutting approach, he'd stop and yell directly into the customer's ear, "Fer good Christ's sakes, Sonny, could yah stop flinchin and figgitin and sit up in yer chair! I been doin this a good long time and I ain't kilt anyone yet!" And with that, he'd zoom over the head a couple of times more, and he was done. He'd turn, grab his crooked mirror, slap it into the patron's hands and snarl, "Have a good look Sonny, and let me know if it's to yur likin, or maybe you'd wanta be consultin your other barber jist ta see if I done it right!"

By now, the customer knew that it was too late. As he carefully slid the cloudy mirror into view, his eyes told him what he already knew, deep down in his gut. There wasn't a single strand of hair left on his entire head! Old Philbert had had his revenge!

Old Philbert passed on to that great, big barber shop in the sky not too long ago, and we now have a new, very efficient barber. However, with Philbert's death, we lost a beloved town character, and the old barbershop is jist a regular barbershop now.

I felt sad upon hearin about Philbert's demise, and as I thought about the ending to this story, I had to laugh, knowing Philbert; I could jist imagine him arriving in Heaven armed with his faithful clippers, rusty scissors and hair encrusted cape. He'd probably take a quick look around, and then he'd walk right up to Jesus or St. Peter, take a good long look at their flowing tresses, whip out his plastic cape and say, "Say, I ain't seen you around before. What'll it be sonny?"

GREAT UNCLE HAL

Mother's uncle, Harold Sutherland, was a tall gaunt man with a fringe of flaming red hair and piercing blue eyes. He was as Scottish as a person could get and damn proud of it too. He and his wife Cassie owned and operated a small family farm on the Goding Road about a half a mile down the road from our house. Aunt Cassie and Uncle Hal as we called them were the limelight of our lives. When things got too boring at home, we could always be found at their house listening to or being involved in some aspect of their daily life.

Uncle Hal had a number of what Aunt Cassie called "bad habits." She was constantly harping at him about one thing or another. Uncle Hal didn't jist smoke, he smoked! Smoking was his passion and his life. He especially loved Camel cigarettes, and he smoked them one after another. If you looked around and saw a cloud of blue smoke, you knew that Uncle Hal wasn't too far away. He often claimed that he'd discovered a new insect repellent that absolutely killed all the mingies and black flies that followed us around in swarms. And with a constant cloud of blue, cigarette smoke hovering around his head, we believed him! He was also known to tip a glass or two on occasion, but probably his worst habit was his decided gift for profanity. If there was a swear word known to man, Uncle Hal probably knew it and did not hesitate to use it. His speech wasn't jist peppered with obscenities, it was saturated with them.

When we were young, Aunt Cassie and Uncle Hal had already been married for quite a while and their favorite pass-time seemed to be arguing. It was not uncommon for us to go outside on a lovely spring morning and hear a complete obscene phrase come drifting up over the hill like a shout from Hell. They fought verbally like a couple of banshees. I can vividly remember hearing the following one morning.

"You bald headed old son of ah whore, I thought I told you to get tha spare tractor parts yourself tha next time you went to town!" Most people would have been shocked to hear such language, but we had become so accustomed to their salty speech that we jist accepted it as normal.

Along with all his other bad habits, Uncle Hal was "gifted" with a unique sense of humor. You never knew what he was going to do or say. It didn't matter who you were either, everyone was at his mercy.

Uncle Hal and Aunt Cassie lived together fifty-odd years and no one could ever understand the success of their marriage. It seemed to outsiders that their main objective in life was to make each other miserable because they would do the most horrific things to each other. However, if one took the time to look beyond the pranks and jokes, you would find a deep and abiding love for one another.

They had an old fashioned wood burning, cook stove in their kitchen and this stove was a constant source of irritation and friction between them. Aunt Cassie was a wonderful cook, and she would have the stove all banked at jist the right temperature to bake apple pies. Uncle Hal would come in from working in the fields with one demand or another and Aunt Cassie would have to drop everything to go and get what he needed.

Uncle Hal would invariably go to the cook stove to check and see how it was burning, and he'd lift the cover, stir the fire around, throw in a few more sticks of wood, adjust the damper and grumble that "damn wimmen didn't know how to build a good fire!" By the time Aunt Cassie had returned with what Uncle Hal had been looking for, her lovely apple pies were reduced to a non-recognizable burned mass and the verbal insults would begin. She'd call him a nosey, interfering old bastid and he'd respond by telling her that she was a "twit" and a piss-poor cook to boot! We didn't need to go to the movies with entertainment like that!

In those days, they didn't have the luxury of a modern bathroom, but here was an outhouse adjacent to the barn that Uncle Hal commonly referred to as the "shit house." This innocent looking structure was the scene of much retaliation on their part.

One retaliation that I recall, in particular, was when Aunt Cassie got wind of a rumor that Uncle Hal had spread a story all over town about her. It seems that he'd told everyone that he'd come home one afternoon and found Aunt Cassie with one of her tits caught in the wringer of her washer. He allowed that if he hadn't come home when he did, Aunt Cassie would have been walking around lopsided for the rest of her life! Upon hearin this story, Aunt Cassia was outraged! She burned and smarted about this insult for quite a while, and then she came up with the ultimate "payback" plan.

Nearly every night after supper, Uncle Hal would gather up his Field and Stream Magazines or the latest Red Sox scores and disappear into the outhouse for an hour or two, depending on the season. Having memorized his "outhouse" habits over the years, Aunt Cassie called and personally invited everyone that she could think of to come for supper jist before the Fourth of July when she would have plenty of company around to witness her retaliation. She cooked and planned everything right down to the last detail and right on cue, after eating his fill, company or not, Uncle Hal gathered his newspaper and lit out for his favorite abode.

Aunt Cassie waited until she heard the outhouse door slam, and then she sent all the guests outside and told them to be real quiet. Then she took a handful of firecrackers and hurried around the barn to the back of the outhouse. She lit the firecrackers and hurled them in under the toilet seat where Uncle Hal was so happily ensconced. People talked for months on end about how they never thought, that a man with his pants down around his ankles and covered with shit, could move so fast!

Another time, when Uncle Hal had gone on his favorite sojourn, Aunt Cassie took their new Polaroid camera and crept down to the outhouse. She yanked the door open, and there he was Camel cigarette in one hand, a Field & Stream in the other and his pants down around his ankles. She gleefully took his picture, and once she'd gotten it developed, she mailed copies of the picture to a relative in Massachusetts and had it made into a jigsaw puzzle. Then, jist for spite, she mailed copies of the puzzle to all their friends and relatives.

Uncle Hal loved us kids, and he loved to drive us crazy too. We never knew what he was going to do to us next, but he always had time for us too. If he was going to town, he'd stop and see if any of us kids wanted to go with him. He'd take us to the northern Maine fair in

Presque Isle every year, and he always took us fishing with him on the Aroostook River.

He used to take me with him sometimes when he sprayed or cultivated his potatoes. He'd drive his tractor and sprayer up the dirt road to the sprayer hole that was located in the potato field behind our house and once the sprayer was filled, he'd stop by our house to pick me up. I'd sit in front of him on the seat and steer the tractor while he sprayed the fields or cultivated the potatoes. I remember it was a very sad day for the both of us when he announced one day that my rear was getting too big, and we couldn't share the tractor seat any more.

As I think back, it must have been a charming sight to see an old, bald headed farmer driving an ancient, beat up red, Farmall tractor up and down the potato rows with a small blond haired child sitting happily on his lap, steering the tractor.

One day when I was about thirteen, my sister Helen and I went to visit Aunt Cassie and Uncle Hal. Because Aunt Cassie was quite well-endowed in the breast department, Uncle Hal often used this topic to get Aunt Cassie's goat. On this particular day, he was teasing her about her "floppy tits" as he called them. She was happily mixing dough to make biscuits for supper, and he looked over to where we were standing by the door, winked at us and then he told her that she'd better be careful because he didn't want her tits dragging in his biscuit dough. She jist ignored him and with a wink at us, continued mixing her bread. When he saw that his barbs weren't going to get a rise out of her, he turned his attention to us.

Uncle Hal liked to sit with his chair tipped back on its two hind legs and smoke and read the paper. One hand, that had been permanently stained yellow by the cigarettes he chain smoked, held his constant Camel cigarette, and the other hand grasped the Bangor Daily News. The sunlight from the kitchen windows would glance off the top of his baldhead and turn his remaining fringe of red hair a bright gold. His glasses rested on the tip of his nose, and every now and then he would rub the small skin cancer on his lower lip with the thumbnail of his left hand.

Suddenly, he thrust his newspaper aside, got up out of his chair, hitched up his pants and strolled over to the medicine cabinet. He opened the door and withdrew a small, square, green can. Then he turned to where we were standing and solemnly handed it to me. With a very straight face, he said, "Now Tooter and Helen, if you girls want tah have huge knockers like Aunt Cassie, then you'd better rub this ointment on them every night, jist like she does." I looked at the can. It was a can of Bag Balm! Aunt Cassie turned around and looked at us and said, "And by the way girls, it's also very good for hemorrhoids!" And she gave Uncle Hal a knowing look. He suddenly scooped up the newspaper and sat down very carefully in his chair. Over the years, I often wondered if perhaps I shouldn't have heeded his advice about the Bag Balm.

Years later, after I'd married, and I'd come home from Connecticut with my husband for a short visit, Uncle Hal came careening up our drive to my mother's house. He hopped out of his pickup and hurried into the kitchen. Upon spying my new husband sitting at the table, he reached into the worn-out pocket of his overalls and withdrew his wallet. He opened it up, thumbed through the bills and withdrew a dollar. He looked at me and then at my new husband for a couple of minutes, and then he slapped the dollar down on the table in front of my husband and said, "I've been taking care of her all these years and now she belongs to you! Jist be sure that you take damn good care of her!"

Uncle Hal left this worldly place quite a while ago, but deep in my heart I know that he's still watching over me from above. And when I look up and see the clouds rushing all around, I figure that it's jist Uncle Hal giving everybody hell up there in Heaven....

THA WARDEN

Sonny was awake long before the clock on his nightstand told him it was time to get up and his inner clock had never let him down. Even though it was the middle of June and getting warmer, he hated to part with his extra blankets. He slid out from under the heavy homemade quilts that his wife had made before she'd died and stumbled to his feet. He nearly tripped over the dog that lay, still sleepin, on the rug at the foot of his bed and he stopped to rub old Percy's ear with his foot before continuing on his way to the toilet. He had a big day ahead, he was on his way up to the Allegash and his heart pounded a little faster as he thought about the long trip and all that lay ahead of him.

He'd packed what little he needed the night before and he liked to travel light. His Maine warden's truck was filled with gas and he'd checked the tires and oil and it should make the long trip up to the Canadian border without any trouble. He quickly ate a stale chocolate doughnut and gulped down a mug of lukewarm coffee, then he set the empty mug in the sink, ran a little cold water over it and his kitchen chores were done. Sonny checked his watch against the kitchen clock and headed for the door. "Come Percy!" He commanded, snapped his fingers and the old dog moved across the floor like a young pup to where Sonny was standin by the open door. Percy was a "ridin" fool and had never liked to stay home ever since the day that Sonny had rescued him and Sonny always took him along on a stakeout if it was at all possible. He liked that old dog's company a lot better than he liked most people. "A hellava lot better if tha truth be told," he thought to himself.

He and old Percy had been together nearly five years now and Sonny often thanked his lucky stars that some lame son-of-ah-bitch from away had abandoned the dog up in the woods along the Reality Road. He and old Percy had fit from the start and he couldn't imagine his life now without that dog.

Sonny waited by the sagging porch steps until Percy had whizzed on every last thing in the immediate area and then he scooped the dog up and slid him onto the worn leather of the passenger seat. Percy sniffed a couple of times and laid his head down on his paws. Sonny knew that Percy would be sound asleep before he'd gotten half a mile down the road.

He gunned the engine of the warden's service vehicle a couple of times and watched in the rear view mirror as the bluish, black smoke billowed from the rear exhaust, then he pulled out onto the Garfield Road and he didn't waste any time payin attention to the posted speed signs either.

The old truck picked up speed as he rounded the sharp corner near the Ashland Aroostook River Bridge and Sonny gunned it a little more as he headed on up the road. Old Percy nearly fell off the seat at the increase in speed and he let out a small whine of protest as they flew over the yes mam's and pot holes on the deserted Portage road.

Ever the warden, Sonny was always on the lookout for game in the fields and for out of season hunters and he let his eyes slide over the growin potato fields. As he rounded a corner in the road he had to smile to himself as he passed the Alcott Farm on the left hand side. Old man Alcott had been so pissed off by all the would-be-hunters from away, taking pot shots at his dairy cattle, that he'd bought a replica of an eight-point buck and had placed it at the end of his field, jist to see how stupid some people could be.

All the locals knew that the buck was a fake, but all those hunters from over to Loring Air force Base and the other fools from out of state didn't and over the last couple of years, this fake contraption had given the inhabitants of Ashland many a good laugh. Folks said that upon closer inspection, at the close of huntin season, they found that the buck was so full of bullet holes, it was a miracle it was still standin. "That son-of-ah-bitch must be so full of holes that it's jist like a sieve," Sonny laughed as he rounded a sharp corner in the road.

As they flew down over the long hill into tha small town of Portage, he eased off the gas a little and coasted past Dean's Hotel, Steven's

Grocery Store and the rest of the small, sleeping settlement with hardly a sound. He glanced out the window to his left and saw Portage Lake sparkling off in the distance, jist as the sun came slowly over the eastern horizon. He slid his shirt sleeve back and checked the time; it was now jist a little past five. He was ahead of the game time-wise and it had been a while since his last visit up north and he was more than ready.

He gave the truck a little more gas and sailed up over the hills and on past the tiny settlement of Buffalo. He shifted himself a little more comfortably in his seat and let his mind slide away like the land all around him. He loved this old truck, yes sir he did! He and that old truck had traveled many miles all over tah hell and gone on the back roads of Aroostook County. He'd been offered a newer model jist last year, but he'd turned it down. This truck might have a lot of miles on it, but he knew all its idiosyncrasies and oddities and besides, he could fix jist about anything that could go wrong with it too. "Not like all them friggin new things that looked all shiny and cream puffy on tha outside and ain't worth tha powder ta blow em to hell!" He thought to himself. "Jist give me an old truck any old time and that's good enough for me! We don't need any ah them new-fangled foreign jobs, now do we Percy?" He reached out and cuffed Percy gently on the back of his head and the dog didn't even open his bloodshot eyes. He'd been down this road many times before.

Jist as he was about to pass through Soldier Pond, Sonny reached up and flipped his ever-present sun glasses down over his deep brown eyes and looked at the landscape all around him. There were acres and acres of abandoned fields that used to be cow pastures and the gardens of the early settlers, but now were overgrown with trees and witch grass. Patches of brilliant yellow buttercups intermingled with clumps of bright red and orange Indian paint brushes, danced in unison in the early morning breeze. "Ought to be some mighty good strawberrin in those fields," He thought to himself as he remembered his mother's old sayin. "Where the paint brushes grow, so do the wild strawberries." Mother was long gone now, but it seemed that she came back to him each day, in one way or another.

The road twisted and turned and the land fell away, way down below the road on the left for miles and miles. There were acres of uncut dried-out hay, swaying gently in the early morning wind. "It looks jist like an ocean of gold," He said to himself. And being a man of the woods, he'd always loved the woods better than the ocean. "At least I know all the creatures that live in them woods," he thought to himself, but he wasn't too sure jist what kind of creature he might find in the deep, dark blue. He'd take the northern Maine woods any old time.

A little further up the road, off in the distance, he could see the shimmer of clear blue water as the rays of the early morning sun glanced off the numerous lakes and ponds that surrounded him.

Feelin the heat buildin in the cab and hearin Percy begin to pant, Sonny rolled down his side window and inhaled deeply. The air was filled with a myriad of scents that he was long accustomed to. There was the fragrance of living things like Indian paintbrushes, strawberry blossoms, Pine trees, Spruce trees and wild grasses. The smell was fresh and cleansing.

He loved to drive too and he drove at a steady pace. The sound of his tires hitting the pavement had a sound all their own and if you listened carefully, it almost became a kind of hypnotic music. The miles slid away and the name places of the old towns slid past as well. Winterville, Eagle Lake, Wallagrass and Soldier Pond. Towns whose early inhabitants had helped build this great state of Maine. "Now these towns are mostly jist names on my map," He thought to himself because most of the farms and old homesteads were abandoned as folks were lured away to the southern industrial cities of Bangor, Lewiston, Auburn, Portland, Boston and Hartford lookin for a better job and a better life for themselves and their loved ones.

Jist before reachin the outskirts of Fort Kent the elevation changed and his heart rate changed too. He always got this same feelin when he reached this spot. The terrain changed from rollin pastureland to higher rollin hills and deep valleys. He was so high up that he could see still pockets of fog lyin in the valleys far below. He always stopped for a couple of minutes when he reached this point in his journey, because he always felt as though he had driven straight into Heaven.

Again, he pulled the truck over, turned off the ignition and heard the ticking sounds from the hot motor as it began to cool off. He opened the door, stepped down and waited for the dog to crawl across the front seat to where he stood. He lifted the dog down to the ground and waited for Percy to relieve himself against the front tire, before walking across the deserted road to the other side. He always stopped here, somewhere between Heaven and Fort Kent. It was a place that he loved most in the whole of Aroostook County. In his long career as a game warden he'd had more trips than he could remember past this very spot and he always had to stop and be jist for a little while.

Sonny pulled his cigarette makings out of his shirt pocket and quickly rolled himself a fresh one. He stuck the limp cigarette in his mouth, lit it and drug the strong yellow smoke deep into his lungs. Then he let the smoke slide out of his nose and watched it as it drifted slowly away on the warm breeze.

Sonny shifted his deep-set brown eyes from left to right across the horizon and liked the idea that there wasn't another living creature around for miles. Well, not that he could see anyway. Being a natural loner, he'd always liked the sound of silence.

Cigarette reduced to a glowing husk and the need to be, satisfied, he ground the butt into the dirt with his heel and walked back to his truck. He turned, snapped his fingers and hearin the familiar sound, old Percy's head appeared in the grass by the edge of the road and he ambled slowly in Sonny's direction.

After a couple of sniffs, Percy lifted his leg and sprayed the front tire again and then Sonny lifted the dog into the passenger seat saying, "Thanks a friggin lot Percy. I jist washed this friggin truck and you have to go and mess it all up again." But he really didn't mind, he jist wished he was an old dog too and could do all the things Percy could do, that's all.

He still had a ways to go before he could stop for the night. He was on a mission. This was his job and he loved every bit of it. The long rides, the long hikes, the investigations, the intrigue, the entrapment and finally the arrests. He loved it all.

There had been rumors and whispers comin down the road from Fort Kent and the Allegash for a long time now, that finally couldn't be ignored. He'd been summoned down to the State House in Augusta in tha early spring and had his ears burned and his ass kicked by the head of the Fish and Game Department about the going ons in the Allegash and this trip couldn't be put off any longer. According to the locals, there had been a lot of first class poachin going on and other hinted at things and now it was time to find out jist what was takin place up there in that rural section of "God's" county.

He drove through the Main Street of Fort Kent until he reached the outskirts of the town and pulled into the diner where he always stopped to eat, when he found himself up in this neck of the woods. It was a small mom and pop operation and the owners, Marie and Lou Morin, prided themselves on serving good, wholesome food at a reasonable price. By now the people around this area knew him on sight and they never called him by his given name of Sonny. They always referred to him as "Tha Warden," and this suited him jist fine.

He pushed the door open, walked in and over to the table where he always sat when he was there. Jen, the only waitress, looked up when she heard the door open and recognizing him, gave him one of her cheeky smiles and a slight wave. It wasn't too long before she was sauntering with a "come hither" sway of her ample hips across the room to where he sat.

Upon reaching his table, she put her supple fingers into her pink mouth and pulled a piece of her bubble gun out and then let it slowly slide back into her open mouth. Then, she reached out and slid her fingers across the nape of Sonny's suntanned neck and gave his neck a nice little squeeze. Jist feeling her cool fingertips against his skin gave Sonny a thrill that ran from where her fingers rested at tha base of his neck all the way down along his sweatin spine. He liked that feeling, he liked it a lot! It had been a long time since anyone had touched him like that or had touched him at all, for that matter.

He leaned back against her hand and looked up at her as she stood there looking down at him. "Well, well, well," She murmured in a low, seductive voice. "To what do I owe this honor, Sonny boy? Missed me so much that yah jist couldn't stay away any longer?" And as she bent closer, an overwhelming wave of heavy perfume from her amply endowed chest engulfed him.

As tempted as he was by the overt sexual invitation, Sonny laughed and shook his head because he knew better than to play ball in that field. Not only was she married, but her husband had beaten the hell out a young state trooper who had tried to pick a few berries a while back and he was still recuperatin. It was temptin, but jist not worth the trouble.

Jen shifted her cheekful of bubble gum to the other side of her mouth and ran her pointed pink tongue across her lips. Seein this, Sonny had to shift in his seat as he felt his sensual side react to her open invitation. Seein that she was makin him uncomfortable, but he wasn't about to bite, she laughed and became all business. "So," She began. "Since I don't suit your fancy, what is it that you really wanted when you stopped here?"

Sonny rubbed his hand across his forehead to remove a couple of drops of sweat and replied, "I jist wanted a black coffee, a couple of Marie's ploys, en a couple of pieces of bacon." "You're a man of habit that's what you are." She replied as she scribbled his order on her pad and then she walked away to tell them in the kitchen what he wanted.

Sonny leaned back against the cracked leather seat and breathed a little easier. Now that Jen was put on hold, until the next time, perhaps he could git down to some real business, his business and the reason he was really here, poachin.

It wasn't too long before she was back with a loaded tray of hot coffee, three ploys and a rasher of bacon. Seein all the food piled on his plate, Sonny looked up at her. "Now Jen, what have I done to deserve all this?" She shifted her hips a couple of times, leaned against him and sighed. "Oh my God!" She exclaimed. "This man of the friggin woods doesn't have a friggin clue, but I'd sure like ta be tha one ta teach him!" She turned to go and then it was as though she couldn't resist one last try, "Maybe I'll jist git myself a little huntin license and a little gun and meet you someday out there in tha deep dark woods and then we'll see jist how good at findin things you really are!" With that threat hangin over his head, she walked away, hips swinging, breasts jiggling and a trail of strong perfume lingerin in the air behind her.

Sonny was glad that in all the years he'd know her, he'd never succumbed to her seductions. "If a man was ever foolish enough to git involved with her even for a one night stand, he'd still come out ah loser." He thought to himself. Then, he turned to the task at hand and soon he was enjoying the repast that he'd been dreamin about for the last couple of months.

The ploys were their featured item on the menu and they were always the same, damn good! They were soft and crisp at the same time. As he cut into them with his fork, the cream and strawberry filling oozed out and seein this, his mouth began to water. He forked some into his mouth and his palate was filled with all kinds of sensations at the same time. There was cinnamon, sugar, butter and vanilla along with the taste of cream and strawberries and a lingering taste of the real cow's butter that they'd been fried in. It seemed almost sinful to taste all these things at once.

As he chewed, he kept his eyes lowered because he could feel Jen's green eyes on him as she watched him covertly from her station across the room. She'd always been on the make for as long as he'd known her and she was gittin a little long in the tooth if the truth be told, he thought. Then he mentally chided himself. "You're no spring chicken either, yah old dog!"

Jist as Sonny gulped his last ounce of coffee, Jen again reappeared at his elbow. Seein that she was holding something wrapped in a paper napkin in her hand, Sonny raised his eyebrows in question and looked up at her. "Well," She said. "I jist looked out and saw your old dog lookin out tha window of your truck and I wanted to make sure that he got to eat somethin too." With that, she handed him the bundle. Sonny didn't have to smell it to know that old Percy was goin to have a real good lunch today. Sonny nodded his head in a thank you, slid his bill off the table and headed for the cashier.

After payin his bill, he picked up the change and walked over to his table and slid a couple of dollars down next to his plate then he turned and with a slight wave in Jen's direction, he walked over to the door and went out.

Surprised that the sun was jist beginning it slow decent on the western horizon, he walked quickly down the steps and over to the truck where Percy sat waitin. He wrenched open the battered door, stepped up onto the runnin board and slid into his seat. Percy, smellin the food, nudged Sonny's hand while he unwrapped the meat. Sonny waited until Percy had eaten it in a couple of quick bites and then he let the dog lick the remaining juice off his hand. Satisfied, the old dog immediately lay down on the seat and fell back asleep.

Sonny wiped the dog's slobber off his hand on the side of his pants and turned the switch. The truck roared to life and they flew out of the parking lot, leavin a trail of blue-colored exhaust in the air behind them. Jist as they hit the main road, Sonny glanced in the rear view mirror and could jist make out the outline of a figure standin in the door of the diner. It was Jen and she had her hand held up in a farewell gesture.

It wasn't too long before the salty meat that he had jist eaten made both him and Percy thirsty and Sonny reached behind the seat and withdrew his thermos of cold water. He took a long swig and laughed as he saw Percy eyein him with soulful eyes, as though he wasn't goin to share the drink. Sonny poured a good helpin into the thermos cover and held it for Percy to drink his fill.

When the dog had finished, Sonny patted his head and said, "Okay, you old duffer. You've been fed and had a good drink. Now do us both a favor and go back to sleep!" Old Percy, as though understandin his command, dropped his head onto his paws and soon there were loud snores, interrupted by long, foul smellin farts, emanatin from Percy's side of the truck.

As he drove slowly along the winding road of Route 161 headin west towards the Allegash, he tried to make a mental plan about how he would handle this particular assignment. He marveled to himself jist how much everything had remained unchanged since the last time he'd driven thru this area. He'd been up here last spring and it still looked tha same. "Small towns don't change all that much except to git smaller as people left, called south, by tha promise of a better life." He thought to himself. He shook his head at the thought of it and to tell the truth, he didn't envy any of them fools when they came roarin home in the summer drivin their new vehicles with their wives and kids in tow. "They may think they have it made in the big cities, but their heart always calls them home," jist like his old grandmother always said.

The miles fell away behind him when he realized with a start that the sun was slidin towards the western horizon. "Might as well find a nice, quiet spot ta spend tha night," he thought to himself as his tired eyes began scanning the edge of the road for a place that he could pull into and camp without being too obvious. After all, wardens aren't tha most welcome people to have snoopin around, especially in this neck of tha woods, now are they?" he asked old Percy as he rubbed the still sleepin dog's head with his hand.

Spying an old tote road off to his right, Sonny deftly downshifted and turned his truck into the overgrown logging road and winced as he heard the branches of the regrown trees scrape along the whole length of his truck on both sides. "Guess I'll be needin another paint job when spring rolls around ah-gin," he said to himself as he deftly maneuvered the large truck around rotted tree stumps and huge boulders. Spyin a small opening in the dense overgrowth, he quickly turned left and eased the truck to a stop.

Feelin tha movement cease, Old Percy pulled his shaggy head up off the leather-covered cushion leavin a patch of drool on the seat where his head had been. Spyin that present on tha seat, Sonny dug in his back pocket to find his handkerchief and quickly wiped the spot before it sank into the seat lining. "Thanks ah friggin lot!" he said to tha dog and Old Percy, feeling that he'd been praised for doin something good, pulled himself upright and licked Sonny on tha right side of his face. Sonny brought his green shirt sleeve up to his cheek and wiped the slobber off his face. "Guess we won't be meetin any wimmen here in tha deep, dark north woods anyway, will we Percy?" With that snide comment to tha dog, tha warden quietly opened the door and dropped to tha ground without makin a sound.

He turned, motioned for tha dog to come and waited till Old Percy had high tailed it into the deepening dusk to squirt a hello to every bush or tree that he could mark. Sonny walked a short distance down the rough road and was surprised when he heard the sound of runnin water jist ahead. "Jaysus, I didn't realize that tha friggin river was this close to tha road." He said to himself. "I know that Canada is jist across tha river, but I never realized that it was this close." He made a mental note to check his map when he got back to tha truck.

He walked on for another five hundred feet or so and then he saw the St. John River as it flowed northeast towards Fort Kent and the border beyond and was amazed that at this point, the river was so low, that a person could easily see the river bottom and the reeds growing there. "Probably wouldn't even reach up to my waist if I tried to walk across to tha other side." He thought to himself.

He brought his sun-burned fingers to his mouth and blew a soft whistle once and it wasn't too long before the old dog came waddling down the trail behind him. Sonny didn't even look back, knowin that the dog would come to his side jist as sure as shootin and there he was, lickin Sonny's hand. "Good dog!" Sonny said as he patted Old Percy's head. "Now lets git us a quick wash and a drink and then git settled for tha night. We've got a lot of work to do in the mornin."

Sonny quickly stripped off his clothes and waded into the slowly movin river and marveled at how good the tepid water felt on his skin. Old Percy didn't have to be told twice, he waded out till only his head and tail could be seen and then he swam back to where Sonny lay soaking in the murky water. After washing the dust and sweat off, Sonny snapped his fingers to git the old dog's attention and then he waded back to shore, smilin to himself as he heard the dog slowly paddling behind him in the water.

After wiping himself off with his shirt, Sonny quickly dressed and headed back up the trial towards his truck and supper. He dug out a can of dog food and dumped it into Percy's dish as the old dog pushed him impatiently aside to get to the food. "Looks almost good enough for me to eat too," Sonny told the dog as he tried to decide what he'd have to eat. Finally deciding on a left over cup of coffee and a stale sandwich, he wolfed it down and then set about makin himself and Percy a bed for the night.

He quickly cut some branches off a fir tree and lay them under a bush next to his truck. Then he flipped his sleepin bag across the branches and his bed was ready. Old Percy didn't have to be told what to do next and he ambled over to where the makeshift bed lay and settled his ample body across the softest parts. He shifted himself slightly to get more comfortable, let out a long sigh, a couple of loud farts and fell asleep. Sonny, hearin and seein all of this, shook his head and laughed silently to himself. "Sure must to be great ta be an old dog," And then he had to laugh again because he really was gittin to be an old dog too. He'd be 49 this comin July. The last thing he did before turnin in was to call headquarters to let them know where he was jist in case they needed him, or he needed them.

After tha long day of drivin, Sonny thought he'd fall asleep rather quickly, but try as he might, every time he felt himself slidin towards sleep, the old dog would whimper or fart or thrash in his dream, causin Sonny to wake. He'd reach out and pat the dog on the back until his dreams subsided and then tha warden prayed for sleep, that didn't come.

His mind was like that sometimes. After attendin a meeting that was especially important, he'd digest the information all tha way home and when he'd get home, he'd replay all tha pertinent facts over and over in his mind until they finally made sense to him. That was the way he always made his cases stick, head work, plain and simple. "So, what exactly, are we lookin for here? Is it poachers, is it druggies? Jist what tha hell is really goin on up here in tha wilderness?" The whine of a huge fleet of Maine mosquitoes descended upon Sonny and he gave up analyzing the situation, to try and cover his head from the onslaught. Carefully zippin the sleepin bag over his head, Sonny knew that this was goin to be a long, hot night because he'd been down this road more times than he could count. He smiled to himself as he felt Percy thrash and shift in reaction to the mosquitoes' fierce bites. "I feel real sorry for yah Percy but there ain't no room in this friggin bag and it's too hot to sleep in here too." And then he finally drifted off to sleep.

Mornin came early and it was a still tired warden who shifted the old dog off the top of his ratty sleepin bag and crawled out. He swore to himself as he massaged the kinks out of his back and legs, sleepin out in the wilderness never did get any softer. Old Percy opened one sleepy eye and seein that all was well with his unkempt master, snuggled deeper into the sleepin bag and ignored Sonny.

Feeling the call of nature, Sonny relieved himself next to a large hazelnut bush and walked quietly down the overgrown trail to the slowly moving river. Stooping, he splashed water onto his face and then he wiped himself off on his shirtsleeve. Looking around, in the early morning light, he noticed that nearly directly across the river on the Canadian side, there was an opening in the overgrown riverbank that matched the opening right where he was standing. Surprised by what he hadn't noticed in the waning light of the night before, this time, he looked around more carefully.

Seeing that the ground beneath his feet had marks like a boat or canoe had recently been pulled up out of the water onto it, Sonny felt a jolt go up his spine as he realized what he had jist seen. He quickly stepped back into the overhanging bushes so as not to be seen so easily if anyone happened to be watching from the other side of the river.

Thinking back over the past couple of weeks, Sonny tried to remember the last time it had rained. "Whoever it was that hauled that boat up out of tha water, must have done it very recently," He thought to himself. "I didn't know it, but me and Old Percy might jist have found tha exact place that them fools are crossin into Maine with whatever it is they're bringin with them."

Moving quickly, he reached behind him and tore a small branch off a bush and using an old Indian trick, he reached down and swept away all evidence of his boot tracks in the soft ground. Then, he turned and hurried back up the hidden trail to where his truck was still parked. He had to laugh to himself as he saw that old Percy had crawled into his sleeping bag and the only part of him that was showing was his long, matted tail.

Sonny knelt down and peeled a reluctant Percy out of the bag and carried him to the truck. Knowin that old Percy would need to relieve himself, Sonny slid the dog down his leg till he was standin and waited for the dog to finish, then he gathered him up again and thrust him onto the seat and gently slid him over to the passenger's side.

Sonny's heart was racing and he was sweating slightly at the thought that he jist may have found the place where all the contraband was being smuggled in. He threw his sleeping bag into the back of the truck and quickly picked up the branches he'd laid on the ground for their bed and chucked them behind several large bushes. Looking around, he didn't see anything that might give away the fact that he'd been there all night and he hoped that his tire tracks would be obscured by the heavy undergrowth of the logging road.

He jumped into his truck, quickly picked up his citizen band radio and called headquarters. Waiting impatiently for them to answer, Sonny ran through all the facts once again in his mind. Finally, a very sleepy voice answered and he related what he'd jist found and what his exact location was. Then, he told them that he was going to get tha hell out of there and move his operation down the road a piece till it got dark and then he was heading back to see if anyone would attempt to cross later on that night. He told them that he'd call in after he'd made camp and let them know his new location. Headquarters told him not to do anything until he'd heard from them and he agreed that he wouldn't, but promises are meant to be broken and he had no intension of keeping his promise either.

He started the truck and after several attempts, he got it turned around and he drove slowly and carefully back down the logging road till he reached the highway. Quickly looking both ways and seeing no traffic coming, he eased the old truck out into the road and took off towards the Allegash thankful that it hadn't rained recently and his tracks in and out of the site shouldn't be noticed by anyone.

After he'd gone a couple of miles, he began looking for another place to stash the truck where it wouldn't be easily noticed. Finally, he found jist what he was looking for. Off to the right side of the road, there stood an abandoned weather-beaten barn with one of the doors slightly askew. He reached over and patted old Percy on the head and said, "We've found jist tha right place to stash tha truck." And he pulled off the highway and drove down the grass-filled driveway up to the barn.

It was obvious that there hadn't been a human being around the building for a very long time and Sonny didn't waste any time wrenching open the doors and moving the truck inside. Seeing that he had only inches to spare when he closed the doors, Sonny was grateful that he'd found a place like this so easily as he helped Percy down and they walked all around the building as the dog relieved himself on every bush he could find.

Sonny quickly opened another can of dog food and fed Percy and while he was eating, Sonny wolfed down some of the food that he'd packed for himself and called it good. He had too many other things to work out than to worry about food. He needed to notify headquarters of his new location and he needed to come up with a plan to gather information about who was crossing the river and how he was going to arrest them when they came. He had a lot to do.

He made the call and found that they were trying to find a couple of other wardens from the area to help him and that he was expected to keep in close contact with headquarters about his plans and doings. Sonny made the necessary small talk to keep headquarters pacified and hung up with the promise that he'd keep them informed should anything change. Then he made a makeshift bed for Percy on the damp floor of the old garage and then he settled himself into his driver's seat to think and plan his next mission.

Knowing that old Percy would begin howling right on cue whenever there was a full moon, Sonny had purposely waited till after the moon had waned before he had decided to make this trip. "At least I don't have to worry about tha dog howling and announcing to everyone who might be in the area that we're here." He thought to himself as he readied himself for the walk back to the place where they'd parked the night before.

He pulled on an old moth-eaten sweater and tucked his pants legs into the top of his boots. Then he strapped on his holster and slid his gun into it, and he was ready. He grabbed his radio and flashlight and walked quietly to the sagging barn doors and pulled one open and winced as the rusty hinges screeched in protest as metal rubbed against metal. Hr turned to see if there had been any reaction from Percy, but the old dog still lay on the sleeping bag that Sonny had thrown on the dirt floor. "That old dog could sleep thru a thunder storm," Sonny smiled to himself as he eased the door shut. "He should sleep right through till I git back." And he headed quickly up the driveway to the road.

Sonny, always athletic and in good shape, quickly took off in a half-run half walk, back down the deserted road towards his destination. He covered the distance in a short period of time and was thankful that he hadn't met another person or vehicle the whole time. He turned into the logging road and quickly walked back to the edge of the slowly flowing river.

He looked at his watch and saw that it was nearly nine o'clock and then he settled down behind a large bush to wait to see if anything might happen. As the sound of the water lapping against the shore and the night wore on, Sonny found himself nodding off every now and then and finally, looking at his watch again, he saw that it was quarter to three, he decided to give the stake out a miss. He walked quickly out to the road and jogged back to where Percy still lay sleeping peacefully in his sleeping bag.

As Sonny pulled the door open, the hinges again sang their protesting song and this time, old Percy sat up and howled right along with them. Sonny hurried over to him and shushed him by patting him on the head and then he took him outside to relieve himself. Then he and the old dog went back inside to sleep.

Along about noon, the old dog, hungry and wanting company, lapped Sonny's still-sleeping face a couple of time and Sonny, overwhelmed by the dog's fetid breath, woke and knew that was all the sleep he was going to git for a while. He got up and gave the dog some food and then called headquarters to tell them about the stakeout.

Headquarters again insisted that he wait till they could send some other wardens to help him and Sonny lied again and told them that he would, but they both knew that he wouldn't. Sonny spent the rest of the day between napping and humoring old Percy. It seemed that the dog was always on the "wrong side of tha door." If he was out, he wanted to be in and if he was in, he wanted to go out. Sonny was going to be very happy to have this stakeout over and headed back down the road to Garfield that's for friggin sure.

The second and third night's stakeout were a repeat of the first with the exception of a violent thunder shower arriving in the middle of the night on the third, leaving Sonny soaked and royally pissed off as he headed back down the road towards his truck and dry clothes. "If something doesn't happen by tonight, I'm going to have to drive into town and git some food for me and Percy," he thought to himself as he walked back to camp. "Some of them ploys sure would taste good long about now and old Percy sure could use a good hamburger," he told himself as though he needed an excuse to go back to the diner.

Old Percy had taken to their new sleepin routine of sleeping in the daylight hours without batting an eye. Once Sonny had changed his wet clothes and had crawled into his sleeping bag, the dog would immediately lie down next to him and go to sleep too but no matter how tired Sonny was, his mind would constantly review the prior night's stakeout over and over again. "If they are crossing at that point, they'll have to be making a run agin pretty soon," Sonny told himself over and over until he finally slid off to sleep.

On the fourth night, as Sonny was running down the road to the stakeout point, he had a gut feeling that tonight was going to be tha night. Being mostly Indian, even though most of the "Campbell" folks steadfastly denied that part of their heritage, he knew to trust his instincts and he was more than ready. "If they're goin to come over tha boundary tonight, I'll be waitin!" he told himself as he dropped his backpack to the ground and slid into the same hole under the bush where he'd spent so many nights before. He reached down and pulled a large branch in closer to his body and looked at his watch, eleven thirty-five. "Now let's see what happens," he said to himself as he settled back against the tree trunk. "Let's jist wait and see."

It didn't take too long before the mosquitoes, no-see-ems, mingees and every other blood-sucking insect known to man had found him and he stifled the urge to yell as they found every available piece of skin to drill into. Feeling as though his very body was on fire, Sonny shifted his clothing every which way to try and keep the friggin things off him, but after years of being in the woods, he knew that he jist had to bite the bullet and wait it out. Morning would come soon enough or at least he hoped it would.

Long about two thirty, Sonny came fully awake when he sensed or heard a small "thunk" as though something heavy had run against a more solid object. He brought his head up and listened carefully again, but there were no sounds to be heard. He slowly stretched and checked to see if his gun was unobstructed and he lifted his head to have a look towards the opening in the trees and then what he saw made his blood nearly stop. Standing almost directly in front of him were two men and they were intent only on dragging a small raft up onto the riverbank. Sonny slid down on his haunches and tried not to look in their direction. To make matters worse, the small sliver of moon, glinting off the river, hit him directly in the eyes, obscuring his view of what was on the raft.

As the two men struggled to pull the raft onto the shore, he heard them talking back and forth in French and every now and then an English expression or swear word was thrown in and Sonny cussed the fact that he wasn't bi-lingual. But he did hear one word being mentioned over and over again as they untied the bundles and removed the water tight wrappings. The name he kept hearing was "Sammy". "Sammy who?" that was a questioned he'd like answered.

Finally, the raft was empty and the men hurried to move the bundles up the trail to a more protected area under a large tree that had been struck by lightning at one time or another and the top half had fallen to the ground and made a natural hiding place for the stash. Sonny strained his mosquito bitten ears to hear what they were saying and then he heard a French word that he recognized, "tomorrow," Sonny breathed silently "Tomorrow night, they will come to pick up the stash," and he smiled to himself. Tomorrow couldn't come soon enough, that's for sure and he settled back into his hole till the men had left.

Waiting until he heard the raft thud against the opposite shore, Sonny extricated himself from the insect-riddled hiding space and hurried to where they'd hidden the stash. Brushing aside a large branch that was covering the bundles, Sonny quickly reached into the opening and withdrew one of them.

He lifted the package and sniffed it and was surprised to find no smell. "That's funny, I thought for sure that it would be marijuana," he thought to himself as he sliced open the string that held the package together. Reaching into the package he withdrew another small bundle about the size of a candy bar. Again, he lifted the smaller package to his nose and sniffed, and again, nothing. "Well, I guess it must be cocaine then," he thought as he stuffed the smaller package into his shirt pocket as evidence. He pushed the larger bundle back under the deadfall and after making sure that everything was hidden jist like he'd found it, he loped off out to the road and breaking into a real run, he ran with a light heart and feet, down the main road to where old Percy lay waiting.

As soon as he'd taken the old dog outside to sniff and urinate, Sonny put a call through to headquarters to tell them about the latest happenings. He could feel the excitement of an impending drug bust come over the wire to where he was sitting amidst the drone of a myriad of blood-sucking vermin and he was relieved when the sergeant told him that by tomorrow, he would finally have all the backup he would need. After making the call, he doled out the rest of Percy's food and the old dog after wolfing down the small portion, nudged Sonny until he gave him half of his dried-out doughnut too. Sonny, feeling sorry for the dog, rubbed his head and said, "Don't you worry old soul, by tomorrow night, you and me will have all the food our bellies can hold, I promise you that." Then he pulled his smelly sleeping bag up over his head and tried to quiet the racing of his heart so that he could get some rest.

Sonny slept the sleep of the dead and it was Old Percy's insistent nudging and whining that finally caused him to wake. He pushed the dog's slobbering tongue away from his face and sat up to see two other game wardens sitting in the shade of the barn. Surprised that he hadn't heard them come in, Sonny pulled himself out of the sleeping bag, to apologize to them for not being awake when they'd arrived.

After several minutes of good natured kidding about their having been able to outsmart tha "Indian," Sonny and the other two wardens got down to business about the upcoming night's stakeout. Having worked with the two men before, it didn't take the three of them long to decide on how best to handle the raid. Then, remembering the package that he had taken from under the tree at the stakeout site, Sonny pulled it out of his shirt pocket and handed it to one of the men. He sniffed it and hefted it jist like Sonny had done and then he slit the string and opened it. He wet his index finger and stuck it into the powder for a second and then he put it on his tongue. He let the taste linger on his tongue for a second or so and then spat onto the dirt floor. "Yup," it's cocaine all right and it's my guess that it's very good stuff if you like that kind of stuff, that is." He quickly retied the package and placed it in his knapsack. After all the details had been reviewed, one of the wardens opened his backpack and handed Sonny some packages.

Sonny smiled as he recognized what the food was had where it had come from and upon sniffing the food, Old Percy sat back on his haunches and waited impatiently for his share. Sonny divided up the bacon and ploys with the dog and commenced stuffing his belly full of the wonderful food. The two wardens talked quietly with him as he wolfed down the first fresh food in five days and waved aside his offer to join him knowing full-well that he was only trying to be polite.

Finally, having pushed aside his knawing hunger, he wiped his mouth on the back of his shirt sleeve and thanked the two men. One nudged the other and said, "Oh, it wasn't us who thought about you and your stomach, it was your girlfriend down tha road." Then, upon seeing the look of recognition slide across Sonny's face, at the reference to Jen the waitress, the two men laughed until Sonny's naturally tan face had returned to its regular color.

The three men stayed inside the barn, talking quietly or napping until the sun had just begun to set and then it was time for the stakeout to begin. When the moon was just a sliver in the eastern sky, they hurriedly checked their equipment and made a last call to headquarters and they were off.

As they jogged along the deserted road, they discussed different aspects of the impending arrests and it was then that Sonny asked them if either one of them spoke French. The older warden slowed down a dite and turned and looked at Sonny like he hadn't a brain in his head. "Have you ever known a Pelletier who wasn't French?" He asked. Sonny had to laugh because he'd forgotten the man's last name. "Well, that's good because those two guys were speaking French last night and I could only understand one or two words." "What were the words?" Pelletier asked. "One was tomorrow and the other was a name, Sammy." Sonny answered. "Know anyone by the name of "Sammy" in this area?" "Now that you ask, I do," the other warden answered. "There's a guy who works for the Border Patrol and his name is Sammy Marquis and he pretty much runs the border station here in Fort Kent." Sonny slid his eyes sideways at Pelletier and they looked at each other as they digested this piece of information. "Interesting," was all that Sonny said as they jogged along.

As they approached the clearing where the stakeout was going to take place, Sonny, having trained himself to always check out the area before committing himself to any operation, glanced quickly around and across the road. He was startled to see the shape of a Maine State Trooper as it slid behind a concealing bush directly across the road. "Shoulda known," he thought to himself. "Them guys down to Augusta really want all of tha glory, especially if they don't have to do any of tha hard work!"

Knowing that the pickup would be made by someone comin up the main road, the three wardens walked down the logging road till they could see the place where the drugs were hidden in the tree and positioned themselves across the road and settled down to wait. The hours crawled along and the insects made a concerted effort to eat, suck or bite their way through the men's clothing until the wardens thought they would go insane. Because the smell of fly dope might give their presence away, none of the men had applied any, much to their regret.

Suddenly, the sounds of a couple of atv's coming up the road at a pretty fast clip, alerted the wardens that something might be happening. The men took out their guns and slid back into the darkness to wait. One of the atv's flew on past the stakeout point, but the one bringing up the rear, slowed and turned into the tote road until it reached the lightning struck tree and stopped. The man turned off the vehicle and slid to the ground. He checked his watch and then walked directly to the tree where the stash was hidden. He lifted the large branch jist like Sonny had done and satisfied that the drugs were still there, turned back to his atv.

The next sound they heard was the other vehicle returning at a much slower, quieter pace and it too turned into the tote road. As it slid to a stop behind the other, the two men quickly pulled out some large sacks from the makeshift boxes attached to the back seat of the atv's and began thrusting the packages into them.

At the same instant, Sonny and Pelletier stood up and turned on their high beam flashlights and focused them on the two men. "Put your hands over your heads!" Pelletier commanded. "You're under arrest!" The two men hesitated for a couple of seconds and seeing that they were overpowered, they froze where they were and it was all over in a heartbeat.

As the two suspects were bundled into the police cars and the drug bundles were confiscated and counted, Sonny looked at his watch and was surprised to see that it was only nine forty-five. As the three wardens walked back down the road to the deserted barn, they talked back and forth about how easy this one had gone down. Not at all surprised that the two men they'd arrested were only nineteen and twenty-one, Pelletier commented that he sure could use a cold brew if they were interested.

Sonny thought about how he must look and smelled and decided that he'd give it a miss. He couldn't wait to git the old dog rounded up and into the truck and headed down tha road towards home, a hot bath and a good night's sleep. "After all," he told them. "It's pretty bad when your own dog won't sleep with yah!"

Martha Stevens-David

THA MANURE SPREADER

Hugh McHatten stopped the tractor jist short of the barn doors and swung around in the seat to look back over the field that he'd jist dressed. He jist loved this job. Yes-sir, there was something about spreading manure that made him feel good. Some people would say that this was a nasty, smelly job but Hughy didn't care. There was something about loadin the spreader right to the top and then driving back and forth across the empty fields and seein the manure flying out the back onto the ground. He jist loved it! After all, it didn't cost him nothin; it was poor man's fertilizer.

Hughy had been born on this country farm in Aroostook County, Maine and was the youngest of three sons. He was the one who really loved this land and he was the one who'd stayed home to help his parents as they got older. Finally, when his father was unable to farm any longer, Hughy was the one to take over. Farmin was hard, thankless never-ending work and it would discourage the hardiest of me, but Hughy never got tired of it.

When the first touch of winter came howlin up the State Road and "Tha County" was covered with three feet of snow, most folks put their feet up and slid their arm chairs a little closer to the wood stove. But Hughy would take this lull in stride and he'd begin reviewin his plans for crop rotations for the comin spring.

He'd pour over the new seed catalogues and farmin bulletins from the Aroostook County Farmer's Co-op to learn what new farmin techniques might have been introduced during the past year. Maine Seed Potato Growers had sent him a news bulletin about a new potato cultivar that was supposed to be the answer to a farmer's prayers. The Aroostook County Co-op had been experimentin with this potato seed for the past five years at the co-op farm in Presque Isle and they'd had some very good results so far.

This hardy potato seed was supposed to be blight free, resistant to all the ordinary potato pests and best of all it was supposed to be able to withstand the short, cold growin season of "Tha County." If this was true, that meant that a farmer could begin plantin a lot earlier in the spring instead of havin to wait around until the ground warmed up. Hughy made a mental note to call around to some of his neighbors and ask if any of them were plannin on buyin and plantin some of this amazin seed.

Hughy made the most of this time-off in the winter. He'd head for the barn right after breakfast and spend his days doin all the little jobs that he'd had to neglect during the busy farmin days of spring, summer and fall. He'd tear apart whatever machine had broken down, repair and grease it and get it ready for the comin spring. A farmer's life in "Tha County" is ruled by the capricious seasons. Spring is the time when he puts all his thoughts and energy into preparin his land for plantin. Summer is the season that claims him body and soul because once the crops have begun to grow; he is their slave until they are harvested in the fall. And winter really doesn't leave him alone either, because it's then that he must make his plans for the comin spring.

Every farmer has a favorite piece of farmin equipment that he loves for many reasons. Maybe it's because this piece of machinery is easy to use or maybe it's simply that it makes his life easier. For Hughy, the thing that he loved most was his John Deere manure spreader and that was because of the family history attached to it. The spreader had belonged to his grandfather, his father and now it had been passed on to him. There was somethin about that long, green smelly machine that he'd loved since he was a small boy.

The McHatten's had been farmers for generations and it was a well-known fact that they always took good care of their farmin equipment. His grandfather and father before him had taught him by example. "If you take care of your equipment, your equipment will take care of you," was their motto. When most farmers parked their tractors for the weekend and never touched them again until the following Monday, the McHatten's were different. They'd rise bright and early jist like any other workday and spend the weekend repairin and cleanin their machinery for the coming week.

Hughy knew his machinery inside and out and there wasn't too much that he couldn't fix himself. Once in a while, the old conveyor bar on the manure spreader would jam and he'd have a hellava time gettin it workin again. Sometimes one of the blades would break and he'd have to call over to Aroostook Farm Machinery in Presque Isle to get replacement parts. Because his spreader was so old, the salesman, upon hearin who was on the line, would put him on hold, hopin like hell that he'd jist hang up and call someone else to try to get the replacement parts for his friggin antique machine.

When he was done spreadin manure for the season, he'd wash the spreader carefully and oil all the movin parts. Then he'd walk all around the wondrous machine and check it over very thoroughly. If any of the paint seemed to be flakin off the sixty year-old machine, Hughy would sand down the area and then repaint the spreader so that it looked jist like new.

Hughy took a lot of ribbing from his neighbors about this old spreader. Sometimes, when he was dressing his fields near his home on the State Road, cars would pull over to the side of the road and people would get out to have a closer look at the antique machine. Hughy would casually drive over and stop so that they could have a better look. He'd proudly and patiently answer all their questions about the spreader and he was never too busy to talk to them or have his picture taken with it either.

Every once in a while, he'd drive over to Presque Isle and stop in at Aroostook Farm Machinery and checkout the newest models. He'd walk around and even lay down on the ground to have a better look at the under carriage of the spreader. "Can't even come close to tha one I've got," he'd say aloud to the hoverin salesmen. "Betcha this one won't last sixty years." He'd lift the price tag and glance casually at the amount that was printed there and with a snort, drop the tag as though it had burned his hand. "Fifteen thousand dollars!" The price would burn a hole in his mind. His spreader had cost only ah hundred dollars when his grandfather had bought it back at the turn of the century and it had paid for itself many times over. "A feller would be a hellava long time payin for a new one," he'd think to himself as he took the road for home.

The years went by and then came a day that Hughy would remember forever. It had been a hot, dry summer, the summer of sixty-seven and it had nearly been the end of his farmin career. Nothin seemed to go right that year and he should have had an inklin when in the spring the friggin snow hung around forever. He'd rushed, but it was the second week in June before he'd finally gotten everything in the ground. Then, everything flew to hell! It seemed as though Mother Nature was all ass-backwards that year.

First, there was no rain for weeks and then it rained for weeks, then it turned hot, and then hot and dry. Then, when the potatoes finally started blossomin, he noticed that the seed that he'd planted wasn't the seed that he'd wanted. When he went out to spray one mornin, he noticed that some parts of the field had blight while other parts of the field were full of potato beetles. Another part of the field was full of wild mustard and in another part, the potato tops were all burned as though there had been a frost. He didn't know what to do first, spray, dust, pull the mustard or blow the whole friggin field to hell. So he did everything, he sprayed, he dusted and then he cultivated. He wouldn't have minded so much if the potato seed had been his favorite Green Mountains, but they'd sold him the wrong seed and he hated those jeezely Russets!

Fall arrived and the harvestin was finally done and he thought to himself that it was lucky he'd survived. It was his habit at the end of harvest to go out and dress the fields with fresh manure in the fall to get a little head start on spring. He hitched up his old Farmall tractor and backed it into the barn. He set the tractor on idle and hopped off to hookup the manure spreader. Then, he drove the machinery out behind the barn and spent the morning and afternoon loading the spreader with manure and spreadin it on the fields.

Sometimes, the wind would shift direction and a strong gust would carry the manure in the opposite direction and small clumps would pelt him on the back of the head and all down his back. He'd shrug the stuff off and think to himself that it could be a whole lot worse. "Ah man gets pelted with one kind of crap or another all his natural life. If a man has to be covered with shit," he thought to himself, "At least, this is tha good kind."

Jist as he was about to spread his last load of the day, he noticed that his mother had stepped out onto her front porch and was waving for him to come over. Since the spreader was still nearly full and he would have to complete the job in the morning anyway, he stopped the tractor where it was right next to the road and left it there for the night.

At around seven-thirty that night, jist before he hit the hay, Hughy went out onto the front porch to have a last look around. He could barely make out the outlines of the tractor and spreader in the field down the road from his house and he felt a little guilty about leaving his precious equipment unprotected out there in the elements.

The next morning, he was up at the "crack of the crack" as they say in "Tha County" and he ate a quick breakfast and headed for the field. He looked up at the sky, checked the weather, looked to see if the moose had pulled down the fence again and checked to see if all the cows were there. He did everything but look in the direction of his farmin equipment.

When Hughy was about twenty feet away, his eyes saw, but his mind didn't register, the fact that his tractor had been moved and his manure spreader was gone! He couldn't believe it! He walked over to the place where he'd left it and looked down at the grass. Yes sir, he could make out the marks of a vehicle that had driven down into his field, hitched on his precious spreader and driven away with it! He was outraged! He wanted to find the rotten son-of-ah-bitch who'd stolen his spreader and wring his neck with his manure-stained hands!

Hughy left his tractor where it was and headed for the house as fast as his old legs could carry him. He grabbed the phone out of his wife's hands and called everyone he could think of in "Tha County" to be on the lookout for his spreader. Then he called the Maine State Police barracks in Houlton. When he told the dispatcher that he wanted to report a stolen manure spreader, the dispatcher laughed like hell until Hughy threatened to come down there and "pound the piss outta him." Hughy really got hot when the friggin dispatcher asked him if he thought they should put an "all points bulletin" out on his spreader. Hughy thought for a minute and said, "Go right ahead and do that because that old John Deere spreader was an antique and it's probably worth more than you make in a year!" The dispatcher didn't seem to think that everything was quite so funny anymore.

Hughy tried everything he could think of to find his precious spreader, but it was not to be found. Finally, pissed-off, angry and sad, he made a huge sign and took it out and drove it into the ground next to his property on the State Road. It read:

WILL THA SON-OF-AH-WHORE WHO STOLE MY
MANURE SPREADER PLEASE BRING IT BACK
"YOU CAN KEEP THA MANURE!"

THA TRUCK

Sammy and Tib had lived next door to each other all their lives. Their mothers had gone into labor on the same day and they'd been born jist three hours apart. The doctor had spent the day of November first, nineteen forty-four, running back and forth between the Baker and Maclean houses waiting to see which baby would arrive first. The boys had heard the story of their births so many times that when anybody brought the subject up; they'd tune them right out. They were downright sick of hearin about it.

They were closer than brothers and they even began to look alike, as they grew older. They had the same hair color that they wore parted on the left side and when they'd finally gotten old enough to have facial hair, Tib showed up on Sammy's doorstep with the beginning of a beard and was surprised to find that Sammy was growing one too.

Some of the old folks around town said that they were joined at the hip and if you saw one coming down the street it was a pretty good guess that the other wasn't too far behind. If the truth be told, if you happened to view them from behind, it wasn't easy to tell jist who was who. If it wasn't for the fact that both their mothers had unimpeachable reputations, some folks would have spread the rumor around that somebody had "jumped the fence."

When one of them took sick, the other one knew that he was going to catch something too. If one had a toothache, the other one would begin rubbing his jaw in the exact same spot. There was the day that Tib fell off a ladder and broke his leg. Before he'd even heard of Tib's unfortunate accident, Sammy took to his bed with a terrible pain in his leg. He lay there for three days jist waiting for something awful to happen to him too.

As the boys grew older, they reached the age when most men take a wife and they did what everyone really didn't expect, they married sisters. Then, each family gave their son a plot of land right next to the other. When asked if they'd planned it that way, both men looked at each other and shook their heads. It wasn't too long before both men were mired in life in the way that only a wife and family bring.

The two families interacted every day in some shape or form. Sammy and Tib always planned it so that all their vacations were together. They went hunting and fishing every year in the spring and fall. The only real difference between the two men was that one was a lot more ambitious than the other.

Sammy longed and struggled for all the "finer" things in life while Tib was quite content to jist be. Tib took a night job out to Pinkham's Mill and lived his life in the slow lane while Sammy was always rushing to and fro, hustling the almighty dollar. Sometimes he worked three jobs and weeks might go by without either one setting eyes on the other even though they lived right next door. Tib spent most of his off days in the company of his old dog Skippi, hunting of fishing or jist laying around his house playing with the kids and the dog. He was content to live life jist the way it was.

But Sammy was the exact opposite. He wanted things, he needed things. He had dreams and he wasn't content in the slightest. Sammy laid awake nights, thinking and planning how he was going to get what he wanted in this world and he wasn't afraid to work for it either. Sammy pined and longed for a new truck. He wanted it the way a man sometimes wants a lover. It had to be candy apple red and it had to have four wheel drive too. He didn't believe in credit cards and wouldn't allow his wife to have any either. If she whined or begged to have jist one, his standard reply was, "I'm not going to have one of those friggin, jeezley things and that's that!" He didn't believe in having bills and he was going to pay cash for the truck come hell of high water!

Every time Sammy got close to realizing his dream of buying a new truck, one of the kids took sick or taxes went up or some other God-awful thing happened and he had to set his dream on the back burner once again.

Finally, after working overtime, holding down three jobs and saving for ten years, Sammy finally had enough money. He went over to the Presque Isle Savings Bank, got a cashier's check and with a determined look on his face, he marched himself into Jake's Auto Sales on Main Street. He walked up to Jake Stevens' desk and sat down. He looked Jake right in his clear, blue eyes and said, "I've got a cashier's check in my pocket that could have your name on it, if the price is right!"

Jake, used to dealing with thrifty Mainers, used his tried and true, best deal-sealing tactic. He turned in his chair, wrenched open the door of the small refrigerator located on the floor behind him and reached inside. Withdrawing a couple of beers, he broke open an ice-cold Budweiser and handed it to Sammy. "Okay Sammy, what are yah lookin for?" Sammy took a long swallow of the cold beer, burped and said, "I want an F100 Ford truck with cream-colored leather seats and all tha trimmings. It has to be a four wheel drive and it has to be candy apple red!" Jake thought for a moment as Sammy rambled on. "It has to have "Ford" mud flaps and a vinyl bed liner and I want a wiper on tha rear window too."

When Sammy finally wound to a stop, Jake looked at him and said, "Tell me Tib, what's tha amount on your check?" Sammy squirmed in his chair for a moment and finally, he pulled the check out of his pocket and looked at it. "That's for me tah know and you tah find out," he said coyly. "Jaysus Tib, give me a break will yah. I need to know what your bottom line is before I can show you anything," Jake replied.

Sammy shook his head. "No offense Jake, but you guys are all tha same. Once you find out how much I'm plannin ta spend, you'll try tah foist all your old junkers off on me." Seein that Sammy wasn't going to budge, Jake said, "Let's go out to tha lot and have a look around and see what I have." Sammy set his now empty bottle of beer on Jake's desk and headed for the door.

They walked round and round the lot and Sammy jist couldn't seem to find the truck he wanted. Tired, Jake glanced at his watch and said, "Jaysus Tib, we've been around this friggin lot so many times that we're beginning ta wear out tha tar. Why don't you jist tell me how much you're willin ta spend and when I go down ta Bangor to tha auto auction on Friday, I'll look for a nice truck for you." Sammy looked at Jake for a couple of minutes and then he mumbled, "Not more-n twelve." Finally hearing the figure, Jake laughed and headed for the office because he now had a figure to work with.

Friday finally rolled around and Sammy was jumpy all day with anticipation. Every time the phone rang, he'd run over everyone else to get to answer it first. Long about five o'clock, when he'd jist about given up on hearing from Jake, the phone rang. Sammy listened closely for a couple of minutes and then his face lit up. He dropped the phone on the desk, grabbed his jacket and headed for the door. Jake had found a truck!

It was a nineteen sixty-three, red F100 and it was cherry! Sammy danced round and round the truck, never taking his eyes off it for a moment. He opened the door, stepped up on the running board and carefully slid into the soft, leather seat. He felt as though he'd died and gone to heaven! The "new" leather smell slid up his nostrils, around inside his head and was imprinted on his brain. He slid his hands over the steering wheel and across the dash. Yes sir! It was real leather! He slid his body down into the soft, upholstered seat and breathed in the leather smell. This was the truck all right! Jake turned on the overhead light and glanced at the dash. The odometer read 12,000 miles. "Shit, that ain't bad," Sammy thought to himself, "only a year old, why it's barely broken in!"

Sammy slid down out of the seat and dropped to the ground. He walked all around the truck and ran his hands over the bright, shiny red paint, examining every detail. Satisfied, he turned to Jake. "So," he asked nonchalantly, "What's tha deal with this puppy?" "Well," Jake answered, "It's a great deal really. It belonged to an old guy who loved trucks jist as much as you do and he'd only jist bought it last year and then he dropped dead. Go Figure! I guess his bad luck, is your good luck!" Sammy eyed Jake for a long moment. "I'll know jist how much good luck she is when you tell me what you want for her and don't be tellin me that tha old geezer dropped dead in tha truck or anything horrible like that."

Jake started selling! He walked all around the truck with Sammy close behind. He discussed tha tires, tha springs, tha engine, tha exhaust system and tha paint job. He could see that Sammy was a goner. Jist to push the sale a little harder, Jake unlatched the hood of the truck and swung it upwards. "Have a look at this baby, Sam." Jake commanded "Have you ever seen a prettier sight in all your life?"

The huge engine was an engineer's dream. The monster took up every square inch of available space and wires ran every which way. To some men, the smell of gas and oil is the same as an elegant, expensive perfume is to a woman. The two men stood where they were, jist tryin to take it all in. "I tell yah Sam, with this engine and tha four wheel drive, you ought to be able to climb Mt. Katahdin with no worries." Seein the look on Sammy's face, upon hearing that oversell statement, Jake quickly amended his sales pitch. "Well." he said sheepishly, "Maybe Haystack."

"I'll tell you what I'm goin to do Sam," he said. "I'm goin ta let you have this truck jist as she stands for fifteen thousand! En, you can drive her home tonight, how's that?" Jake turned in time to see the light go out in Sammy's eyes.

Sammy reached into his shirt pocket and pulled out the bank draft. He read across the row of figures printed on it and turned to walk away. Jake, seein a sale going up in smoke, hurried over to where Sammy stood. He deftly reached out and slid the bank draft out of Sammy's fingers, grabbed him by the arm and headed him towards the office. "Now, Sam, lets not be too hasty. I know that you love that truck and I'd sure as hell hate to see some little Christer, buy her and stove her all ta hell! Let's go git us another cold brew and think about it."

About an hour and half and a six pack later, the deal was struck. Sammy was the owner of the cream puff Ford and he was also the owner of a Ford Motor payment contract to the tune of twenty-five hundred dollars. He was going to have one hell of a time explainin this one to his wife.

Sammy was in like, in love and loony when it came to that truck. He knew the inner workings of that machine better than he did his wife! He bought a diary and wrote down every time he changed the oil, filled her with gas, rotated the tires and how many miles he drove daily. He installed a heater plug in the block so that the engine and the oil would be nice and warm before he took her out in the cold Aroostook County mornings.

Worried about rust and corrosion, he took to stoppin at the Ashland Town Garage to hassle the sanding crew about how much salt they were mixing with the sand when they sanded the icy roads. He'd head for the car wash as soon as he noticed a fine film of dust on the paint. He jist loved that truck!

His wife, now royally pissed off that he paid more attention to the truck than he did her, told all the neighbors that she was going to extend their bedroom so that she and Jake and the truck could all sleep together in the same room. Maybe then she'd get to see him more often!

He had a cleaning routine that he practiced religiously. He waxed; he dusted and vacuumed on a weekly basis. His wife, seein him headin out the door with her new vacuum cleaner, remarked to her mother that she jist might add a little chrome and red paint to her living room and kitchen and maybe he'd clean that up too!

He snuck a bottle of his wife's favorite perfume, Quadrille by Balenciaga, out of her bedroom and sprayed the cab and floor mats with it. His wife, when she discovered what he'd done with her expensive perfume, was furious and he placated her by saying that he'd sprayed the truck with her perfume because it reminded him of the way she smelled. After hearin the halfhearted compliment, she eyed him silently for a couple of seconds and let it slide. But later, when she was telling the story to her best friend she said, "I wanted to tell him that his cologne reminded me of a scent too, and the animal is black with a white stripe down its back!"

Every time he went for a drive and took anybody with him, to keep the floor mats pristine, he'd make them put plastic bags on their feet. If his wife and kids protested, he'd reach across them, open the door and point. They got the message real quick! No bags, no ride!

It had been one hell of a winter, the winter of nineteen sixty-four, especially for "Tha County." The normal snowfall for that neck of the woods usually was about one hundred inches each year but the arctic winds had dipped down from Canada and brought the cold and the swirling, heavy snows along with them. "Tha County" was inundated with one Christer of a snowstorm after another. By April, winter still lay heavy across the greater part of Aroostook County and Sammy received a phone call that was to forever change his life.

Sammy hadn't seen much of Tib for about a month and when Tib called that Friday morning, Sammy was really glad to hear from him. "So you old bastid, what's new with you?" He asked. "Nothin much"

Tib replied. "I was jist wondering if you might like ta go ice fishin before tha ice goes out on Squa Pan Lake?" "When were you thinkin of goin?" Sammy asked. "Well, how does tomorrow mornin strike you?" Tib said. "The only problem is, my Christly old truck has shit-tha-bed and we'd have to take yours." Anxiety, about his truck, slid through Sammy like a bad case of the trots. His mind reeled and raced, trying to come up with an answer that wouldn't offend his oldest friend.

"I know what you're thinking, Sam" Tib hurried on, "But, I'll be real careful and try not to get your truck dirty. I talked to a couple of fellers out to tha mill yestiday. They said that the road into Squa Pan Lake is plowed out nice en smooth en they caught a whole mess of smelt there a few nights ago and they was real good!" Tib rambled on and on and Sammy, feeling his heart strings over ride his brain, caved. Jist as he was about to hang up, he heard his old friend say, "Oh and by tha way, I hope you don't mind, but I've gut to bring Skippi. The vet said the other day that he's getting too fat and he needs to run ah little. See yah." And he hung up before Sammy could say no.

Sammy slid into bed and lay there, but he never did close his eyes. His mind skipped from one horrible scenario involving his truck to another and each one was worse than the one before. He'd been up for hours by the time Tib ambled through the snow to his house. His truck was all warmed up and ready to go, but Sammy refused to let Skippi into the truck until Tib had taken him into the garage and dried all the snow and water off his coat. Then Sammy made Tib put his jacket on the leather seat before he'd let the dog up onto the seat. Sammy started to hand Tib a couple of plastic bags for his feet, but stopped when he saw the look in his best friend's eyes. "Jaysus Tib, are yah nuts or what? It's only a truck for Christ's sake! Tha next thing I know, you'll be wantin to put sandwich bags on Skippi." Sammy leaned forward a little and looked past the large dog. Tib, seeing the hope in Sammy's eyes, laughed and said, "Forgettaboutit, Sam."

It was a little after six when they finally made it to the turnoff at Squa Pan Lake. Sammy stopped and downshifted into four-wheel drive. The truck geared down and sailed up the roughly plowed road like a corncob through butter. It made Sammy proud to think his pride and joy handled so well, but he jist couldn't rid himself of that anxious feeling.

Feelin sweat break out on his hands, he reached into his pocket, pulled out an old rag, and carefully wiped the water off the leather steering wheel. Seeing this, Tib turned his face away and smirked to himself in the passenger side window. "If I ever git tah be that friggin foolish about a truck, I hope ta Christ somebody shoots me," he thought to himself.

Suddenly, the truck ground to a halt on the frozen road. "Tib!" Sammy looked over the dog and yelled in his best friend's direction. "Could you puleeze wipe the drool off Skippi's lip? I don't want his slobber all over my cab en my leather seats!" "Jeeze Sam, will yah cool it. It's jist a little dog slobber for God's sake!" And he reached up and stroked the old dog's head. Sammy grimaced as he watched the dog lick Tib's face and lips. "Jayus, ain't I glad, that I'm not your wife! I'd hate to have ta kiss you!" "Kiss this!" Tib said and he lifted one buttock off the seat and patted it.

Sammy pulled into the turn around and carefully backed the truck out onto the frozen lake. He stopped when he was about thirty feet from shore and cut the engine. They sat there for a moment and all they could hear was the ticking of the motor as it cooled down. Then Tib opened the door and the dog took off in a frenzy of excitement and freedom. The excited dog slipped and slid as it tried to adjust its feet to the glassiness of the frozen lake. Tib took a small piece of wood out of his pocket and threw it across the ice to the dog. Skippi caught the wood in his mouth and quickly brought it back to him. "There ain't nothin like a small stick to make an old dog feel like a pup!" Tib laughed. When Skippi brought the stick back to him, he threw it again and started unloading the gear. "That foolish dog will keep that up all day if I keep throwing it to him," he said.

Sammy glanced at his watch and made a mental note to pry Tib off the lake by ten o'clock, fish or no fish! The sun had been up an hour before Sammy even noticed and there was no heat in it at all. Every once in a while, its pale light slid through the heavy clouds and the strong winds sent the light snow skittering across the frozen lake. Tib put his frozen fingers to his lips and blew a shrill whistle and the dog came bounding back across the frozen water.

Tib reached into the back of the truck and drug out his auger. He set it on the ice and began turning the handle. The auger slid and danced on the densely frozen ice and he had all he could do to hold it in place. After a couple of tries to get the drill to bite into the ice, he stopped, and said, "Jayus Tib, I never thought I'd have such a hard time ta dig a hole in this ice! It must be twenty inches thick!" "Well Tib," Sammy answered, "You wanted to fish, so let's get on with it. It's colder than zip's ass out here and gettin colder too!" Tib repositioned the machine and bore down on the ice again, but as before, the bit jist skittered and danced on the frozen surface.

"Did yah think ta bring an ax or a hammer?" Sammy asked him. "Jeeze no Tib, I didn't think I'd need one." "Well, we might as well pack it up and head for home then. We can't get to tha fish and I'm about ta freeze to death!" Tib looked at him for a moment and then a smile slid sideways across his face. "Not ta worry, old friend, not ta worry" and he began rummaging around in his knapsack.

Sammy, wondering what his friend was talking about, stepped back and waited to see what Tib was up to. "I always practice tha Boy Scouts commandments religiously," he grinned at Sammy. Seeing the question on Sammy's face, he explained. "You remember, don't you Tib, tha Boy Scouts motto, "anticipation," "preparation" and "awareness." That's my motto too! And Sammy, boy am I ever prepared!" With that declaration, Tib whipped out a long, round red-wrapped cylinder. Sammy stepped a little closer and then he stepped back when he recognized what it was that his friend was waving around his head.

"If we can't drill down to them little fishes, we'll jist blow them tha hell up out of that frozen water! Hell Sam, we'll have more fish than we can eat in a matter of minutes, with this ole boy!" "Wait a minute, Tib. You know it's against tha law to use dynamite ta catch fish." Tib looked his best friend in the face. "I won't tell if you don't." he giggled. "Besides, who's going to know? There's nobody around for miles. If anyone hears tha boom, they'll jist think it's ah jet breaking tha sound barrier over ta Loring."

Tib dug in his pocket and finally found his lighter. He flipped it open lit it and then he stuck the dynamite's fuse into the flame. Tib drew his arm back to throw the lit stick of dynamite and Skippi, thinking that he was throwing a stick for him to fetch, took off at the same time. The dynamite and dog flew across the ice in perfect synchronization. Skippi leapt into the air and caught the stick of dynamite in his mouth. He skidded to a halt and with ears up and tail jist ah wagging, turned around and proudly headed back towards them with his trophy.

Disbelieving what they were seeing, Tib and Sammy screamed and danced in panic. Tib's eyes were bugging out and he was flapping his arms and screaming at the dog. "No! No! Skippi! Drop tha stick! Skippi my boy, drop the friggin stick!" "No! Skippi! That's a good dog! Drop the stick!" screamed Sammy. The more they yelled and screamed, the more confused the dog became. He looked from one screaming man to the other and mistaking their actions for anger, he took off on a dead run for the only protection afforded him, the truck! He scuttled under the truck with the lit dynamite stick clutched firmly in his mouth. He crawled underneath until jist the tip of his nose stuck out at the very edge of the pickup. The smoke from the burning dynamite stick curled up past his nose into the frigid air.

Sammy and Tib, seeing where the dog was lying, stopped dancing and yelling. They began backing up as fast as they could go. Tib stopped running long enough to check the time on his watch and it was all over in a huge bang! Immediately following the dynamite blast, the truck's fuel tank blew and Sammy and Tib were peppered with pieces of shrapnel from the truck and the truck or what was left of it, was consumed by roaring flames.

Sammy turned and watched as his beloved truck became a fireball. He wiped a hand across his face and sank to the frozen surface and sat there. Tib jist stood where he'd stopped as though rooted to the spot. As the smoke cleared a little, they could easily see pieces of the truck strewn all over the frozen lake.

Tib could only look at the mangled truck in shock. "Skippi, poor old Skippi! He was my buddy, my best friend. I've had him since I was a kid. I'm sure gonna miss that old dog! Tib began to cry. Sammy could only sit where he was and then he was cryin too. But he was blubbering about his truck. Finally, Tib wiped his eyes and tried to comfort his friend. "Holy bloomin Jaysus Tib, did you see how high that sucker went? When that blew, it musta lifted twenty feet off the ground! Who'da thought that one little measly stick of dynamite could do that much damage?"

Sammy looked at his friend for a long moment and when the anger and shock had dissipated a little, he said. "I jist want you to know Tib, that I'll never be able to replace that truck!" Tib, feeling jist a tad insulted, looked down at his friend. "I don't know what you're pissing and moaning about Sam. All you have to do is call Ford and they'll have you a new truck as soon as they receive the insurance check! But, I'll never be able to replace old Skippi! And I've seen him a hell-of-ah lot more than I've seen you since you bought that friggin truck!" With that, oblivious to the frozen track of tears on his face, Tib set off across the lake towards the road. It was going to be a long, cold walk home....

UNCLE RON

Uncle Ron was the kind of man nobody really understood. He was, well, jist a little different and that was putting it mildly. He stood about five feet eight inches tall and all of his life he weighed around one hundred forty pounds. His hair was a light; reddish brown and his eyes were the color of muddy water. It was really his laugh that got your attention though. He had a way of laughing that made you question not only his sanity, but your own as well. His laugh began with a high pitched giggle and ended somewhere up close to a scream. Hearing it made the fine hairs rise up on back of your neck like the hackles on an angry dog.

Uncle Ron worked at a variety of jobs throughout his lifetime but his usual occupation was that of a carpenter and his work was easily identifiable around town. He was seldom asked to help with the finish work or any job that required attention to detail though. Unlike his uncle, Barney, who was a master carpenter, Uncle Ron could have been a good carpenter too, but he jist didn't give a damn about details.

When nailing a board onto a two by four, if he gave one of the nails a huge slam with his over-weighted hammer and the nail bent over, he wouldn't stop and try to straighten it out or jist pull it out, discard it and pound in a new one like the other workers. He'd continue pounding on it until he had not only pounded the bent nail out of sight into the wood, he'd pound away at the nail until he had huge hammer marks pounded into the wood as well. The foreman, when inspecting the job at the end of the day, knew not only by sight but also by feel, what section of the building Uncle Ron had worked on that day.

He was usually given jobs that didn't matter all that much because they certainly weren't ever going to be seen by anyone. They didn't trust him to saw anything either, because he couldn't ever saw anything straight. So, he got to pound a lot of nails in his forty-odd years as a carpenter.

When we were kids, we used to love to visit Uncle Ron. His small house was jist as strange as he was, but Uncle Ron was very proud of his house because he'd built it all by himself.

His house looked like a very simple four-room house from the outside and if you viewed it from a distance, it didn't look too bad either. But as you got closer, it seemed to have lines going in every direction. The crookedness of the house and its unplumbed lines pulled your eyes every which way. His siding boards generally started out pretty straight, but by the time he'd nailed the other end of the board onto the frame, it was all crooked. He never bothered to try and figure out what had caused the distortion; he simply nailed the next board on right where the other one ended.

We used to drive Uncle Ron crazy with questions about his house. They would all go a little like this: "Uncle Ron, why is your front door handle so small?" Answer: "Well, it still opens the door doesn't it?" "Uncle Ron, Why don't you have any steps for your backdoor?" Answer, "Well, I know there ain't no steps out there and besides, I never use that door." "But, Uncle Ron, what if a stranger comes to visit you and he opens the back door and falls out on his head?" Answer: "Well, I don't let no strangers in my house, so I guess I don't have to worry about that, now do I?" "Uncle Ron, why don't your cupboard doors open and close properly?" His reply, "Well, if they don't close too tight, I don't have to work so hard to open them."

Uncle Ron always answered all of our questions very patiently. He had an expression that covered everything he'd ever attempted in his life; "Shit-ah-God-damn, good enough!" That was his stock reply when our questions got to be too tiring, too technical or too personal. We never could figure out if he really knew the reasons why things had turned out the way they had, or if he had ever even thought about it.

We had a very large family and Uncle Ron somehow took it upon himself to build all the females in our family a "hope chest." We always knew that when high school graduation time rolled around, Uncle Ron would pull up in the driveway with his usual run-of-the-mill hope chest loaded on the back of his old, green pickup   Some of the hope chests would be straighter and some would be more crooked. Some would be shorter and others would be longer. Some would be full of knots and others would have the knots all knocked out of them. Some would have a beautiful shine to the finish and other would have all kinds of dead insects stuck in the still tacky varnish. Uncle Ron jist couldn't seem to get it right and it didn't matter to him one iota.

There used to be a contest in our family to see who got the best and the worst one. If we dared to complain to Uncle Ron that the lid didn't quite close properly, he'd scurry out to his truck and amidst the sounds of tools being thrown all over the place, he'd shout, "By gorry, I'll fix that in a jiffy!"

He'd run back inside with a five-pound sledge hammer dangling from his fist. Then, he'd lift the heavy hammer high over his head and bring it down with a glancing blow on the corner of the offending lid. Sometimes, the force of the blow would close the lid so tight that it could never be opened again in our lifetime! Other times, the heavy blow would shatter the lid, sending large ugly cracks streaking across the wooden lid.

Uncle Ron would whip his faded red cotton handkerchief out of his shirt pocket, wipe it across the shattered lid a couple of times and exclaim, "There, it's all fixed! Jist as good as new!" "But Uncle Ron, now it's all cracked!" We'd whine. And then came his standard reply. "Shit-ah-God-damn, good enough!" "Besides," he'd cackle, "If you leave tha lid open all tha time, no one will ever notice." Or, "Hey, jist chuck a couple of old quilts over the top and no one will even see tha cracks!" Then he'd giggle and laugh to himself as we all stood around looking at the too long, too short, to big, too small, insect studded, cracked, tacky lidded hope chest.

Uncle Ron wasn't ever to find fame in the field of carpentry like Uncle Barney did. Nor was he ever to find happiness in love. He was to marry twice and shack-up three times, but none of his romantic liaisons ever worked out for him.

The first lady Uncle Ron was to marry came from Oklahoma. When asked about her, he told folks that she was tall, lean and mean. She was a no-nonsense kind of woman and when she spoke in her soft southern accent, Uncle Ron said that her words may have sounded soft, but they were "edged in steel." Their union produced two children in a relatively short period of time and for a while things seemed to be going all right for them.

Until, one morning, Aunt Laura showed up at our door with all her things packed in her car. When mother opened the door, her sister-in-law burst in and she quickly told mother that she'd had enough! She said that she was taking the kids and going back to Oklahoma. She stated that she had taken all she was going to take from that slimy, little pervert and that was that! She said good-bye to mother and left and that was the last we ever saw of her for a very long time.

Later, when all the furor of their break up had died down a little, we finally worked up the courage to ask mother what a "pervert" was. She stopped washing the dishes, swung around from the sink and looked at us for a long moment with a deadly light shining in her deep brown eyes and then she told us that we had better mind our own business if we knew what was good for us.

When the Japanese conflict broke out, Uncle Ron and a lot of our other relatives and other town folk hastened down to the county seat at Houlton to volunteer their services for God and country. Uncle Ron was swiftly inducted into the army and after a quick basic training; he was immediately shipped to Japan.

Hearing the news of his induction, folks around town joked that they sure hoped that he could shoot a hell-of-a-lot better than he could pound nails, while others said that tha army must really be scrapin tha bottom of the barrel to have taken Uncle Ron so quickly.

Every now and then a soiled, hastily written letter would arrive from Japan and all the relatives would gather at grandmother's house to hear what he had to say. Uncle Ron didn't write much and the few scribbled lines started off okay, but the final sentence wound up slanting downward off the bottom of the page. It seemed that everything he did, turned out crooked somehow. He wrote that he was busy most of the time, shootin, shittin and shakin and he didn't bother to say in what order either.

When Uncle Ron finally returned from Japan, he brought a surprise along with him, a wife. He'd married a Japanese girl by the name of Rica. She was petite and dainty with long, blue-black hair that was cut in bangs straight across her pretty white forehead. She looked jist like a lovely little Japanese doll to us. They settled down in his crooked little house and we thought that surely they'd live happily ever after.

We didn't see too much of Aunt Rica and when we did get to see her; she couldn't speak enough English for us to really talk with her. We asked Uncle Ron how he managed to communicate with her. He jist laughed his high pitched laugh and said that for the things he wanted, he didn't have to talk too much. "Anyway," he said. "Most gall-darned wimmen talk way too much most of the time and it's good to have a wife yah can't understand."

For a little while, Uncle Ron was the envy of the entire male population of Ashland and the surrounding areas. Especially after other servicemen returned from Japan with tales of how the Japanese wives took care of their men. When pressed for details about their private life, Uncle Ron merely giggled his high-pitched giggle and headed for home in a hurry. A lot of the envious men around town were heard to comment amongst themselves that it was too darn bad that the Japanese War was over because they would certainly have joined up too!

After about a year of nuptial bliss, we were surprised to hear that Aunt Rica had departed Ashland for greener pastures. Folks sat many a long winter's night around their wood stoves, tryin to make some sense of this latest departure. Everyone agreed about one thing and that was that Uncle Ron was a hellava nice guy. Why was it that he jist couldn't seem to keep his wimmin? Nobody had an answer to that.

It was often repeated around town that as she boarded the Trailways bus for Boston, Aunt Rica was heard to utter a long, mean epithet aimed directly at Uncle Ron. It was half in broken English and half in Japanese, roughly translated, it sounded like she said, "Ruck Roo Ron!" Whatever that meant.

Uncle Ron pretty much stayed by himself in his little crooked house during the rest of his years. He was seen around town with several women from time to time, but none of them seemed to want to stay with him too long. But he never really gave up the chase.

In his later years, it wasn't uncommon for us to see his old, green pickup go streaking down the Masardis Road past grandmother's house on a Saturday night heading in the direction of town. He, like all the other unattached males around town, would park in his favorite parking space in front of Saint Mark's Catholic Church or the Ashland Hardware Store. He'd turn off the motor and slide down real low in the seat until jist the top of his bald head showed. He'd stay there checking out all the local girls until they rolled up the streets around eight o'clock and then he'd head back up the Masardis Road, streakin by the place where he'd been born, hell-bent for home and bed.

Uncle Ron passed away a few years ago and when I finally heard the sad news I was living in Australia. I had a good cry and then sat down to write this story. I figured that even though Uncle Ron had been a little strange, he really was a kind and gentle person at heart. And when his soul came drifting slowly up to heaven, St. Peter would carefully review his story about how he'd lived his time on earth and reach the inevitable conclusion, "Shit-a-God-Damn, good enough!"

THA SALESMAN

By the time Charley David Rose finally made his way into the world, his parents already had four girls and had given up on ever having a boy. Need-less-to-say, he was more than welcome! His father had longed for a son so bad that every time his wife was "carryin," he demanded to be allowed to name the child in advance. Hence, all his daughters had boy's names. They were Jackie, Ronnie, Dana and Billy. Folks, upon hearing his daughter's names, laughed and said that, that jist showed what a fool he really was. Did he really think that by naming the kid in advance, it might have some effect on its gender?

As the years flew by and Charley grew, he never had a serious thought in his head, ever. Right from birth, he'd sailed through life without a bump or scratch. He'd even missed all the normal childhood diseases, the measles, mumps and chicken pox. He couldn't recall ever having had a sniffle. He was charmed all right and that was all there was to it. He was a "God-child" and there wasn't anything that he couldn't do or wasn't allowed to do.

Charley was more than spoiled and his parents didn't care who knew it. To their way of thinking, a spoiled child was a happy child and a happy child was a child who was well-loved, if you get my drift. By the time he was ready for school; all the teachers had been given notice that Charley wasn't to be spanked, reprimanded, scolded or anything of that sort. If the teachers had a problem with Charley, then they were to call his parents and his parents would take care of the problem. "And we all know what his parent's will do about it," all the teachers laughed. "Nothin!"

Charley had a lot of "firsts" in his young life. At the age of six, he was the first kid to have his very own snowmobile. He was the very first kid in Aroostook County to have an A.T.V., a hunting rifle with a real scope, and a motorcycle, all before the age of thirteen. He was the first kid to learn to drive with his father's permission before he was of legal age. He was also the youngest kid in "Tha County" to smoke, drink and discover girls.

Charley never gave the slightest thought that all these firsts might not be so good for him or even how hard his mother and father had worked to get these things for him. He didn't spend one second of his self-absorbed life worrying about the health or happiness of another human being and least of all his parents and his siblings.

By the time Charley had graduated from high school, with barely passing grades, he had no clue about what he really wanted to do with his life. He'd spent all of his formative years being catered to by his adoring family.

His parents were tha kind of parents who felt that the good things in life had passed them by and they spent all their lives trying to make sure their son got all the fun and goodies that they'd missed out on.

On graduation night, Charlie's father handed him the keys to a brand new bright red, nineteen sixty-three F-100 Ford truck and not only had he filled the tank full of gas; he'd also filled a plastic barrel in the back of the truck with every kind of alcoholic drink imaginable. He smiled at his narcissistic, handsome son, gave Charley the "good old boy" pat on the back, slid a handful of condoms into his shirt pocket and said, "Go git em son!"

The next couple of months passed in a blur as Charley wove his way through the liquor, the girls and "Tha County." He could always be found with a new girl-riding shotgun by his side. Charley didn't seem to have too much trouble attracting the girls, but he had a real hard time keepin them. When he'd finally come up for air and noticed that the girl who'd last been riding in the seat next to him was now a totally different girl, he never even questioned it. He simply reached up, slicked his Elvis Presley styled red hair back with the palm of his hand, grinned in her general direction and said, "How yah doin hon?" And off he'd go, with a new drink in one hand and a new girl in the other. Life was good to Charley Rose.

Charley lived life to the fullest and he never missed a dance! He came home late and got up late and he was always met with adoring glances. His father was always waitin to hear of his son's latest exploits and newest conquests. When folks, mentioned anything detrimental that they'd heard about Charley, to his parents, they were met with such a wall of denial that they jist gave up. You couldn't make someone hear what they really didn't want to hear and that was that.

Finally one day, upon hearin the rumor that Charley might have gotten one of the local girls "in tha family way," his father was the first one to deny it around town. But once the news of the "coming event," spread throughout "Tha County," Charley soon found himself without the constant flow of female companions like he was used to. Suddenly, he wasn't so "cute" anymore and he wasn't such a desirable son-in-law to be anymore either.

Once Charley refused to acknowledge the fact that he'd fathered a child and hadn't owned up to it, he was "persona-non-grata" in many of the households in "Tha County." But that didn't bother Charley too long. He jist set his sights for a wider range and took himself over the Canadian border to the small French villages nestled along the Saint John River Valley. "Alla them little French girls still think I'm pretty cute," he told his father with a shit eatin grin.

Jist about the time the first hard frost hit "Tha County", Charley had a wakeup call that he couldn't ignore. At about two-thirty one afternoon, Charley heard the phone ring in the kitchen. He roused himself up out of an alcohol induced sleep long enough to see what time of day it was and then he slid back into his nice warm bed. Suddenly, he heard his mother down in the kitchen, scream and drop the phone and the next thing he heard was the sound of her feet as she came running up the stairs towards his room.

She burst through the door and collapsed on Charlie's bed. "Charley! Get up!" she screamed at him, as she clawed past the blankets till she found his shoulder. Charley jist lay where he was in his warm little nest. For the first time in her life, his mother struck him. She reached over and slapped him real hard on the side of the head and this time, Charley finally paid attention. He rolled into a sitting position and wiped his hand across his face. He turned and was startled to see that his mother was sweating and crying.

She shuddered and wiped her face with the back of her hand and said, "That was tha mill who jist called. They said that your father had some kind of attack and they're takin him over to tha hospital in Presque Isle. They want us to meet them there right away." Charley looked at her with a blank expression on his face; he didn't have a clue as to what she was saying.

It was then, that Mrs. Rose finally saw what a flawed human being her precious son really was. He didn't have enough feeling for another human being to care that his father, who'd done so much for him all of his life, might be dyin. Anger surged through her like a flame and for the first time in her life, she yelled at him. "Git your lazy ass out of bed, git dressed and make it snappy! I need you ta drive me over to Presque Isle to tha hospital. I'll wait for you downstairs!" With that directive, she flew down the stairs to get ready.

To give credit where credit's due, Charley did feel a little niggle of concern about his father, but it didn't last very long. He heaved himself off the bed and ambled over to the over-flowing closet to pick out something to wear. He finally withdrew a shirt and a pair of designer jeans and put them on as he made his way slowly down the stairs to the kitchen. His mother was all dressed and waitin by the back door for him. "For God's sake Charley, will yah hurry up! Your father might be dead before we get there!" She clawed the kitchen door open and ran across the porch towards his truck.

Charley, finally compelled by the urgency of her last remark, hurried to join her in his pickup. He flew down the Presque Isle Road towards the hospital, and he skidded to a stop in the parking lot, helped his mother out of the vehicle and ran behind her into the hospital. After what seemed like hours, a doctor finally made his way towards them as they sat waiting in the Emergency Room.

After much hemming and hawing, the doctor finally admitted that his father was lucky to be alive and if he made it through the next twenty-four hours, there might be a chance for a fairly good recovery. But, he would never be able to work again! His heart had sustained too much damage. Charley couldn't believe it! His father had always worked. Why he'd even worked two jobs most of his life. His father was a workhorse, make no mistake about it. To Charley's way of thinking, his father lived to work!

As his father slowly got better, Charley felt remorse for the first time in his life, but it wasn't remorse for his father who had worked so hard all those years, mainly to give him all that "stuff." It was remorse that his father would never be able to work again and wouldn't be handin out presents to him any longer either. Now he would have to go to work himself. Yes sir! Charley was one flawed human being that's for sure.

The war in Vietnam was escalating and reports of the daily deadly battles were raging across the television screen on a nightly basis. After watching the CBS Evening News one evening and not knowing that Walter Cronkite had put a "spin" on that particular edition, Charley got to thinkin that he jist might take himself down to Houlton to the Army recruiter's office the next day and sign up. The longer he watched the news, the more convinced he was that he should join the good ole United States Army!

He got up out of his father's old chair, walked into the bathroom, flicked on the light and looked at his reflection in the mirror. He slid his hand over his Elvis haircut and tried to imagine how his red hair would look in an Army butch. "Not too friggin bad!" he grinned at himself in the mirror. "Once I git that nice, green uniform on, I'll have tha chicks eatin outta my hand in no time! Yes sir! The Army needs one good man and that sure as shit's gonna be me!"

When the Army recruiter saw Charley walk into his office the next morning, he thought he'd died and gone to Heaven! This was the best lookin specimen that he'd seen come out of "Tha County" in a long time. This kid looked like he'd jist stepped out of a military recruitment ad. Red headed, broad shoulders, six feet two inches tall, perfect, white teeth and clear skin. He was an ideal recruit for the Army. The recruiter didn't waste any time either and the deed was done. The old Sergeant waived the normal waiting period and Charley was inducted into the Army before he knew what had happened.

Due to the war and the urgency for replacements, Charley was only given a seventy-two hour leave and he spent that in a fall from grace, mowing a drunken swath through Aroostook County. He hadn't had the backbone to tell his parents what he'd done, so he stayed as far away from home as he could get for the next few days.

The morning that he was to leave for basic training, he slid out of bed, ran for the shower and a quick shave. His father, an early riser out of necessity and habit, was shocked to hear Charley's feet hit the floor above him at a quarter to five. He felt a slight niggling of apprehension slide through him as he heard Charley come down the stairs. "Maybe he's finally grown up. Maybe he's goin ta look for a job!" He thought to himself as Charley came rushing into the living room.

Also surprised by Charley's early appearance, his mother came to see what was goin on. "Mornin son," she said. "I don't think you've ever made it up before tha sun since I brought you home from tha hospital. Would you like some hot biscuits and scrambled eggs? How about a hot cup of coffee?" She didn't wait for him to answer, but hurried into the kitchen to get him some breakfast.

His father looked at his son for the longest moment as his old heart pounded in his chest and then he said in a quiet voice. "Must be a mighty beautiful girl waitin for you, for you to be up so early this mornin." Charley, walked over to the living room window, drew aside the curtain and looked out into the driveway where his dusty Ford F100 was parked.

"Dad, I've gut something to tell you and you ain't goin ta like it." Charley heard the rattle in his father's chest as he struggled for breath, as he tried to imagine jist what friggin mess his only son had gotten himself into now. "I joined tha Army last week, en I'm leavin today." Upon hearin this shocking announcement, his father made a chocking sound as he involuntarily expelled the air from his tortured lungs. Finally, Charley turned around, but he couldn't meet his father's shocked gaze, as his dad sank into the chair behind him.

"Dad, you know I ain't done nothin but fool around since I graduated over a year ago and now it's time for me ta be a man. I've gut to do this dad, I jist have to!" His father gave a strangled gasp and Charley heard him say something that sounded like, "I knew it all along, but I jist wouldn't believe it! My son is nothin, but a God-damned fool!" With that, his father dropped his head into his hands and began to cry. Hearin the sounds coming from her husband, Charley's mother came running back into the room. And that was how they found out that Charley's lazy ass now belonged to the United States Army.

By eleven-thirty that morning Charley had boarded the Greyhound bus in Presque Isle for the trip to Fort Dix, New Jersey for his basic training. He still didn't have the slightest clue as to what he had gotten himself into. After all, he'd been living in the Kennedy "Camelot" era for a long time and "make love not war" was his motto.

Forever egotistical, he got up a time or two, before the bus left the station, to lean out the window to wave goodbye to his parents and to all the folks that he thought had come to see him off. A slight teariness slid into his eyes as he looked around and saw all the familiar faces looking back at him. "Never thought I'd made such an impression on all these folks," he said to himself as he leaned a little further out the window to wave goodbye once more.

Little did he realize that folks weren't there jist to see him off, many were there to see if the rumor they'd heard about his joinin the Army was really true! A couple of old jeezers, who'd seen fightin in World War Two and the Battle of Bataan and lived to tell about it, nudged each other as they saw Charley board the bus. "It won't take too long before the military tears that little bastid a new arsehole!" one old soldier said to another. "Ayah, but I don't know who I feel sorrier for, Charley or tha Army!" the other old man replied and they both had a good laugh over that one.

A lot of worried fathers, fearful that small children with red hair and resembling Charlie, might begin showing up in "Tha County", heaved a giant sigh of relief that night, because they hoped it was going to be a good long time before "Tha County" girls, again saw the likes of Charley Rose.

When the long, Greyhound bus drew to a stop in front of the military barracks in Fort Dix, New Jersey, Charley waited until he was the last one to get off. When he'd finally ambled to the front of the bus, he bent down and checked out his reflection in the driver's rearview mirror. Then he slicked back his hair with the palm of his hand, grabbed his bag and sauntered slowly down the steps of the open door.

Jist as he was about to step off the bus, a Sergeant came up to the door and seeing Charley standing on the last step, he stopped. "Well," "Well," "Well," what do we have here? Ah good ole boy from "Tha County"? Well, sister, let me make your acquaintance. I'm Drill Sergeant Michaud and I've been waitin for you all my life! Did yah have a nice trip down from potato country? Were yah well taken care of?" the Sergeant asked solicitously. Charley, used to being catered to at home, smiled and started to answer when the Sergeant's friendly demeanor suddenly changed.

The seasoned military man leaned up closer to where Charley was standin until his nose was jist brushin Charleys. "I don't care if yah were tied by your testicles to tha bumper of this bus and they drug yah all tha way down here, yah little asshole! I don't like prima donnas and I don't like tha expression on your smarmy, stoopid face! Now git your ass off this bus and git in line with the rest of em!" And he jerked his head in the direction of the other men waitin behind him. His fetid breath smothered Charley for a couple of seconds and it was all he could do to breathe.

Charlie's head swirled with the insults and outrage and he stumbled as he made his way off the last step of the bus. The Sergeant, noticing the stumble, screamed at him again, "What's tha matter farmer? Still think you're dancin across a potato field? Git your sorry ass in tha back of tha line over there!" Humiliated, Charley finally found the end of the line and slunk in.

By the end of the first week, the Army knew jist what they'd bargained for and he wasn't the bargain they'd first thought. No matter what they'd thrown at him, Charley wasn't able to do it. He couldn't shoot, he couldn't run, he couldn't climb, he couldn't swim and he couldn't think. They gave him test after test and he failed them all.

Worried, the Drill Sergeant placed a call to the Houlton recruiter to double check on Charley. "Are yah absolutely certain that this old boy wasn't drafted? Are yah positive that he actually volunteered?" he asked.

Thinking that Charley was using reverse psychology and deliberately trying to outsmart them by failing every exam, they turned him over to the shrinks. After a battery of questions and tests, the shrinks came up with the final diagnosis. Charley was suffering from a syndrome called "Narcissistic Personality Disorder."

The shrink called Charley's unit and the Sergeant waited with baited breath to hear what was wrong with Charley. When the doctor had finished his technical spiel, the Sergeant asked. "What tha hell does all that mean? Put it to me in everyday language, doc!" "Well." The shrink replied. "To put it plain and simple, he's been pampered and spoiled all his life and he's never had to do anything he didn't want to do. Now, we, tha Army, are making demands on him that he can't meet and he isn't faking. He really can't do what it is that we want him to do. You'll never make a soldier out of him. You might jist as well cut your losses and do tha Army a huge favor. Send his ass home!"

It didn't take the Army too long before they realized that Charley was like a rotten apple. All beautiful and shiny on the outside, but rotten to the core on the inside. And that was that, Charlie's Army career lasted exactly fourteen days, six hours and thirteen minutes and it wasn't too long before Charley was on another Greyhound headed north, with a manila envelope stuffed in his pocket. Inside the envelope was a paper and written on it was the notation, "Unsuitable for Military Duty - 4-F."

Charley's arrival home was exactly the opposite of his leaving. When the bus pulled into the depot in Presque Isle, the only person at the station was an old wino who was looking for a free ride on to Madawaska. Charley, used to having a vehicle at his disposal, couldn't think what to do next. Finally, he wandered over to the station window and asked to use the phone.

His mother, surprised at hearin his voice on the other end of the line, called his father to the phone. "How's tha weather down there in New Jersey?" his father asked. "Don't know dad," Charley answered. "What do you mean you don't know? Are yah too busy learnin ta be a soldier ta look outside and see?" "No dad, I can see alright and all I can see is an empty parkin lot." His father felt like he was havin a conversation with two different people. "Yah mean they don't have a lot of trucks and tanks and planes all over tha place?" his father asked. "Dad, tha only thing that I can see is tha back ass of a big old greyhound and that's about it!" Charley replied. His father was perplexed. "I don't git it son, what tha hell is tha Army doin with a dog? I thought you was trainin ta be a paratrooper?" "Naw dad, that's tha Air Force. Jesus dad, could you jist come and git me?" Hearin this, his father couldn't think for a moment. "Come and git you? Jesus son, I ain't never been further than Bangor in my whole life, en I don't have tha slightest idea how ta git ta New Jersey, en besides, why would you want me ta come and git you? Don't you still have another five weeks of basic?" "Dad, listen ta me for once, will yah. I'm over ta tha bus station in Presque Isle. Could you jist come and git me?" With that admission, Charley's voiced faded away.

His father couldn't believe his ears! Had his precious son failed his physical? Was there something wrong with him? Question after question slid through his addled old brain. "Sure! You betcha son, I'll be there in a jiffy," and he hung up.

Charley glanced at his watch, seven twenty-five. "Tha old man won't be here till about eight thirty by tha way he drives," Charley thought to himself as he headed to the Westmorland Hotel Coffee Shop that was located jist down tha block.

After Charley was home a couple of days and the excitement of his return had faded somewhat, there was much discussion amongst the family about what to tell the neighbors about his sudden return. It was decided that they'd jist say that Charley had a "symptom" and that he'd received a Medical Discharge. Talk and speculation by the townspeople, about Charlie's illness and sudden discharge, slid around town like grease in a fryin pan and folks never tired of discussin Charlie's problem.

"Did yah say that tha Rose kid had a bad heart?" One asked another. "No! No! All I heard was that he had ah "syncope" or "symphony" or somethin. He had ta take a medical discharge. Tha Army didn't want him, what with a "bad ticker" and all." The story was told and retold so many times that it became so jumbled up, that folks couldn't make heads nor tales of it. In the end, nobody including Charley, knew exactly what was wrong with him and why he'd really received a Medical Discharge.

Charley, still enamored with the idea of being a soldier, took to wearin his uniform all over "Tha County", until one of the old Army retirees, who'd fought in both the Second World War and the Korean War, stopped him on the street in Madawaska and told him that if he didn't stop wearin that friggin uniform, he was going to pound the piss outta him. After that, Charley still wore his army pants or shirt, but never at the same time.

Things settled back into the routine that Charley had had before he'd gone off to join the Army and it wasn't too long before the shit hit the fan. Charley hadn't even been away long enough to say that the kid wasn't his and her father was soon walkin behind him down the aisle.

As the minister said the hurried vows, Charley's mind slid away to the battlefields of Vietnam. Folks said that he said his "I Do's" but Charley never remembered sayin them.

Charley and his new wife promptly moved in with his parents and he quickly took up where he'd left off. Once again, Charley was the little, spoiled pampered kid that he'd always been. The only difference was, now he wasn't little and he certainly wasn't a kid. He was married and waitin for a kid of his own to arrive.

Being newly married didn't make too much difference to Charley. As the days slid by, one into another, he picked up right where he'd left off, runnin all over to Christ and gone, lookin for what, he didn't know. His young wife, annoyed at being left alone all the time with his old, adoring parents and knowin that he'd been spendin his time with other wimmin, packed herself up and went home to her parents. It didn't take too long before Charley was served with a "Notice of Support" order.

One night in early November, when the roads were greasy with new-fallen snow, Charley finally came face to face with reality. He'd been partyin over to Fredericton, New Brunswick and had decided to make the long drive home, even though he was already "three sheets to tha wind." He made it all the way home okay, but he forgot to slow down as he turned into the driveway. When he'd finally applied the brakes, it was too late and his truck slid right into the front porch bustin it to hell and gone!

His father, hearin and feelin the terrific impact and terrified by the sound of breaking wood, came stumbling out of bed to see what had happened. All he saw was Charley in the driver's seat and his truck imbedded in the porch up to the front door sill. When Charley's alcohol addled brain settled down, he looked up and saw his father's shocked face starin back at him thru the front door window.

Charley, lookin for tha humor of the situation, yelled to his father, "Jaysus dad." "My brakes musta locked and I slid right into tha porch." His father pulled some of the debris away and drug Charley from the truck. He helped him into the house and pointed him in the direction of the stairs. "Charley, you go and have a good night's sleep and we'll have us a talk in the mornin." Charley gave his father his two fingered Army salute and stumbled up the stairs towards bed.

"In the mornin," turned out to be four thirty in the afternoon before Charley finally made his way down the stairs. His father, seein that Charley was all set to head for the door, called him into the kitchen. He pulled a chair out and motioned for Charley to sit. "Son, you know that I've always done my best for you, don't you?" Charley looked at his father and was surprised to see how old, gray and tired he looked. "Yah dad, I know all that you've done for me." "Well son, you know that I never minded, not one little bit, but now tha doc says that I ain't gut too much time left and I'd like to know that when I leave this Christly place, you have a nice future all lined up for you en yours." His father stopped for a moment to catch his breath and let his little talk sink in. "So, I've cashed in a bond that I took out when you were born, en it's all yours. I hope that you'll use it wisely ta help you prepare for your future." His father handed him a check and Charley had to wait until the tears in his eyes went away before he could read the amount written there. "Pay to the Order of Charlie David Rose the sum of Five Thousand Dollars." Charlie tried to thank his father, but his father jist waved him away. "Son, take this check with my blessin, ta my way of thinkin, you don't owe me a damn thing." He reached out and grabbed Charley's shoulder, gave it a good squeeze and then he shuffled off across the kitchen floor and out the door. Still clutchin the cashier's check in his fist, Charley sat in the chair and thought about what he was going to do with all the cash.

His father hoped that Charley would take the money and go to school and get some trainin and he was happy when he learned that Charley had taken himself off to the North East Tractor Trailer School in Boston to learn to be a truck driver. But Charley soon found that driving an eighteen wheeler was a lot more complicated than it seemed and he was soon back in "Tha County" with no truck driver's license and half of the money gone. Then, he tried growin potatoes on a small patch of land his uncle owned on the Garfield Road, but the plantin, cultivatin and the sprayin soon put the run to his ass. Next came guidin for sports in tha Maine woods, but after having to be rescued by the warden's service several times, the wardens finally told him that if they had to come and rescue him one more time, well you get the picture.

Then a job at Pinkham's Lumber lasted about three months. Next, he tried to convince the school board that he'd make a good bus driver, but after they'd checked his drivin record, they wouldn't have him either. He took a job on the night shift at the plywood factory over to Presque Isle, but pullin all those splinters out of his fingers was pure hell! The next job was at McCain's potato chip plant in Easton, but smellin all that grease eight hours every night, clogged up all his sinuses. There was a short stint as a cab driver, but he lost that job when he forgot that he was a driver and not part of the party goers. Charley jist couldn't find a niche, no matter what he tried. He was expert of all and master of none.

Charley floated around "Tha County" like a dandelion seed in the wind. His good looks and great smile often got him a foot in the door, but it wasn't too long before he was standin on the other side. "A complete waste of good skin" was the general consensus of the hard workin folks in "Tha County".

The winter of sixty-seven was a hellacious one. Folks were droppin like flies from one kind of flu or another. Mr. Rose was the first one to go and heartbroken and lost, Mrs. Rose was soon gone too. Charley, bereft, adrift and in a state of shock, soon found himself at the lawyer's office for the final readin of the will. Mr. Stevens had been his parent's lawyer all their lives and after glancing at a list of documents on his desk, he looked sorrowfully at Charley. "Son, I want to tell you that I'm awfully sorry"… Charley looked up at him and waited. "I'm awfully sorry, but I've carefully reviewed your parent's estate and after the sale of tha old house, there will be jist enough money left to pay off tha rest of their debts." Charley stared at the old lawyer in disbelief. "But that can't be!" He exclaimed. "My dad and mother worked hard all of their lives and dad made good money! Why, most of the time, he even worked two jobs!" Mr. Stevens nodded his head. "That's true Charley, but do you realize, that during all that time, he wasn't able to save a penny, no matter how hard he worked." Mr. Stevens looked meaningfully across his desk at Charley, but Charley still didn't get it. The old lawyer finally shook his head and said, "Charley, let it go, there isn't anything left, at all." And then he said the hardest part, "My advice to you and you ain't goin ta like it, is ta go out and find yourself a job. Any kind of job and tha sooner tha better!"

Charley went whinin to his sisters and one after the other, they turned him down. They really didn't have any sympathy for him. He'd always been tha golden boy, while they had to work for what they wanted. Their answer was always the same. "No!" He couldn't move in with them. "No!" He couldn't borrow any money. "No!" They weren't going to cosign a loan for him. He'd always had more than they'd had. That was their final answer. The worm had turned; Charley was finally on his own.

Charley, a parasite from birth, soon found wimmin, a lot older and a lot more time worn, with a little money put aside, who were more than willin to have a young, good lookin man in their bed, for a while. But Charley, incapable of a real feelin towards anyone other than himself, wasn't a kept man for too long. He had so many addresses in such a short span of time that the post office jist stamped his junk mail and bills "General Delivery" and threw it in an old box on the floor in a corner of the Ashland Post Office.

The years passed and Charley found that he was mortal after all. His red hair receded across the top of his head until he couldn't even see it any more unless he turned around and his belly grew until his feet disappeared entirely from view too. He was no longer the mean, lean, lovin machine. Those days were gone for good. Charley was middle aged and loosin ground fast!

Charley took to hangin out at the bar at the Westmorland and as the old hotel grew seedier and seedier, so did Charley. Then one day, one of his older lovers made him an offer that he couldn't refuse. She'd pay for him to go to the Morrison Sales Institute in Boston, if he'd agree to move in with her. Charley didn't hesitate for a minute, he knew how to be a hired lover and he knew a golden offer when he saw it. Less than a week later, for the second time in his life, he was on a Greyhound bus headin south.

Charley took to sales like a kid to puppies. He was in his element! He flew through the six-week course and soaked up the sales techniques like a sponge. Armed with several freshly signed "diplomas" he headed north with a new confidence and zest for life. He was going to sell and he was going to become the "super salesman" of "Tha County." As soon as he got back to Presque Isle, he grabbed his belongings and ditched the old bag. He was finally on his way!

Dressed in the old bags, dead husband's suit and armed with business cards and a briefcase, Charley quickly landed a job at the "Maine Mobile Home Center" jist outside of Presque Isle on the outskirts of the Caribou Road. The owner was a blousy, bleached blonde, several years his senior and a widow to boot. Charley could see the writin on the wall! Tha Gods were kind! He moved into an office that was only slightly shabbier than the trailers that he'd be sellin. Life was good! For the first time in his life, Charley felt that he had a callin. He had the Morrison sales technique down pat. He could talk a potato farmer into buyin his own potatoes. Yessir! He was that good!

The first thing Charley did after sweepin and cleanin up his office was to pound nails into the sheetrock and hang all his sales diplomas on the walls. Then, he went over to Woolworths and bought himself a huge picture of a deer standing in a field. He hung it on a long wall across from where he sat and then he set about rearrangin his desk and sales area.

He drug a small table into his office and placed it along the wall that had a small closet right next to it. He had everything situated so that, when seated, everyone in his office could see the picture of the deer and all his diplomas too. And he could easily reach over and open and close the closet door, anytime he wanted. Now he was ready.

Givin praise where praise is due, Charley was good! He was very good at makin sales. It wasn't too long before folks were buyin trailers they didn't want and partin with all their hard earned potato pickin money in a hurry. Charley was on a roll, but the roll didn't last too long. All those things he'd learned down in Boston soon fell by the wayside and the sales ceased.

Charley was arrogant, that's the word, arrogant. And folks in "Tha County" can't stand an arrogant man. Ah liar, ah snake, ah cheat, ah thief or ah cad, folks might tolerate them, but arrogance, no! Charley couldn't understand what was wrong. "I know how ta sell," he thought to himself. "I have all them diplomas don't I. These folks are jist friggin fools, that's all." And he really believed it. He didn't believe that he could really be the problem.

Folks would drive slowly onto the run-down sales lot and Charley would amble over to the door, coffee cup in hand. He'd lean against the open door way with a shitty little grin on his lips and slowly sip his coffee. When folks hesitantly headed for the front steps, he'd step out onto the porch and shout, "Welcome folks, welcome! Come on in!" He'd step back and with a grand sweep of his hand, as though he owned the whole friggin joint, he'd move them into his office and into some chairs. Then he'd amble over to a dirty window and gaze out into the sales lot for a couple of minutes, leaving the prospective buyer's jist sitting there, staring at his back, perplexed. Finally, he'd turn around, set his coffee cup on his desk and slide into his chair. He'd run his hand over his bald scalp a couple of times, all the while giving the folks the once over. And then he'd begin his sales pitch.

Most folks, thinkin Charley was a real good guy, warmed up to him right away. And Charley, having trained all his life, to separate folks from their money, did the Morrison Sales Institute proud. He could make a sale rather easily, but he never did learn how to close.

Charley's sales plan was rather simple. He first made the potential buyers his "best" friends. Then he walked them around the sales lot until they found a trailer they liked. Next, he'd hustle them back into his office where he'd make them a fresh, hot cup of coffee and write up a preliminary sales contract. Then he'd always make an appointment for six o'clock the next evening. Charley knew that a man, who'd worked hard all day, was tired, dirty and hungry. He'd sign anything in order to get home, have a wash, a good stiff drink and fill his empty belly.

The next evening, Charley would have the customer's sales file all set up nice and neat on his desk. He'd have two pens on the other side of the table so that each buyer had their own for signin the final sales contract. Once the eager buyers came in, after shakin hands all around, Charley would begin applyin pressure. The sad thing was, most of the time, Charley had the sale already made, but he jist couldn't see it. Something happened to him at every closin and it would all turn bad.

Captivated by the sound of his own voice, he'd drone on and on about all the sales he'd made and how great he was, until folks would be sittin in their chairs in a daze. Not hearin a response from them, he'd stop and look at them real close. And then things would fly all to hell. Seeing their glazed over eyes and thinking that they were going to back out of the sale, he'd slam his fist on the desk so hard that the buyers jumped as much as their coffee cups.

"Thanks a lot for wastin my friggin time!" he'd shout. The buyers, bewildered by this verbal attack, would look at each other and wonder what tha the hell was goin on. Charley would lean in real close to them and say; "You don't work for nothin, do you?" Startled, the customers would shake their heads no. Charley would look at them again and shout, "Well neither do I!" And he'd bang his fist on the desk again, causin the customer's folder to jump across the desk in front of them.

If the customer reached into his pocket for the down payment money, Charley would glance at it with scorn and refuse to take it! If the customer asked in a hesitant voice when they were goin to get their home, Charley would glare at them and say in a haughty voice, "The answer is in the question!" Folks didn't understand what that meant either. They'd look at each other wildly and slide their chairs a little further away from the desk towards the door.

Seeing this backward movement, Charley would suddenly point at the large picture of the deer that was hanging on the office wall and yell, "See that deer!" and the buyers would turn and stare at the picture for a couple of seconds and then back at Charley. But he never finished the statement. He'd glare at the would-be buyers for a couple of long seconds and then he'd reach over and wrench open the closet door. In the middle of the closet floor was a tall pile of manila folders.

Charley would hold the closet door open so that folks could see the folders stacked there and then he'd point to the pile of sales files sitting in the middle of the closet floor and say in a deadly quiet voice. "Do you see that pile of folders? Well that's folks jist like you who didn't want to give me my money! Folks jist like you, who will never have a friggin home!"

He'd stare meaningfully at the prospective clients for a moment or two and then he'd sweep their sales folder off the top of his desk and onto the top of the pile stacked on the closet floor. Then he'd slam the door closed so hard that the thin walls of the mobile home office would bend. It wasn't too long after that, that the potential buyers would find their feet headin for the door and they'd be gone. Gravel would fly and they'd be tearin up the Caribou Road towards home as fast as they could go.

Nonplussed, Charley would go into the back room, dump out the

207

remainder of his cold cup of coffee, brew himself a new one and head for the front door. He'd lean nonchalantly against the door jam until another unsuspecting customer drove onto the lot and it would begin all over again.

So, if you are ever visitin in "Tha County" and you find yourself drivin past the Maine Mobile Home Center on the Caribou Road and you happen to see old Charley, lounging in the door way, drinkin his coffee. Don't stop, jist slow down a dite, give old Charley a good old wave and keep on drivin.

DAD & ME

Dad loved to fish and with eight kids, he usually took a couple of us with him every time he went, because he knew that if he didn't, there'd be a lot of sulking when he returned home.

He was like a man who'd won the jackpot when Uncle Pete gave him a green canvas covered "Old Town" canoe, and he'd carted that dilapidated thing home like he'd won the biggest lottery in the world. He'd gone over the boat from stem to stern and not finding too much to worry about, reinforced a couple of ribs, gave the canoe a couple of coats shellac and as we are fond of saying in "Tha County," it was, "shit-ah-God-damn, good enough!"

In the spring, after the water had gone down a little on the Aroostook River, dad would rush home from his daily job at the potato house, hurriedly eat supper, grab his fishing gear and head down the dirt road for the river. He'd back his battered old pickup down to the riverbank, and then he'd slid the long canoe off into the swirling water. He'd step in and hold it in place with his paddle until we kids had jumped in and then off we'd go.

An even older Johnson motor, that had been used and abused long before he'd gotten it, had accompanied dad's canoe. He'd torn that motor apart time after time and try as he might, it never seemed to work properly. If he even got it started, it might take off like a bat out of hell and then jist as suddenly, it would sputter a couple of times and die. Many's the time that he'd had to paddle in the Aroostook River all the way around Uncle Hal's island back to whcre he'd parked his truck at the bridge. I'm sure that if he'd had the slightest notion that someday he'd be able to buy a motor that worked all the time, that old Johnson would have found itself lying on the bottom of the Aroostook River, especially after he'd had to paddle up-currant about five miles to get back home.

Dad jist never knew if or when that friggin motor was going to start. Sometimes, he'd pull on cord of the motor until it gave a few feeble coughs, and die and he'd never get it started. And at other times, he'd choke it a little and it would come roaring to life and in a cloud of blue smoke, off we'd go, around the island and out into the swiftly flowing Aroostook River.

Then dad would head for his favorite fishing place, Trout Brook, which was located on the Garfield side of the river. Jist before we got there, he'd turn the motor off, and we'd slowly cruise into the mouth of the crystal clear brook. He'd reach up, grab a branch of river birch and tie us up. Then he'd quickly thread a brown angleworm onto his hook and drop it into the water.

If dad didn't catch anything right away, he'd quickly take off the worm-encrusted hook and tie on one of his special homemade flies. His tackle box was filled with new flies that he'd spent all winter and spring making and he was anxious to try each and every one. Ever since his father had found the brook way back when dad was a little boy, he'd always had good luck at Trout Brook and considered it his private fishing hole. And he always got a little testy if he happened to be cruising by and saw anyone else fishing there.

In the early spring, after the water had gone down on the flats, dad would always leave the heavy canoe on the riverbank across the bridge on the island side of the river. He had a strict rule for us kids and that was that we weren't ever to touch his canoe, but like all the other rules that he'd made to protect us, that didn't stop us either. We'd wait until we knew for sure that he'd be working up to the Masardis potato house all day, and he wouldn't be driving by our house, then we'd rush down to the river, drag the canoe into the water and we'd be off. We never touched his motor, but we stole that old canoe so many times, that dad would have killed us if he'd known jist how many times we took it. Most of us couldn't swim, and we didn't have any life preservers and we didn't care either.

It was about a mile and a half around Uncle Hal's island and the current, especially if the water was high, could be quite tricky at times, but we didn't even think about that. We'd slide the canoe into the swirling water and off we'd go. Happy and carefree, we'd float down that river jist like a feather on the water, oblivious to the dangers that lurked only a couple of inches away.

One time when I was about eight years old, dad took me fishing with him. When we got down to Uncle Hal's island, he parked the pickup in his usual spot under a tall Oak tree near the bridge. Then he carried all of our fishing gear down the bank to the canoe. He always left the canoe in the same spot, and he could tell immediately if it had been moved. He eyed it closely for a couple of seconds and satisfied that apparently we hadn't touched it, he reached down, tipped it over and a small garden snake wriggled out of the canoe and across my feet.

I was deathly afraid of snakes, and I did a "holy conniption fit" dance at the sight of the snake and it took dad a while to convince me to get in the boat. And then it took dad a while to convince me to stop crying and that the snake wouldn't hurt me. Sniveling and snuffling with a few hiccups thrown in, I asked dad if he was ever afraid of anything.

Dad looked at me for the longest moment and then he replied, "Sure Toots, there have been lots of times that I've been scared, scared tah death, as a matter of fact." "When were you ever scared dad?" I asked skeptically. He had a faraway look in his eyes when he finally answered. "Well, when I was nineteen years old, I was scared tha day I opened tha wood box at home and found my father inside with his head blown off." His eyes slid away from mine, and he looked off in the distance, at the river for a while, remembering that day all over again.

Then he looked at me and asked. "Do you remember when Uncle Herbie died?" I nodded my head. "Well, I was scared when they were dragging this very river down around the bridge in Ashland for his body. And, I'll never forget tha morning up there at tha potato house, when I unlocked tha doors and felt two feet brush against tha side of my face. Old Charley Eastland had hung himself there tha night before. I was always scared to go back into that potato house after that."

Dad scrabbled in his pants for his lighter, paused, lit himself another Chesterfield and then he continued. "And I was really scared when your cousin accidentally shot your brother Walt when we were on a hunting trip up to Moosehead Lake. I had to carry him, and he was bleeding like crazy, down out of tha woods, fearin all tha while that he was gonna die on my back. So you see Toots, I've been scared more times than not.

Always remember, you're not a fool to be scared. Sometimes, you're only a fool when you're not scared." I still remember dad's sage words, but they didn't help all that much, I'm still afraid of snakes!

PRAYERS

Every Sunday, throughout the Ashland area in Aroostook County, Maine the churches of all the different denominations would ring their bells and church-going folks would hurry off to their respective houses of worship. Competition for the lost and sliding souls among the churches was fierce and God help you if you didn't belong to what each group considered the "best" church and the "best" church was the church group you happened to be talking to at the moment.

If you belonged to the Catholic Church then you would never get to heaven or so the Protestants predicted. And the Pentecostal Church was jist a step above Hell according to the Seventh Day Adventists and the members of the Baptist Church were absolutely convinced that they were the chosen ones and so on and so forth.

Each denomination watched the others with the diligence of Nazi Storm Troopers. Whenever a member of another congregation committed an indiscretion and it became public knowledge, the incident was reported, repeated and embellished beyond all recognition. Now, no one actually "lied" because that would have been "unchristian" and a sin to boot, but the line between lying and exaggeration was cut awfully close.

Because Saint David's Catholic Church in Ashland was all alone among the seven non-Catholic ones, it caught an awful lot of hell and criticism from the others. Father Morin had been the parish priest at St. David's for over thirty years and he was generally well thought of by the practicing Catholics in our small community.

When Father Morin's elderly housekeeper died suddenly, the parish council instructed him to find himself another. So, off he went to Boston and when he returned, he had a new housekeeper with him. She was much younger than Father Morin and she spoke English with a lovely Irish lilt. Every few months there would be a new salacious rumor flying around town about Father Morin and his "housekeeper," Agnes McGillicuddy.

Every now and then, the good father would deposit his housekeeper in the back of his old, black Buick and they'd drive regally through town on their way to parts unknown. Tongues would wag and speculation would be rife until they reappeared, seemingly oblivious to all the gossip their trip had caused. Try as they might, folks never really knew jist what the housekeeper's role really was. In the ten or so odd years that the lovely woman lived in the parish house with Father Morin, she was referred to as his wife, his mistress, his lover, his sister, his cousin, his aunt, his girlfriend, somebody else's wife and all of the above.

Another rumor that made its way around town and fostered by members of the Protestant churches was that Father Morin was a secret alcoholic. "Didn't you notice that his cheeks were jist a little too pink?" And, "He seems to enjoy drinking from the chalice a little too much doesn't he?" And "Why is he so happy all the time?" Some people even swore that when he'd given them the Sunday blessing, why, his breath absolutely reeked of strong spirits. And the rumors went round and round.

Some parishioners, known to imbibe on a regular basis, were livid that the "old fart" had the nerve to scold them about their drinking habits. He, a man of God, was drinking more than they were and in church too! Finally, a couple of enterprising altar boys settled the question once and for all. They slipped into the sacristy office early one Sunday morning before mass and opened the closet where Father Morin supposedly hid his "liquor." They found a whole case! A whole case of Welch's grape juice! There wasn't a single drop of wine or liquor to be found on the premises.

When this stunning news finally made the rounds, Father Morin found himself deluged with repentant confessors. "Forgive me father for I have sinned." "And what sin have you committed my son?" asked the good father. "I am guilty of spreading false word against my neighbor." Father Morin eyed the sinner, gave him three "Our Fathers" and ten "Hail Mary's" and "Go forth my son and spread no more," was Father Morin's admonition. Little did the good father know, but he was the person about whom the rumors had been spread.

The parishioners of his parish knew of his innate goodness, but human beings being what they are, that didn't stop them. They complained behind his back that he was too rigid, too lax, too old, too dogmatic or too immoral. No matter what he did, criticism followed him. It was often discussed amongst the parishioners that when father decided to retire, they'd ask the archbishop in Portland to send them a younger, more modern, more enlightened priest.

The day finally dawned when Father Morin heard God call his name and he went flying off to the big Catholic Church in the sky. His flock briefly mourned his demise and then they settled down with baited breath to await his replacement.

Petitions for a new father were sent en-mass down to the archbishop in Portland and a few months later there came to town a young, handsome priest. The parishioners were astounded with this stroke of good luck. He sped into town in a bright, red, ford Mustang with white racing stripes down the sides. He had the body of a Greek god and his silvery blond hair was cut short and held in place with layers of hairspray. He assumed his position with poise and self-assurance that belied his tender age. With the exception of mass, he was never garbed in the traditional black, flowing robes that old Father Morin used to wear religiously.

Father Clark could be found most any time of the day dressed in a white tee shirt and blue, form fitting Levi's. Whenever he moved, the very expensive scent of Pierre Cardin after shave or some kind of body lotion permeated the air around him. He wore black, Rayban sunglasses that were more often than not shoved up on top of his head than on his nose. When he turned his clear blue eyes on you, some of the parishioners said that it was as though he could see right down to your very soul. Others allowed that it was impossible to lie to him when he was looking at you with those clear, blue eyes.

He was the answer to their prayers or so it seemed. His viewpoints on life and the church were so modern that they were too good to be true. He advocated that each man was answerable to his own conscience and should leave the church out of it, if at all possible. He wholeheartedly supported birth control, whatever the reason. He didn't flinch when questioned about abortions or mixed marriages either. He even went so far as to state that divorce might even be the best solution in many cases.

Father Xavier Clark was meant to change the church. He advocated folk masses and supported the mass said in English. He discontinued confessional services on Saturday nights and he opened the parish hall on weeknights to the kids. Dances were held there every weekend.

Each week the parishioners waited to see what new, exciting changes were in store for them. There was a general consensus that, oh yes! God does indeed answer prayers after all. Father Clark is proof of that.

As time went by, little by little, parents began to notice changes in the behavior of their kids. They were spending more and more time at the parish hall and less and less time at home. Father Clark was way too "cool." He understood them in a way their parents never would. Homework didn't get finished, trash didn't get taken out and lawns didn't get cut. All their spare time was spent with Father Clark or at the parish hall. When questioned about their doings there. The stock reply was, "Groovin with Father Clark." or "Oh you know, we rap a little about this and that."

Fathers of teenage girls began to get a little nervous when they heard their daughter's comments about Father Clark. "Gee dad; he's really handsome isn't he?" "I think Father Clark is way too sexy." "Oh dad, do you think you could buy some of that after shave lotion that Father Clark wears?" "Do you think Father Clark will like this shade of lipstick, mom?" Parents began to feel little niggles of apprehension way down in their guts that they couldn't quite shake.

Everything went along pretty much as it was until one day about a year later when the town learned the real truth about why the parish hall and why Father Clark had become so popular.

It was the kind of day in "Tha County" that is seen so seldom that when it does come, people wander around in a kind of daze. The air was a warm seventy-eight degrees, a heat wave for our part of the woods. The soft breeze from the south was filled with the scent of apple blossoms and fresh, green grass. The droning of the bees was the only sound to be heard for miles around. The warm, golden sunshine enticed folks to sit or stand where they were for a little while and jist be. It was the kind of day that hinted or outright promised of better things to come.

It was a Saturday morning at quarter to nine, when everything came to a screeching halt. Mr. St. Pierre, who was head of the Catholic

216

Church Council, was sitting in his sun-filled living room at his home on the Portage Road when the phone rang. He sipped the last of his morning coffee, laid down the morning edition of the Bangor Daily News and picked-up the phone. On the other end of the line was a very agitated Tom Roy, the town cop. Tom apologized for disturbing him and then the cop asked if Mr. St. Pierre could come to the town office as soon as possible. When Mr. St. Pierre pressed the cop for more information, the cop wouldn't say what was wrong. He jist insisted that he had to meet with Mr. St. Pierre on a matter of great importance and that's all he'd say.

Mr. St. Pierre, not amused that he had to dress and leave his chair by the sunny living room window, wondered what the urgent matter was as he drove rapidly up over Station Hill to the town office. As he came through the town office door, the first person he saw was Father Clark, who was slumped in a chair, holding his head gingerly in his hands. He looked up at the sound of the door closing, spied Mr. St. Pierre and without a word of greeting, dropped his head back into his hands.

Mr. St. Pierre stared at Father Clark and was shocked by what he saw. The good father's normally highly coifed blond hair was uncombed and messy. His once white tee shirt was torn down the front and there appeared to be grass stains all over the back. On closer inspection, there seemed to be a line of purple hickeys running down the right side of his neck. His usually immaculate Levi's had streaks of what appeared to be vomit running down the front of one leg. Father Clark burped and Mr. St. Pierre got a whiff of alcohol as the good father's fetid breath wafted past his nose.

Mr. St. Pierre looked questionably from Father Clark to Officer Roy. "I think that you'd better come into my office and sit down Don," the cop said. "My God!" exclaimed Mr. St. Pierre. "What's happened? Has there been an accident? Has somebody died? What tha hell's going on?"

"I really don't know quite how to tell you this Ron," said the cop. "Well, for God's sake jist tell me!" demanded Mr. St. Pierre. "Well, it's like this," the cop said and then he turned to the priest. "Jaysus, Father Clark, I think you'd better tell him." But Father Clark kept his pale face averted. The cop shot him a look of disgust and then he said, "This morning, as I was making my routine patrol along the Portage Road, I came upon Father Clark's car parked at a crazy angle jist off the shoulder on the right side of the road. The passenger's side door was wide open and there wasn't anyone in the vehicle. So, I walked around the car and looked down into the ditch. That was where I found him," and he pointed with disgust at Father Clark. "The good padre was lyin in the grass, nearly stark naked and dead drunk! He had an empty bottle of Chivas Regal in one hand and a rosary in the other."

Upon hearing this shocking news, Mr. St. Pierre looked over at Father Clark. "Jesus!" He thought to himself, "That ain't so bad." And he reached up and wiped his face on his sleeve. The cop, seeing the look of relief on the old man's face went on. "That ain't the half of it," the cop continued with a long look at Mr. St. Pierre. "A little further away was the Morrow girl, naked as a jaybird and out like a light." "Oh my God!" exclaimed Mr. St. Pierre. "What a friggin mess this is!" And he glared in Father Clark's direction. "Where's the Morrow girl now?" he asked the cop. "I've dressed her and cleaned her up a little and she's in my office still passed out. I can tell you one thing though; she's going to have one hell of a hangover come tomorrow mornin!" "I hope to God that that's the only thing she's going to have!" replied Mr. St. Pierre.

After taking the girl home, lying to her parents, and giving Father Clark the lecture of his life, Mr. St. Pierre called the archbishop in Portland and explained the situation as best he could. And it wasn't too long before Father Clark had moved on to greener parishes and the parishioners again waited with baited breath for a new priest to arrive, but this time, they didn't dare to pray.

GREAT GRAMMY IDA

Another hazard about visiting our great Aunt Cassie was her mother-in-law, whom we always called Grammy Ida. Grammy Ida's maiden name was Rafford, and she was Scottish through and through. By the time we were old enough to meander down the road on our own to visit Aunt Cassie, Grammy Ida had reached the ripe old age of ninety-five, and she was all bent over from a combination of old age and arthritis. She walked with the aid of a wooden cane, which she used to hit anything and everything that got in her way, be it kids, animals or inanimate objects.

Her white hair, which she wore pulled back in a bun at the nape of her neck, was so thin that you could see her pink scalp shining through the strands. She wore thick, black, wire-rimmed glasses and when she looked at you, her watery blue eyes were magnified so many times that they appeared three times larger than they actually were. We used to refer to her amongst ourselves as "Grammy Spider" because that's what she really looked like to us. Her arms and legs were reed thin, and she was usually dressed all in black. She constantly had a sweater or small throw draped around her stooped shoulders and her body was round and soft like the body of a spider.

She only weighed about a hundred pounds, if that, and she looked like a gentle breeze would blow her over. Due to her advanced age, most of her facial skin had slipped down around her neck where it had gathered in a huge wattle, and we loved to watch her try and chew gum. The loose skin on her jaw would ripple and jiggle, jist like the skin on a turkey's neck when it ate and overcome by laughter, we'd slid out the kitchen door and collapse in hysterics onto Aunt Cassie's lawn.

She'd worn ill-fitting dentures for years and often, when she tried to talk, the top plate would slip down and rest on the bottom plate, but she'd keep right on talking. One never really knew what she'd said, and she'd reach up and push her upper plate back where it belonged and turn and glare at us like it was all our fault. Though she was old and feeble, her mind was still very sharp, and she always knew who we were and the fact that she didn't like us one bit.

She used to spend most of her days sitting next to the wood stove in the kitchen in her old rocking chair. She loved to read "True Story" and "True Confessions" magazines, and she often dozed off right in the middle of a story. Suddenly, she'd awaken with a start and a couple of snorts, look wildly around her, gather her shawl a little closer about her frail shoulders and then resume reading as though nothing had happened.

Great Grammy Ida had one really bad fault as far as we were concerned though, she didn't like kids, any kids. If she happened to be sitting in the kitchen when we came in, she'd turn in her old rocking chair and glare at us through the heat of the woodstove for a couple of minutes. Upon recognizing who we were, her false teeth would slip and click as she muttered some expletive to herself, and then she'd rock back and forth in her chair until she'd gained enough forward momentum to get up.

Finally in a standing position, she'd teeter back and forth in her tattered slippers until she felt strong enough to walk, and then she'd scurry off across the large kitchen to the sanctity of her bedroom, muttering epithets aimed at us, all the way. She always wore a pair of black felt slippers, and I can still hear the sound her feet made as she scurried across the linoleum kitchen floor to the privacy of her bedroom. It always sounded to me like a drunken crab as it scuttled across the rocks on a beach.

I don't know why we were so afraid of her, but we really were. She rarely ever spoke directly to us when we came to visit. It was her laugh that got to you most though. If something amused her, she wouldn't laugh in a "normal" way like most people, she cackled. The sound of her laugh would cause the hair to rise up on the back of your neck, and you'd suddenly find your feet edging towards the door of their own volition. You got the distinct impression that you were viewing a real live witch.

Her bedroom was located at the northern end of the house, and she commanded an excellent view up over Sutherland's hill to our house. She always knew when we were coming down the road to visit Aunt

Cassie, and she made plans for each and every visit. If no one else was home, she'd lie in wait for us like a general waiting to spring a surprise attack on his enemy.

When you walked into the farmyard in the middle of a sunny afternoon in July, it was easy to be fooled by the serenity of the place. The baby chicks were peeping happily around the hen house. The cows were lying down in the shade of the barn chewing their cuds. The pigs were nestled in the mud behind the barn with their pink ears flopped over their eyes. The chickens were cackling softly to each other in the quiet afternoon. Everything was sleeping or at peace, but not Grammy Ida! She was lying in wait, ready to put all her military tactics into action against us.

Upon hearing our first timid knocks on the back door, she'd open the kitchen door a crack, peer out at us through the screen door and demand. "What do you want?" Or more often than not, she wouldn't even wait to see what we wanted. She'd jist sic their dog Rex on us. He wouldn't bite, but he did put an awful scare into us.

Her other favorite sports were to whack you with her cane or spray us with the garden hose. But her very favorite one of all was to throw the entire contents of her piss pot out through the screen door at us. It was no use goin home to complain to mother about this vile treatment, because she would jist shrug her shoulders and tell us that if we didn't like it, we could jist stay home.

I still remember the many nights my brothers, sisters and I spent lying in bed trying to dream up the ultimate plan for revenge on Great Grammy Ida. Somehow, those plans never reached fruition for one reason or another because we knew that if mother got wind of what we planned to do, she'd tan our asses good, and we couldn't chance that. We always had the comforting thought that every time Great Grammy Ida did something awful to us; "God" would intercede on our behalf, but "God" sure took his own sweet time in answering our prayers.

Great Grammy Ida lived to be ninety-nine years old. And to this day, whenever I go past Aunt Cassie's house, I fully expect Great Grammy Ida to come scurrying out of the house with her piss pot clutched firmly in her knarled, old blue, veined hands, muttering "Where are those little bastids now?" as her ill-fitting teeth jumped and slipped about in her droopy mouth....

Martha Stevens-David

UNCLE

Besides our Great Uncle Hal, one of my other favorite relatives was my grandfather's brother whom we affectionately called Uncle Barney or Uncle. He was really our great uncle, but we always called him Uncle Barney.

He was a big man in more ways than one. He stood about six feet tall and weighed around two hundred and fifty pounds and he had a fringe of reddish brown hair that matched his skin which was the color of burnt mahogany. Uncle had the misfortune of being born with a cleft palate and a hair lip. Surgery may or may not have been available to him, but none was ever performed throughout his lifetime.

Uncle didn't place too much importance on this birth defect however and when you chanced to look into his face, you soon forgot his physical deformity because you were drawn to his eyes. They were the only things about him that weren't old. They were the color of deep amber and they snapped and twinkled and were undefeated. When he fastened them on you, well, you knew that something exciting was about to happen! He had what was referred to as a large barrel chest, a great deep voice and a hearty laugh and he loved nothing better than to sit down and spread some nice juicy gossip or pass on a "dirty" story jist to shock folks.

Very often, after he'd told a story, others would immediately retell it with all of his speech impediments included, which often made the retelling of his story much funnier than the original. Some folks might have felt sorry for themselves if they had been in Uncle's shoes, but not him. He always found something to laugh or joke about, he wasn't one to dwell on what might have been.

Uncle lived about a quarter of a mile down the Masardis Road from his brother, our grandfather Colbath's house. He'd built a small two room bungalow that measured about eighteen feet by twenty feet. Half

222

of the building was reserved as a garage for his pickup truck and the rest of the space was used as his living quarters.

Across one end of the narrow structure, he'd built a bunk bed with two long drawers running length-wise under it, which held his clothes and extra blankets. He'd installed a small wood burning stove off to the side of the room and a sink with a hand pump was built across the other end. Over the sink, he built a long narrow window that looked out onto his driveway and the Masardis Road beyond. He hung some flour sack curtains over the window and that was that. This modest, clean abode was his home.

He'd remained a bachelor all his life and when we asked him about this, he'd laugh and shout at us in his deep voice, "Do you know anyone who's fool enough to marry me?" We didn't quite know how to answer that because all of us kids thought he was pretty great.

When mother took us to visit our grandparents, which wasn't often, we'd beg to go and visit Uncle if he was home. We'd run the quarter mile down the Masardis Road to his house like an anxious husband on his honeymoon.

It was such a delight to visit his small, warm abode. Uncle had been a mule tender in Kentucky during the First World War and when he'd finally come marching home again, he walked with a limp. We all thought he was a bonafied war hero and had been shot in the leg by the Confederate soldiers, but when we asked him about his limp and where all his medals were, he roared with laughter and explained that he hadn't been shot at all, that he'd simply been kicked in the leg by an ornery mule. "Yes sir!" he'd told folks. "I finally met something that was more ornery than me!" and with that explanation, he'd slap his leg and roar with laughter.

The first things you noticed when you opened the door to his small building were the smells of the lineament that he rubbed on his injured leg and the smell of his chewing tobacco. His little ten by twenty foot living space was always immaculate and his bed, which was covered with several colorful patchwork quilts, made by himself or one of our relatives, was always neatly made no matter what time you went to see him.

Uncle washed all his things by hand and he hung everything above his pot bellied woodstove to dry. He'd hang his long woolen socks up by the toes and the water dripping off the drying socks would dance and sizzle across the top of the hot stove. The smell of the wet wool from his drying clothes always permeated the air. He used to laugh and tell us that his socks were always hanging there, ready for Santy Claus.

Because he loved children so much, it was a shame that Uncle Barney never married and had some children of his own. It was bad luck for him, but good luck for us kids. Unlike his brother, our grandfather, Uncle loved kids, all of us kids and there were many for him to love.

Every time mother looked out the window and announced that Uncle was coming, we'd immediately be filled with two very differing emotions, joy and fear. He'd stomp into the house, pull off his old woolen hat and look around the room for us. We'd die a thousand deaths. The smaller kids would run and grip mothers skirts in a death hold, then, overcome with curiosity, they'd peer out from behind her body to see what Uncle was going to do next.

He'd stand there in the middle of the kitchen with his eyes searching for the first victim and then with a mighty roar, he'd pounce! We'd gasp and freeze where we were, struggling to catch our breaths and with our hearts thudding in our chests. He'd swoop us up with his large, square gentle hands and rub our faces hard against his unshaven whiskery cheeks and crush us against him in such a bear hug that our ribs wouldn't unkink for about a week. He'd reach into his coat pocket and bring out a handful of pink peppermints or some other treat that he'd bought in town to give to all of us. Oh, how we loved him! He was our real life Santa Claus. He never came visiting without bringing something for mother or us kids.

When we were fortunate enough to be allowed to go for a visit to his house, we'd run the whole way down the road to see him and upon hearing our first timid knocks, he'd open the door and we'd pour through, breathless and so excited to spend some time with him. His little house held so many treasures for us. Underneath his bed, he kept his battered old violin and after the proper amount of begging and pleading, he'd drag it out and proceed to play it fiddle-style. It was enchanting to say the least. Over the years, we heard his complete repertoire over and over again, but each time, it seemed as though we were hearing the tunes for the very first time. We'd climb upon his patchwork bed and sit quietly with our feet dangling over the edge while he played his tunes and danced around to entertain us.

Uncle was a 'master carpenter' by trade, but he also had developed a keen interest in geology. Over the years he'd assembled quite a rock collection which he'd let us examine whenever we wanted. He even had a few gold nuggets and pieces of silver which he kept in small glass bottles. We'd pick them up and turn them over and over in our grubby hands while Uncle explained exactly what they were and how they'd been formed eons ago. I have loved rocks all my life and I believe that we learned more about rock formations from those impromptu visits to Uncle's than we ever did in school.

Around nineteen fifty-five, there was cause for much excitement in our family. Uncle had been out on another prospecting trip on the land he owned behind his home and came back one day very excited and acting very mysterious. He had a large, heavy burlap sack loaded across his shoulders and everyone teased him about finding gold. He merely looked at them with a gleam in his amber eyes and said, "And don't you think it ain't out there, by Jaysus!"

The very next morning he took himself and the mysterious bag off to the local assayer's office in Presque Isle. Mr. Pike, the assayer, carefully examined the rocks and stated that he thought he knew what they were, but to be completely certain, he'd have to send some pieces off to the Bureau of Mines in Augusta for confirmation. Uncle reluctantly handed over his precious samples and he waited with baited breath for the days to pass and finally the message came that he was to return to the assayer's office.

When he arrived, there was another man, along with the assayer, waiting there for him. The assayer introduced Uncle to a Mr. Jordan who stated that he worked in Augusta for the State of Maine in the Mines and Minerals Division. Mr. Jordan proceeded to inform Uncle that he had indeed made a rare mineral discovery. Uncle, his amber eyes snapping with excitement and suspicion, rubbed his jaw and waited. Then, Mr. Jordan told Uncle that the samples contained a large quantity of uranium and copper with a fair amount of gold mixed in. Uncle nodded his head in agreement, but he still didn't say a word.

Mr. Jordan looked at him for a couple of seconds and then finally he said the words that made Uncle's blood run cold. "Mr. Colbath, do you realize that tha state of Maine holds all tha mining rights to any mineral discoveries made in tha state?" Uncle never took his eyes off Mr. Jordan as he continued, "It is your obligation as a citizen of the great state of Maine to divulge the exact location of this mineral find, to me immediately."

That was all Uncle needed to hear. He hadn't taken orders since he'd been in the Army and he hadn't liked it then and he didn't like it now! He slapped his old woolen cap back onto his bald head and stood up. He looked Mr. Jordan straight in the eye and said. "If you think I'm going to hand my discovery over to those sons-ah-whores in Augusta, you've got another think comin! You want to know where I found this stuff? It's up your ass and turn left!" With that, he yanked his sample-filled burlap bag off the counter and headed for the door. He slammed the door so hard that all the rock samples, which were lined-up in little glass bottles on the assayer's office shelves, danced a merry little jig.

Uncle seethed and smarted for quite a while, but there was no way of getting around the law so he quietly sold his samples to the assayer and with that money he promptly bought himself a new Buick automobile. However, he never did tell anyone, friends or family, the whereabouts of his mineral deposit. He took that secret with him to his grave.

Uncle loved to go hunting and fishing and as he got older, it was often difficult for him to get around as much as he had in the past. Usually, the younger members of the family would take it upon themselves to include him in their hunting and fishing plans. He never lost his enthusiasm for either sport till the day he died.

Uncle was very generous with his time and talent. He was a master carpenter by trade and in the early years, when he was a young man, he'd learned his craft as an apprentice shipbuilder along the coast of Maine.

Since Aroostook County is a long way from the coast, Uncle didn't have many calls to build any boats. Mostly, he built barns, garages, outhouses, potato houses and houses. If he built a house for anyone in the family, he'd make the owners agree not to sell the house to anyone else in their lifetime. It was one of his little quirks. He jist wanted to be sure that the building that he'd worked so hard on and built so perfectly, remained in our family for as long as it could.

When he was well into his late sixties, he suddenly announced one day that he was going to build a 'boat." Whenever he was questioned more closely about his "boat" he'd become very vague and with a twinkle in his eye reply, "That's for me to know and for you to find out, by Jaysus!" And he'd go merrily on his way.

Soon everyone in the neighboring towns had gotten wind of his plans and his progress was the talk of the surrounding areas. His many trips back and forth to town with large loads of lumber caused my father to remark that, "This was going to be interesting to say tha least."

It was a hot, sultry morning in May when Uncle commenced to building his "boat." He checked and rechecked his plans and carefully laid out the lumber. From that day on, he could be found at almost any hour of the day, from sun up to sun down, sawing, nailing, sanding or chiseling away on his "boat." All his old cronies and strangers alike made it a point to stop by Uncle's yard at regular intervals to check on his progress.

As the "boat" finally began to take shape and its true dimensions became obvious, folks would scratch their heads and ask him, "Which ocean did he plan on floating her in?" Uncle would look at the inquirer with a light dancing in his dark brown eyes, laugh and keep on working. Folks began commenting amongst themselves that "Unk's boat was even bigger than his house." Some even dared to hint that he'd "Taken leave of his senses, if he'd had any to begin with!"

But Uncle was determined and he wouldn't be deterred. He cut every rib of that boat with such precision that when it was finally time to assemble it, the pieces fit together like a puzzle. He'd hold his callused fingers against the sanded wood and walk back and forth from stem to stern to see if there were any rough spots that he might have missed. When he'd determined that the sanding was perfection, he began to coat the boat with varnish. He varnished and sanded so many times that folks lost count of the coats and sandings.

As the boat building progressed through one season to another of the long, hot summer, he was molested by every insect imaginable. The hoards of mosquitoes, black flies, horse flies, mingies and no-see-ums were never ending and there would always be a thick black cloud of one kind or another swarming around Uncle's head. When one bit him in a vulnerable spot, he'd forget what he was doing and swing his varnish-covered brush at the spot that was bitten, bleedin or burnin or a combination of all three and by the end of the day, his face, neck and bald head would be covered with globs of dead insects trapped in hardened varnish. Uncle would carefully peel those hardened pieces of varnish off his skin, laugh and say that the clumps were amber and he was going to sell them to all those fancy ladies down in New York City to make jewelry out of and he was goin to get rich!

Finally, the "boat" was completed! Cars, pickup trucks and the like jammed the Masardis Road as all the rubber-neckers craned their heads to get a better view of the "boat." It was huge! It was bigger than his house! The hardened layers of varnish glistened and gleamed in the afternoon sun like a huge diamond in the middle of the Aroostook County forest. Folks, drivin down the Masardis Road, were momentarily blinded by the reflection of the sun off the side of the boat.

After having viewed the "boat," for himself one night, dad came home and made an announcement to mother. "Noah ain't the only one who has an ark! I jist saw another one and it's sitting right in Uncle Barney's driveway." After that, the "boat" was jokingly referred to as "Uncle Barney's Ark."

Upon its completion, there was much speculation about whether or not the "God-damned thing" could even float. Everyone kept pestering Uncle to haul it out to Portage Lake or down to Squa Pan Stream and give it a go, but Uncle Barney couldn't be induced to move her. Uncle never let all the ribbing or jokes bother him either. He'd listen to the good natured banter with a sparkle in his snapping brown eyes, slap his knees and roar with laughter along with everyone else.

The "Ark" remained propped-up in Uncle's door yard for a good many years, through the short summers and the arctic winters and he never did attempt to see if she would float. One day, when I was grown and married, I gathered my courage and asked him why he had never taken her out to sea or at least to Portage Lake. Uncle looked at me for the longest moment and then he said, "Toots, I don't need to know if she can float or not, I jist wanted to see if I could build her!"

Uncle, who was well past eighty and whose health was beginning to fail, continued to live alone in his little house until the very end. Mother tried many times to get him to come and live out his final years with her and dad down at the Colbath family homestead, but he steadfastly refused. He never did install a telephone all the years he'd lived alone, so he and mother worked out an emergency plan. He reluctantly agreed to replace his front door light with a red light bulb. In the event that he ever needed help, he said, he'd turn on the porch light and seein it, mother was to come down right away.

On that fateful night, when he finally decided that he needed help, he turned on the light. Unfortunately, there had been a very heavy snowfall during the night and a snow drift over the front door completely covered the red light bulb. Our sweet Uncle Barney, died as he had lived, alone and proud and very much a man....

THA COP

Ashland might have been called a one horse town by some, but it was also a one cop town. In the early 1960's, Ashland was in desperate need of a new town cop. So, a search was initiated and a man was finally hired who was from "away." The new town cop's name was Rick Morton and it didn't take too long before his nickname around town was "dick" for reasons I shall elaborate on.

Now, as in most small towns everywhere, everyone either knows or is related to everyone else. People have a natural tendency to be wary of strangers and the inhabitants of Ashland were no exception. Everyone discussed the new addition to the police force and the population in general agreed that being a cop was a job akin to cleaning toilets, except that cleaning toilets was a much cleaner job.

Mr. Morton fit into the everyday life of Ashland like a horsefly on a horse's ass. The more he made himself known, the more he irritated and alienated himself. He stood about six feet-two in his stocking feet and he was skeletal thin. He only had a fringe of light brown hair left on his otherwise baldhead, but he had the balls of a brass monkey. Town folks put him down as being an ineffectual blowhard and incompetent to boot and pretty much left him alone. In other words, they didn't interact with him unless they absolutely had to.

He'd been in town for about fifteen months when things suddenly took a drastic turn. Ashland is no worse or better than any other small town when it comes to questions of morality. Husbands cheated on wives and vice versa. But, in a small town like ours, if one is going to cheat, one had better take the utmost care because everyone knows everyone else and usually, sooner or later, any secret is an "open" secret. Some of the well-known philanders around town began complaining to one another about their dislike of the new town cop. When pressed to be more specific about why they disliked Mr. Morton so much, they jist mumbled that they didn't like the "rotten son of ah bitch!" and let it go at that.

This muttering and name calling amongst them continued for quite a while, until one night at a regular meeting of the Veterans of Foreign Wars, one of its members finally admitted why he hated the cop. He said that Mr. Morton had caught him in a "delicate" situation so to speak and from that night on, he'd had to pay the friggin cop every week to keep his mouth shut.

It was like Pandora's Box, once one person talked, everyone talked. They began comparing stories and all the men found that they all had one thing in common besides screwing around and that was blackmail. Morton had his hooks into half of the male population in Ashland for one thing or another. The cop set the rules and he was quite particular in regard to payment too. The "payments" rendered were in the form of illegal moose meat, deer meat, lumber, fish, calves, chickens, pigs, liquor, camping trips and even plain old money.

It didn't take too long before word about the problem with the cop spread around town. The monthly meetings of the Knights of Columbus, the Odd Fellows and the Veterans of Foreign Wars were generally considered a "boys" night out in "Tha County." The members usually spent their time watching stag movies, playing poker, bitchin about their wives and getting royally soused. Now, these monthly meetings were spent in trying to find the best way to rid the town of this terrible scourge.

There is an old Maine saying, "Nothing puts tha fear of God into a man like being hit in tha pocketbook or being rapped in the balls!" In this case, it certainly applied! Men, who stood six feet tall and weighed over two hundred pounds and feared no one, were suddenly reduced to sniveling rats. How could this fat, pompous little bastid dictate to them how they should live their lives? How dare he live so well? How dare he judge them? Who died and left him God? "I thought Hitler was dead!" lamented another.

"Have you noticed how he struts around town like he owns tha friggin place?" they asked each other. "We have to do something!" they moaned. They hated to admit it, but they were scared, deep down gut, wrenching scared! If they didn't continue to meet their payments to that self appointed judge and jury, then they knew that it wouldn't be too long before Morton would see to it that their wives, girlfriends, bosses or whomever they had trespassed against, were quickly informed as to the date, time and person in question.

After much trial and tribulation, they hit upon the ideal way to rid themselves of him. Vigilantes are not only indicative of the old West, they can also be found in the north as well. The "injured" parties decided that if they presented themselves to the rotten little bastard enmass, then he wouldn't have a leg to stand on. They sweated, schemed and planned and finally came up with a foolproof plan.

They invited Mr. Morton to attend a meeting of the Veteran's of Foreign Wars on the pretext that he was going to be getting an award as "Cop of tha Year," and on the specified night, old Dick was there with bells on. He'd gotten a haircut, shined his shoes and even had his best suit pressed. When he'd strutted thru the door, everyone was waiting for him.

When they presented their case, it didn't take Morton too long to catch on, what with a dozen or so angry men gathered around him making threats and calling him names. He tendered his resignation to the town manager early the next morning and left town long before a replacement cop was found. It was thought that he'd moved to a small town someplace down around Vermont or New Hampshire.

Once again, the cheating husbands, the poachers and alcoholics around "Tha County" heaved a sigh of relief. At the next town council meeting it was unanimously agreed that the next candidate to be considered for town cop should be born and bred in "Tha County." "That way," they reasoned, "he'll be used to us and our ways, if yah get my drift," they said to each other with a wink, a nudge and a smile on their face.

The next man chosen to be town cop was indeed from the area. He'd been born and bred in Mars Hill and had attended the local schools. He'd been called up to serve in the military, but didn't believe in killing, so he'd joined the Navy and served his whole tour of duty aboard an aircraft carrier in Southeast Asia. Upon his military retirement, he'd returned to Aroostook County to settle down with his Asian wife and five children.

On the day he was hired, he had a preliminary meeting with the selection committee and they laid down the law about how he was to conduct himself and jist what his specific duties were. He got the message loud and clear. "Jist do your job and keep your mouth shut. Harass tha kids a little to keep them in line. Ride through town once every hour or so to show folks you're on tha job. Hand out a few speeding tickets to tha friggin out-of-staters and tha God-damned Canadian truck drivers and leave the rest of tha populace tha hell alone!"

Skippy the "new" town cop stood about five feet eight and was portly to boot and he took to being a cop like a duck takes to water. He was perfection plus! He took his standard issue cop's uniform over to Presque Isle and had it tailored to fit him and his pot belly. He was as spit-shined and polished as was humanly possible and to complete the picture, whether it was day or night, he had an unlit cigar clamped firmly between his yellow teeth. He soon perfected a slouch while sitting at the wheel of his cruiser that made people wonder if he was awake or asleep as he cruised slowly through town.

Skippy wasn't a "stupid" man by any means. He was what the folks from Aroostook County commonly called an "educated fool." Which loosely translated, meant that he'd finished the tenth grade and didn't know what to do with all that learnin. When confronted with a "crisis," he could cite chapter and verse from the Police Regulation Guide on jist where the "law" stood on every single matter. If the town in general had considered Morton an incompetent person in regards to the law, then they hadn't bettered themselves any in the hiring of Skippy. He had a "coward's" natural ability for avoiding trouble.

If an endangered citizen called him and told him that one of their pissed-off neighbors had fired a gun at them, Skippy would pause, take a long drag on his unlit cigar and mutter, "That's a violation of Code 217, Section 4." "What tha hell does that mean?" demanded the irate caller. "Oh," replied Skippy importantly, "That means it's against tha law to shoot a firearm within city limits." "Well," screamed the caller, "What tha hell are yah goin to do about it!" "According to the Police Regulation Guide," Skippy droned on, "a "city" is defined as having a population of twenty-five thousand and over and I'm afraid that Ashland doesn't qualify as a city." "I don't give a shit about whether or not we qualify as a city!" the pissed-off caller screamed, "Someone's shootin at me!" "If you feel that strongly about the matter Mr. Hafford, why don't you jist give the State Police a call down to the Houlton barracks. I'm sure they'll be happy to help you." And with that, Skippy hung up.

It is a general rule of thumb that kids are a good barometer in regards to people. They generally dislike figures of authority outright, but they took an instant dislike to Skippy, especially after he'd stopped quite a few of them and ticketed them for riding their bicycles too fast down over Station Hill or for hanging out on the street corner in front of Chasse's Department Store too late on a Saturday night. The kids weren't doing anything wrong, but it was eight o'clock and Skippy wanted to get home to watch his favorite television show, Mayberry RFD.

Kids have a long memory and they did everything they could think of to aggravate the hell out of him. His house and automobiles were weekly targets for all kinds of pranks. They spray painted graffiti on his automobile, tied his dog to the bumper of a log truck that was headed for Moncton, Quebec, Canada. Changed his mailing address to Mapleton. It went on and on. Even kids who had never been accosted by Skippy joined in on the harassment of the cop.

The day that began Skippy's fall from grace, was as perfect a spring morning as one could ever hope to have in "Tha County." When his alarm clock rang at five am, he threw himself out of bed and hustled to the bathroom. He hummed a few bars of "Beautiful Dreamer" as he hastily lathered himself with soap, then he rinsed himself off and stepped out of the shower. He dressed, sprayed his dark red hair into place with hair spray until even a tornado couldn't move it. Carefully combed and trimmed his mustache and slathered some of his wife's moisturizer on his face and he was done. He quickly adjusted his custom-sewn uniform so that every detail was perfect and made his way out the door to his cruiser.

He had made plans for the day and he wanted to get an early start. Today was the day that he was going to make history! He was going to break all records! Yes sir! He was going to write more traffic tickets than had ever been written by an officer before in the Town of Ashland!

He'd stayed up late the night before and had carefully laid out his plans. He was going to drive down over Station Hill and park his cruiser about half way across the span of the Aroostook River Bridge that separated the town of Ashland from Garfield Plantation. His plan was to set-up his road block there and catch all those friggin Canadian truckers as they drove their over loaded-rigs across the bridge on their way to Levesque's Mill in Masardis. He knew that the shortest way across the Aroostook River was across that bridge and he couldn't help but catch all of them. He realized that upon hearing about the road block set up on the bridge, some of the overloaded trucks would simply go around the back way though Garfield but that was jist fine with him, he'd catch them later.

The blood-red sun was jist coming over the eastern horizon as Skippy rolled onto the bridge and he drove to the half-way point and pulled the cruiser into his pre-planned position. He parked it so that only one vehicle, going in either direction, could cross the bridge at any time. He got out of the car and walked to the end of the span that bordered the Portage Road and placed his road block sign about twenty feet from the end of the bridge. "Surprise! Surprise! Surprise!" he smirked to himself as he imitated Barney Fife, his favorite character. "Those suckers are goin tah git a surprise today!" He slid his cap onto the back of his head, stroked his new cigar and sauntered back to his cruiser.

The hot sun had risen enough so that it had a glare to it as it glanced off the Aroostook River and up into his eyes. Skippy adjusted his hat, gathered his log book and other items that he needed for this huge task and carried everything around and placed it on the trunk of the cruiser. Then he stood back to await his place in history.

It was a very slow morning traffic wise. A few locals in their pickups meandered by on their way to town and as they slowed down to rubber neck, Skippy, recognizing the drivers, irritably motioned for them to stop rubber neckin and drive on. One of the drivers, who had been harassed by Skippy before, drove slowly past his cruiser and then yelled out the window, "Must be a friggin road block for a runaway dog and he'd be lucky to catch that!"

Suddenly, Skippy's spirits picked up as he heard the familiar grinding of gears as a fully loaded log truck downshifted in its approach to the opposite end of the bridge.

Skippy, cool as a cucumber, opened the cruiser door, slid into the driver's seat and flipped on the red and blue flashers on the top of his vehicle. As the overloaded truck started across the bridge, Skippy could jist make out the driver in the cab, as he struggled to slow down. The huge, dirt-encrusted Peterbilt finally lurched to a stop in the middle of the bridge jist a couple of feet from where Skippy sat waiting in his cruiser.

Skippy eased himself out of the patrol car like a general about to address his troops. He wiped imaginary dust off the visor and carefully readjusted his hat on the back of his immaculately coifed red hair. With his big belly leading the way, he strolled over to the vehicle with slow deliberate steps and walked from one end of the log truck to the other before he approached the surly, sweating driver.

Skippy thrust out his chin, adjusted his unlit cigar and said, "I need to see all your trucking documents tout sweet!" He smiled inwardly to himself thinking how brilliant it had been of him to throw in that little bit of French. Mumbling epithets aimed at Skippy in French, the driver pulled out his license and weight papers and thrust them into the cop's out stretched hand. Skippy went over the documents with finite care, then he announced to no one in particular that he jist might run everything by the State Police Barracks in Houlton, jist to make sure that there were no outstanding arrests or warrants. He looked up at the driver's face that was suffused with anger, made a little mock salute and turned around.

He strolled back to his cruiser and commenced to make the call to the Houlton Barracks. Skippy's needs down at the State Police Barracks had been given the priority rating of being somewhere between a headache and a hemorrhoid. The troopers all tried their best to ignore any incoming calls from the Ashland area because they were sick and tired of having to run up to Ashland every other week or so to take care of Skippy's self-caused problems.

It took an extra long time for the information to come back that the Canadian driver was not wanted in any way, anywhere, for anything. Skippy finally strolled back to the seething, surly, truck driver. Everything would have been fine except, Skippy decided to carry the "investigation" jist a little further. He instructed the driver to turn on his headlights, then his direction lights and then to step on his brakes.

Everything checked out fine. Skippy's dream of his first "big" ticket quickly dissipated like water down the drain.

By this time, not only was the driver hot, sweaty and very thirsty, he was royally pissed off at havin been detained for so long for nothing! He wrenched open the door and swung down from his truck jist as Skippy made his fatal mistake of kicking the left front truck tire. In the next instant, Skippy felt a sensation like the sun going behind a cloud and it was then that he realized that he was standing in a huge shadow.

He straightened up, nonchalantly dusted off his hands and slowly turned around. He inhaled sharply and tried to step back, but it was way too late. The trucker's patience was gone. He had been messed with enough! He loved his truck and when he saw that little prick kick the tire, well, that did it! Before Skippy knew what was happening, he was hanging by both feet, upside down, over the side of the bridge about fifty feet above the fast moving water of the Aroostook River.

It didn't take too long before a crowd had gathered and the incident was the topic of conversation for many months to come. Folks allowed that it was one hell- of-a-sight to see Skippy hanging by his feet over the side of the bridge. The first thing to go into the drink was his hat, then his cigar, wallet, handcuffs, loose change and his gun. The burly Canadian jiggled him up and down like a limp puppet a few more times and every time the driver jerked Skippy up and down, he screamed a French epithet at him. Onlookers, who understood Canadian French, later related that it was too bad that Skippy didn't understand the language because that driver had had a few choice names for him! The crowd held its breath as it waited to see what fate awaited Skippy. A few of the braver onlookers even shouted for the truck driver to "drop tha little scumbag in tha river."

Finally, the trucker reeled Skippy back in over the railing of the bridge and stood him on his feet. He grabbed the teetering Skippy by his crumpled shirt and drug him over to his patrol car where he heaved him into the front seat and slammed the door with such force that it rocked the cruiser from side to side. He stood in the middle of the bridge and glared at Skippy through the car window for a few seconds longer, then he strode off to his waiting truck. He shifted into gear, revved up the engine and slowly roared off in a cloud of dust and diesel fumes. As he passed Skippy, who was still slumped in his patrol car, he leaned out the window and gave him the royal "middle finger" salute that is totally recognized around the world and needs no further explanation.

Skippy slumped dejectedly in the front seat a few minutes longer, then aware that there was still a crowd of rubber neckers standing around to see what was going to happen next. He reached over, flipped on the p.a. system and announced in a shaky voice that anyone who wasn't off the bridge in five minutes would be arrested on a "Code 247A," "Obstructing a Public Roadway." Then he called the town office and requested an extra set of car keys. It was a much subdued Skippy who rolled through town that night and it took a while for some folks to even recognize him. His hat was gone, along with his cigar, sunglasses and his shitty, pious attitude.

Summer turned into fall and things pretty much remained the same around town in regards to Skippy, but he didn't hand out too many tickets to truckers anymore. Although, he still stopped little old ladies and kids and harassed them every chance he got. The kids seethed and smarted and waited for the chance to "get even" and finally they came up with a "fool" proof plan.

The seasons change quickly in this northern county. On a crisp, autumn night when the wind was out of the north and had a slight chill to it and the clouds were scudding across a wan moon, the kids finally had their ultimate revenge.

It was the Saturday night jist before Halloween when the kids broke into the Civil Defense Office and stole one of the dummies used by the Ashland Fire Department for C. P. R. training classes. The fire department had jist purchased a new dummy and folks were startled every time they saw it because it was so realistic and life-like. The volunteer firefighters often sat the dummy in the passenger side of the fire truck and took it with them when they went out on calls. It used to give folks a real start when they'd stop to talk to the firefighter and discover it was a dummy that they'd been talking to for fifteen minutes.

The kids took the life-like figure down to Sheridan and hung it by the neck directly in the middle of the Bangor and Aroostook train trestle bridge that crossed over the Sheridan Road. They figured that the first person to see it hanging there would take it to be a "human" who'd committed suicide and rush off to call Skippy.

At about ten forty-five that night, Mr. Poitraw, having bent a few elbows at Michaud's Restaurant in Ashland that whole evening, was very carefully making his way home. As he rounded the sharp one hundred-eighty degree turn, his headlights flashed on a gently swaying figure hanging by its neck from the trestle. Mr. Poitraw stifled a scream and hastily crossed himself as he careened down the Sheridan Road, past the slightly swaying figure towards home. He flew up his drive and with a scattering of gravel, came to an abrupt stop jist inches from his garage doors. He crawled out of his car, stumbled up the stairs and into the house. He had to dial the number three times before he was able to reach Skippy. "Skippy, you've gut tah come quick!" Mr. Poitraw moaned. "Skippy, some poor fool has gone en hung himself from tha Sheridan train trestle! "Are you certain you saw what you say you saw?" Skippy asked. "You bet your sweet ass I am!" screamed Mr. Poitraw. "I fought in W.W. Two en I know a dead man when I see one!" Skippy glanced at his watch and sighed when he noticed that it was nine forty-five. He was going to miss "Dallas" again this week.

The kids hiding in the tall grass near the bridge laughed as they heard Skippy's cruiser coming at a snail's pace down the Sheridan Road. Skippy drove up slowly with lights flashing, siren howling and gun drawn. He didn't even get out of the cruiser. He saw all he needed to see. He rolled down the cruiser window and pointed his flashlight up in the "dead" man's direction. He adjusted his new sunglasses, flicked his radio on and proceeded to place a call to the Houlton State Police Barracks.

By now, most of the inhabitants of the small town of Sheridan had arrived to see what tha hell all the commotion was about. They could see tha "poor" soul still hanging by his neck and Skippy sitting in his patrol car, sucking on his soggy cigar, calmly filling out his police report in triplicate.

Everyone gathered around and stared up at the gently swaying dummy. "Jaysus Skippy, you could at least cut him down!" Another one of the onlookers asked. "Are yah sure that poor bastid is dead?" "What are yah goin to do about this?" demanded someone else. Skippy didn't lift his eyes from the sheets he was slowly filling out; he shifted his ever-present cigar from one side of his mouth to the other. "It's covered under Section 221, Paragraph 6 of the Penal Code." Skippy replied smugly. "What tha Christ does that mean?" Asked one man. "It's out of my jurisdiction." Skippy replied. "Yah, we know, Skippy," They all replied in unison, "It's a matter for tha State Police!" Skippy calmly rolled up the cruiser window, turned on his radio, leaned his head back against the head rest, closed his eyes and sucked on his unlit cigar.

About forty-five minutes later, the crowd heard the sound of sirens coming up the Frenchville Road at a pretty fast clip. The onlookers grew quiet as two state police cruisers rolled to a stop and the "real" cops stepped out. The officers didn't even glance in Skippy's direction as they proceeded to make their way over to the victim. They stood and gazed up at the swaying body for a couple of minutes and then Trooper Walker climbed up to the train trestle and withdrew his knife from his pocket. He yelled for everyone to stand back and then he proceeded to cut the body down. The "body" landed face down on the ground with a dull thud! Skippy, hearin the sound the dead body made, shuddered and turned his face away from the grisly scene.

Trooper Walker slid down the grassy embankment and walked over to the body, knelt down and gently turned it over. He shone his flashlight into the face and the unblinking plastic blue eyes stared back at him. He dropped the dummy back on the ground, stood up and walked quickly over to Skippy's patrol car. He reached down and opened the door so swiftly that Skippy nearly fell out. Trooper Walker grabbed Skippy by the arm and propelled him over to the body and he shoved Skippy's head down to within an inch of the dummy's face and bellowed, "The next time you report a "dead" body, you'd better make God-damned sure that it's a dead body or the next dead body will be yours!" You got it!" With that, he dropped Skippy on top of the CPR dummy. Folks later said that it jist goes to prove the point that one dummy can't even recognize another!

DAD—DEEP SEA FISHIN

Where we lived in Aroostook County, Maine, it was about the same distance to any large body of water no matter which direction you went. If you traveled west, you'd run into the Great Lakes. If you went North, it would be the mouth of the St. Lawrence that you ran into first, and if we went Southeast, sooner or later, we'd finally run into the vast Atlantic Ocean.

We were truly "woods" people. We were born in the northern Maine woods, and we died in them too. Oh, it's not like we didn't have any large lakes, rivers or streams all around us. We did, but we never really knew how huge the Atlantic Ocean was until we saw it for ourselves when we were many years older.

When we were growing up in "Tha County" in the fifty's and sixty's, dad would go hunting and fishing in the familiar places all around us that didn't entail traveling too far from our rural home. So, in the spring of "55," when he came home after working in the potato house all day and announced that he might be goin "deep sea fishin" sometime later on in May, mother, as well as the rest of us, was quite taken aback.

We had jist sat down to a supper of mother's homemade bread, fried potatoes and roast chicken when dad made his startling announcement. All of us kids, upon hearing this stupendous news, stopped shoveling our food into our mouths and looked at each other. Dad was going to tha ocean! This was amazing to say the least! We knew the general direction of where the Atlantic Ocean was in reference to our home on the Goding Road in Ashland, but we'd never known anyone who'd actually gone there.

Mother, laid her fork down in her plate, took a sip of tea, and cast her brown eyes on dad and waited to hear what he was going to say next. Dad, lifted his bald head and looked around the table at the seven pairs of blue and brown eyes looking back at him, smiled and said, "Well, me and Raymond and Carl was talking at lunch, and we decided that we'd like tah give it a try. Raymond has a brother who lives down to Lubec and his place is right on tha ocean. He has a boat that he'll take us out in, and we could spend the whole day fishin and come back tha next." Dad waited to see how this news was going to sit with mother, and he slid his bright blue eyes in her direction and waited.

Mother forked another mouthful of chicken into her mouth, chewed for a couple of long moments, and then she said, "Well, if you're only going tah be gone overnight, that won't be too bad. I guess I could manage if these kids don't give me too much trouble." And with that pronouncement, she looked around the table at all of us. Mother was from the old school, and she'd kill you jist as quick as she'd look at you if you were misbehavin. We all nodded our heads that we certainly wouldn't be giving her any trouble, no-sir-ree, no trouble at all.

The rest of the evening was taken up with dad's plans, and we all sat where we were, eatin mother's amazing "Stevens' Special" chocolate cake, mesmerized by dad's exotic talk about goin deep sea fishin in the ocean. It wouldn't have been any more shocking to us if he had announced that he was goin to Africa or to the Far East or even the moon. It seemed a lifetime and a world away to all of us Stevens' kids.

Dad explained that he'd have to chip in about fifty dollars which would cover his portion of gas, food, the rental of the boat and their overnight lodging. Mother, upon hearin the amount of money needed, winced a little, but then capitulated, "Well, I have a little more than that put aside for school clothes for tha kids, but I guess we have all summer to save up again, don't we?" And with that last remark, she looked at all her children still sitting at the table. We knew what was in store for us because we'd already been down that road many times before.

Whenever dad's meager salary didn't cover a sudden expense, we were called upon to help find the needed funds in any way we could. It didn't matter how old you were either. If you had two hands and were reasonably healthy, you did as your parents asked. There was no ands, ifs or buts. We didn't have to worry about the other kids laughing at us as they saw us walking along the back roads pickin berries, dragging sacks half-filled with bottles and cans or selling freshly picked fiddleheads.

Back then, most of the families that we knew were in the same situation as ours, too poor to have anything put aside for a rainy day and too many mouths to feed. The problem was that we had to stake out our territory first, because most of the other kids would be out there jist like us, looking for anything that they could turn into a money-makin proposition.

Once approval had been garnered from mother, dad set about making his deep sea fishin dream come true, and we set about replenishing mother's saving account. If dad was working in the potato house up to Masardis, Jake, me, Bub and Helen would get up early and leave with him. He'd let us off at the Bangor and Aroostook Railroad tracks that separated Squa Pan from Masardis and we'd pick up bottles and cans along the roads all the way back home. On days when we had school, the other kids would tease us after having seen us dragging our burlap sacks along the road behind us. It really used to piss Jake off if all the "church goin" kids made snarky remarks about us "havin the best territory" to find bottles and cans in because that meant to all of us Stevens' that all the "real" alcoholics and drinkers lived in our immediate area.

Jake wasn't a fighter by any means, but Bub would take on all comers, and he usually won too. He had a fiery temper to match his dark auburn hair, and he had a mouth to match. He usually went around with his fists at the ready, a curled lip and an attitude to match and most people left him pretty much alone. But sometimes I was glad when he stood up for us and took care of the snooty kids whose father didn't drink, and they didn't have to pick bottles by the side of the road, and they would finally mind their own business and leave us tha hell alone.

Days passed and before we knew it, it was time for dad to leave. He'd packed his fishing stuff days before and all he had left to do was have a bath, pack his clothes and be off. The night before, mother, not used to having dad go off for any length of time without her, fixed his favorite meal. In all the years they were married, she still couldn't understand how dad, whose whole life revolved around potatoes, still loved the taste of potatoes more than anything else. He wasn't particular about how they were cooked either. Fried, boiled, baked, mashed or raw, it didn't matter to him. If it was a potato, he'd eat it.

So, she built up the fire in the old Glenwood cook stove and greased the top real good. Then she peeled some red potatoes, sliced them real thin and cooked them on top of the stove until they were nice and crispy. After sprinkling a little salt and pepper on them, she'd scoop them onto a plate, and that was it. Depending on the time of year, she'd serve them with a slice of pan-fried deer meat and some homemade pickled beets or fiddleheads. Dad, with a nice glass of his home-brewed-beer, declared this to be a feast! That night, he was one happy man, because come mornin, he was goin deep sea fishin!

Before dad sent us off to bed that night, he and Jake and Bub had a lengthy discussion about what he might catch in the deep, dark sea. Jake had been readin a lot ever since dad had announced that he was going to the great Atlantic Ocean, and he had a lot of ideas about the kind of creatures that lived in the sea. He and Bub had argued long into the night for weeks about what dad might catch and bring back. Jake thought that dad might catch a giant squid or an octopus, but Bub was adamant that he would catch a giant whale or even a shark. Hearin all their views about deep sea creatures, dad laughed and said, "We'll jist have to wait and see."

Early the next morning, we heard Raymond arrive and toot for dad, and he was off. We were so excited for him. We nearly drove mother crazy by running in and out of the house every hour or so asking what time it was. She finally gave up and sent us to bed early jist to have a little peace and quiet for herself.

The next day didn't go any faster than the first, but we knew that by supper time that next night, dad should be home with all his sea monsters. Mother, seeing the writing on the wall and child worn and weary, sent us four older kids across the swamp to our grand-parents to while away the afternoon. We didn't like visiting our grandfather all that much so we took our sweet time getting there. We tossed rocks into the small stream that ran across the dirt road, we picked flowers and played hide and seek. Upon arrival at their home, we visited with them awhile, ate a few of Grammy's Colbath's wonderful doughnuts and headed for home. We couldn't wait for dad to get back.

Finally, around six thirty, we saw Raymond's dusty, green pickup coming down the dirt road in a cloud of dust, and they pulled up in our driveway. Jake and Bub tumbled out the door and off the porch, hitting and punching each other, eager to get to dad first. When they'd gotten up to the passenger side door, Jake looked up at dad, and his big grin slid off his freckled face. Bub, a close second, stared at dad, and he too stopped smiling.

Dad opened the pickup door, slid down to the ground and holding on to the side of the truck, walked slowly and carefully as though his legs didn't work quite right, around to the back of the vehicle. He didn't look like the same man who had left us only twenty-four hours earlier, either. His usually tanned skin was a sickly white and there were black circles around his blue eyes. His normally clean clothes looked like he'd slept in them and other bad things had happened to them too. There was a smell emanating from him that we'd never smelled before, and we gagged a little, as the wind blew it up our noses. We were used to fishin smells and huntin odors, but these smells were altogether different.

He turned and said, "Jake, hop up there and git my things and take them inside." He walked around to the front of the truck, thanked Raymond, and then he headed slowly for the house with Bub right behind him. "Dad!" "Dad!" Where's all tha fish? Where's all tha sea monsters?" Bub beseeched in a loud voice. Dad reached behind him and rubbed his calloused hand across Bub's head. "Hang on a little Bub, and I'll tell you all about it later on" With that, he headed for the house with the rest of us trailin along behind him.

Mother, watching all of this from the front porch knew things hadn't gone at all like dad had expected. She welcomed him inside and sent the rest of us outdoors until she could talk things over with him. We hung around the porch door hoping to overhear something that would give us a clue about what had happened to dad and the big, wide ocean. Every now and then, we'd hear a roar of laughter from mother and after hearing this a couple of times, we figured that dad's trip couldn't have been too bad after all.

Finally, as the sun was sliding towards the western horizon, mother came to get us, and we hurried inside, but dad was nowhere to be seen. We had a million questions for mother, and she merely shushed us and told us to get washed up and go to bed. She said that our questions would jist have to wait till morning because dad was already in bed, and he was very tired. She didn't look too concerned, and she did have a small smile playin around the edge of her mouth. She told us that with a good night's sleep, dad should be feeling a lot better by morning.

Morning finally came and we descended on dad like a pack of hounds. He had made it from his bed to the living room and was sitting back in his old chair with his bald head lying against the back of it with his eyes closed. Mother, hearin us come flying down the stairs, hurried into the living room and motioned for us to leave dad alone, but he opened his blood-shot blue eyes and looked at us, and he knew that he might as well get it over with. We all sat on the floor around him, and he began telling us the story of his encounter with the ocean.

Dad said that after leaving home, they drove about five and a half hours before they reached the fishing village of Lubec. Dad declared that he could smell the water long before they'd reached it and when they'd finally gotten to Raymond's brother's house, he already knew that he wouldn't like the ocean. Jake, mystified by this statement, jumped up and demanded to know what was wrong with the ocean. Dad motioned for Jake to sit down and said, "Jake, tha ocean ain't a bit like the rivers or lakes that you've been fishin in all your life. It smells! And I don't like that smell one bit!" "But what does it smell like dad?" Jake and Bub asked. Dad thought about it for a minute or so and then he said, "To me, it smells like rotten fish and tha smell never goes away. It's in your nose for as long as you are on or near tha salt water." With that explanation, Jake and Bub looked at each other, wrinkled their noses and agreed that they wouldn't like that smell either.

"But dad, where's all your fish and sea monsters?" Bub asked. Dad shifted in his chair and as his memory took him back to the day on the boat, you could see his belly roil up under his union suit, and he had to swallow real hard a couple of times before it stopped. Mother, seeing his reaction, hurried to the kitchen to get a pan and a rag. Dad coughed into his old red handkerchief a couple of times, wiped his lips, and then he continued.

"We had a real nice supper at Raymond's brother's house, and I slept pretty good that night too. Raymond's sister-in-law woke us up at four-thirty for breakfast and to appease mother he added, "But her biscuits weren't nearly as good as yours mum." Hearin this compliment, mother's dark skin glowed a dusky pink, and she looked real pretty sittin there on the arm of our old couch.

Dad looked at us and asked mother for some aspirin, and then he continued. "We walked down to the pier and loaded our fishin gear onto tha small boat, and we were off. We went out about a quarter of a mile into the ocean before we dropped anchor. I put some cut fish onto my hook and dropped tha line into the water alongside the boat and waited, but nothing happened. After about an hour of this and no bites, we all reeled in and changed our bait, but by then the sun was pretty well up, and it was gittin hot too." Raymond, sick of not catchin any fish, asked his brother to try another spot, and we went out a little further and we still didn't git any bites."

"Suddenly, tha wind shifted out of tha southeast, and large waves began pushing tha boat this way and that and I felt my belly begin to feel bad. Then, I saw Raymond being sick over the side of the boat and the next thing I knew, I was sick too." Upon hearin this, Jake and Bub looked at each other. This was news to them! Dad being sick when fishing! They couldn't believe their ears!

Dad, remembering all the ways the small craft had shifted to and fro in the choppy water, burped and held a washrag to his mouth and waited before he continued. "From that point on, all of us were sick. First Raymond, then me and then Carl. We upchucked until there wasn't anything left to upchuck. We were seasick and it was tha most terrible thing I've ever had, en I never want to see tha friggin ocean again!" "But dad" Jake exclaimed, "How big is the ocean anyway?" Dad looked at him and said, "I want you to go outside tonight and have a good look at tha sky, Jake. The ocean is nearly as big as the sky." Jake's eyes widened with the thought of how large the ocean really was. "From now on," dad said. "I'll stick to tha lakes, rivers and streams right here in good, old Aroostook County. They're good enough for me!" With that final announcement, dad laid his tired old head back against the chair and closed his eyes.

Upon hearing dad's final declaration, all hopes of him taking them deep sea fishing when they got bigger, slid from Jake and Bub's mind and the light in their eyes went out. No sea monsters, no sharks and no giant squid. They'd have to be content to catch a few chub, some suckers and maybe, if they were real lucky, maybe a trout every now and then.

Mother, seeing that dad was really worn out and still sick, sent us outside to play and Jake and Bub sat on the end of the porch to try and digest all this information. Mother said that they discussed the pros and cons of deep sea fishin for a long time and then, still not wantin to give up the dream, she heard Bub say to Jake, "Maybe dad caught a really huge sea monster, and it scared him so bad en he didn't want to scare us, so he didn't bring it home!"

THA TIP

Soon, it was nineteen sixty-three and I was a senior in high school. Dad, knowin that I wanted to buy some graduation pictures, took me aside one day and said, "Toots, I know that you have your heart set on buyin some graduation pictures, but I'll tell you, like I told all tha other kids, if you want any, you'll jist have to buy them yourself. I jist can't afford it." At that time, dad was only earning about fifty-four dollars a week working for Maine Seed Potato Growers and he was lucky to have that.

Then one night, dad came home from work and told me about a job up in the Maine woods workin for a "sportin" camp on Fish River. I contacted the owners and got the job. It was only for two months, from March till the end of May, and I would have to clean the cabins, make the guest's beds and help serve and clean up after the meals. Because my grades were good, I got permission from my teachers and off I went. I was due to graduate on June 12th and I really needed the money.

The time flew by and we spent the first three weeks getting the cabins cleaned and ready for the guests. The main lodge was on an island in the middle of the lake and it was surrounded by ten guest cabins. These cabins could sleep as many as five guests and it was my job to see that five of the cabins were cleaned daily, the beds made, the bathroom scrubbed and everything kept in reasonably tidy condition. Guests were usually flown in and out by seaplane, but as the season wore on and the woods dried out, they could come in by a rough dirt road that had been made thru the northern Maine wilderness to the lodge.

Guests came and went over the weeks and I enjoyed my work there, but I never really interacted with any of them all that much because I was shy and they were usually off fishing or out doing other things when my work was over. We had to be up by five am and I was always ready for bed as the sun went down. Quite often, jist before I fell asleep, I could hear the laughter coming from the main cabin and knew that the guests were socializing with the owners and the other guests.

Since I shared the cleaning of the ten guest cabins with another girl, I only had to worry about keeping my half of the ten clean. One cabin that I remember in particular had four men of varying ages staying in it.

Sometimes, as I hurried from one place to another, we would meet on the small trails, they'd smile at me and say hello and that was about it. Other times, the men would be sitting on the front porch of their cabin drinking a few beers and talking and a string of profanity would come flyin thru the cool, spring air that would have put even a Mainer to shame. I wasn't absolutely certain which man had uttered the words, but I do believe it was the younger man. Generally though, I saw very little of the four men because they spent most of their days out on the lake fishing or talking in the main lodge late at night, long after I had gone to bed.

The five weeks passed in a whirlwind of work and early one morning, I heard the plane as it made its landing approach for the lake. This meant that guests were either arriving or checking out. I hurried down to the main lodge and saw that my four guests were leaving. They all shook my hand and when it came to the taller, younger man's turn, he drew me aside and pressed some money into my hand. Surprised, I looked at him and he said, "This is your tip. We may not have caught very many fish, but we sure did have the prettiest chambermaid in Maine!" With that sweet compliment, he winked and then he turned and was gone, following the other three down the path to the plane. I looked at the money he'd given me and it was three, ten dollar bills.

As I slid the tip into my pocket, the owner's wife came up behind me and said, "I hope you keep that money because the person who gave it to you is very famous." I looked at her in surprise. "Do you know whose cabin you cleaned all this week?" I shook my head no. "Well, it was three editors from Life magazine and the younger man who gave you tha tip, he was Ted Williams!" I was both shocked and surprised! Here I was on a tiny island in a remote lake in the wilderness of northern Maine and Ted Williams had been here too!

Finally, my job was over and I headed back to civilization and boy did I ever have a story for dad! When I got home that night, I handed him my thirty dollar tip and told him the story. Upon hearin his hero's name, dad gaped at me and a light appeared in his tired, blue eyes. He looked at the money lying in his work-worn hand and once again he tried to give it back to me. "No dad, please keep it, I really want you to have it and I have enough money for my pictures too."

As I turned away, happy that I'd finally been able to give him something that he would treasure, he sat down in his chair with my tip still clutched in his hand. Mother later said that it was years before dad parted with that money and then it was only because he had to. His old truck had finally shit-tha-bed and he needed to replace the engine.

Dad is long gone now, but he remained a loyal Red Sox fan and a Ted Williams admirer until the very day he died on May 2nd, 1982. I jist hope that when his tired old soul finally got to Heaven, there was a Red Sox game going on up there and his beloved Ted Williams was coming up to bat....

Martha Stevens-David

THA B.T.B. CLUB

For as long as they could remember the five men, Walt, Leroy, Jake, Leo and Pete, had been best friends. From their very earliest days, there was something about the five of them that had drawn them together. Maybe it was because their mother's had always been friends too, but if you asked any one of them, why they were all friends, they didn't have an answer for it. It jist seemed natural for all of them to gravitate to one another.

As soon as they'd been old enough to go outside on their own, there was no stoppin them. They'd be at each other's houses until the mother that had gotten all of them that particular day, got tired of them and off they'd go, to one of the other guy's home. The really odd fact about them, that people often forgot, was that they'd all been born in the same month, in the same year, but in entirely different places. And if the truth be known, they were more like brothers than friends.

In the very early years, little things cropped up that would splinter and divide the group for a while. Sometimes it was a piece of candy, a toy truck or plane that they fought over and when they got bigger, it might have been a bike, a fishing pole or something equally as foolish as that. If one had trouble, they all had trouble.

Then came the day that they discovered girls and this was the time that really tested their unity. But after a couple of minor skirmishes with the "fairer" sex, the guys decided that as nice as they were, they, the girls, jist weren't worth all the friggin trouble.

Walt was often teased by the other guys because girl's jist liked him. Maybe it was his "duck's ass" haircut or his smooth way of talkin to the fairer sex, but Walt, even though he liked girls too, he always remembered his grandfather's sage advice when it came to wimmin. "Remember one thing Walt, most of them females ain't worth tha

252

powder to blow em tah Hell!" By the time they reached high school, the die was pretty much cast and they knew so much about each other that they were closer then brothers.

It jist so happened that they were all on the varsity basketball team and the coach, Mr. Grant, had his hands full dealing with the five of them. They all took Driver's Education at the same time too and this nearly drove Mr. Davis, the drivin instructor crazy. He was countin the days till these friggin kids graduated! It was June 12th, nineteen fifty-nine and Vietnam was hanging over their heads like a well-tied hangman's noose. The day after graduation, they'd all agree to hike to the top of Haystack Mountain and toss around a few ideas about what they were going to do for the near future.

Because the elevation of Haystack Mountain was only slightly over a thousand feet high, folks really didn't think of it as being a "mountain" and it was often referred to by the locals as "tha anthill." It was a relatively easy climb for even the most inexperienced mountain climber and most people in the surrounding towns had climbed it at one time or another. One of the guys had snuck into his father's storage room and stolen a couple of six packs and another had talked his mother into making some tuna fish sandwiches and a couple of them had even thought to bring along some sleeping bags. They were going to make a day and maybe even a night of it, each testing the other to see who might be brave enough to spend the night on top of tha anthill.

Bright and early the next morning, after stopping at Jimmo's Grocery for some "butts," and a couple of pizzas, the five of them piled into Walt's rattletrap pickup, with three in the front and two in the back, and the squealing of the truck's tires could be heard all over town as he made a quick turn out onto the Presque Isle Road. He floored the gas and they soon left Ashland behind as they flew down the tarred road at breakneck speed. And town folks, upon hearing the sound the truck made as it flew past their homes, gasped, held their breaths and made a silent prayer that they wouldn't have to be picking thosc boys up out of a ditch somewhere down the road.

It wasn't very long before the "anthill" loomed up in the clear air ahead of them and Walt slowed down a dite to make the left hand turn into the parking area at the bottom of the "almost" mountain.

They piled out of the truck and gathering the butts, beer, pizzas and sleeping bags, they pushed and shoved each other in good natured humor as they quickly made their way up the overgrown trail to the summit. Even though it was small by mountain standards, it was always exhilarating to actually stand on the edge of a teetering precipice and gaze off into the clear, blue Maine sky. To look off into the distance and be able to see the "real" mountain, Mount Katahdin, standing proud and majestic in the forests to the south.

It wasn't too long before Walt, always the "real" leader of the group, sent a couple of them back down the ant hill to gather some branches to build them a fire. Before going, the others argued amongst themselves if it was "against the law" to build a fire on the top of Haystack, but Walt stood firm and it wasn't too long before they had a nice fire burning in the early morning sun.

The guys opened the beer, smoked a couple of butts and settled down to enjoy the first real sense of freedom that they'd ever known in their young lives. No more school, no more taking orders from their parents, no more pain-in-the ass jobs like pulling mustard, picking rocks and picking potatoes for the local farmers! No-sir-ree, life was calling them and they were more than ready to answer its call, whatever that might be.

As the feeling of freedom took over and the alcohol loosened their tongues, the guys began talking about their hopes and dreams and plans for the future. As the day wore on and the sun got higher, and the booze ran out, they realized that "freedom" wasn't all that it was cracked up to be. A man still needed to have a job to be able to eat and finding one in Aroostook County in nineteen fifty-nine didn't hold that many options.

Long about four o'clock, they decided to call it quits and it was a very subdued group that made their way slowly down the ant hill. Amidst swearing about the never-ending mosquitoes biting every exposed piece of flesh, bellies grumbling for food, heads aching from too much sun and beer and lungs rebelling from too many cigarettes, they stumbled down the rocky outcroppings; stopping every now and then to watch as a chunk of loose rock fell off into the abyss and thanking God that it hadn't been one of them going over the side.

A month passed and their lives were forever changed. Leo, Walt and

Pete had taken themselves off to the recruiters in Presque Isle and joined the military. Walt and Pete were Army bound and Leo was headed for the Marines training camp in Pendleton, South Carolina. Jake had tried to join the Army too, but his childhood bout with Rheumatic Fever had left him with a heart murmur that the Army doctor didn't like hearin at all and he had decided to join his father out to the lumber mill in Portage. That left Billy and he soon headed for Canada where he figured he could work in the woods or the mines bordering the United States and Canada without worrying too much about anyone looking for him there as a deserter.

As life is want to do, time slipped away as did the years, and the guys slowly, but surely returned home one by one. Walt and Pete came home from Vietnam still alive, but never the same again. Walt had been right in the thick of the fighting in Cam Rahn Bay and suffered from Post Traumatic Stress Disorder among other things. He'd seem jist fine one minute and then something would trigger a memory or a smell that reminded him of the jungle and he'd jump and yell, "Get Down!" "Get Down!" and all hell would break loose until they could calm him down again.

Pete came home more half-dead than alive, after being held captive along the Ho Chi Min trail for the latter part of his service. He wouldn't verbalize his treatment by the enemy, but one could easily see that most of his fingernails had been ripped out and he had multiple scars that he couldn't hide on all parts of his body and he suffered from uncontrollable tremors from time to time.

Leo was the luckiest of the three, he'd been stationed stateside for the duration of the Vietnam conflict on a supply base in Texas and he always felt guilty about that. Jake was still out to the mill and was now the father of three kids. Billy had taken a job in Thetford Mines and had nearly been killed when a portion of the mine he'd been working in collapsed. He was more than happy to return to the daylight and look for a job that required being above ground, even potato pickin seemed like a good idea to him now.

One by one, they returned to the only life they'd ever known and to each other. And it wasn't very long before they were hooked up again and to some, it was as though the war and life had never happened. As in everyone's life, things jist sort of happen; girlfriends happen, wives happen, kids happen, careers happen, marriages happen, everything happens. It seemed as though before they even knew it, the other four had joined Jake in marriage, kids, huge responsibilities and the drudgery of dealing with plain old, everyday life.

They loved "Tha County" as only a county born person could. They began taking fishing trips together every spring and hunting trips together in the fall. These trips had taken them far and wide across the vast timberlands of "Tha County" and it was Jake who finally decided to buy a piece of land up to Musquahook from the Great Northern. He'd scouted the area many times as a hunter and when he found a spring that happily bubbled up out of the ground and after tasting the water, he knew this was where he wanted his camp. They all pitched in to help and it wasn't too long before the two room cabin was all done and their hunting trip soon became an annual event.

The camp contained jist the necessities that a man might need for a weeklong or weekend trip into the north Maine woods. It was roughly about fourteen by twenty with an overhead loft built on one side for sleeping. The lower floor had two windows that overlooked a small porch that ran along the front of the building. The oblong room contained a Glenwood cook stove that Jake had begged off his mother, some cupboards on one wall, a couple of single bunks were built along the side of the room and a makeshift counter with a small sink was built across the other end of the room. It was tight and cozy and that was all they needed. Nothing too fancy here, this was a man's camp.

Now the camp wasn't anything too grand because the guys knew that their wives would want to come along if it was too enticing and the men had made a pact that was always kept upon returning to civilization and wimmen. It was agreed that when asked by their better halves about the camp, they were to exaggerate beyond belief the horrible aspects of the hovel where they'd jist spent the entire weekend. The unrelenting swarms of midges, mosquitoes, bees and hornets, the unending swaths of poison ivy and poison oak. The incessant howling of the large bands of coyotes, wolves and the brazenness of the skunks, beavers, porcupines, wolves, bears and moose that constantly circled and threatened the cabin. And they never failed to point out how terrible it was to have to use the outhouse when the "no-see-ems" were in season too.

The men brought odd items to the cabin every once in a while, like pictures of their kids and wives, a patchwork blanket that one of their mother's had made, a better pillow or a really good book that they jist couldn't leave behind.

From time to time, that distant cabin became the focal point of many of the marital disagreements, with the deserted wives growing ever resentful about the time their better halves spent up in the woods. And it wasn't too long before an angry husband, who'd been drug over the coals at home a couple of times, for one inconsequential matter or another, would pin up a picture of his spouse on the cabin's wall and to get even, they'd all take turns throwing darts at it.

As the years slid by and the men aged and their obligations at home lessened somewhat, they took to the cabin not once or twice a year as in their younger years, but as often as they could run away from their mundane lives. The modest cabin became a place of refuge from the rest of the world in general and their wives and kids in particular. As the large lumber companies made inroads into the northern Maine wilderness in search of better timberlands, they improved the roads and now it was possible for the group to drive right up to the doorstep each time they visited the place.

And as men are want to do, whenever there was an altercation at home, be it wives or kids or bills, they'd throw some grub into a backpack, grab a case of beer and head for the woods. If their wives dared to complain, they'd not jist stay away for the night, they'd make a weekend of it. As soon as the first one arrived at the cabin, he'd build a nice fire, sweep out the remains of the last visitors, place a call by CB to the others and extend an open invitation for the rest to drive on up. Then, he'd sit back, drink a few brews and scratch any place that itched without fear of reprimand or embarrassment by his spouse.

When they'd first built the cabin, they'd christened it "Tha Club" but as the years wore on and their passion in their marriages had cooled and solidified, the name was gradually changed to the "B.T.B Club."

Leo, who was especially good at carving and woodworking, had secretly gone down in his basement at home and made them a lovely sign that he'd sanded to the max and varnished until it hurt your eyes to look at it. When it was finished, he'd carried the five foot by ten inch sign up to the cabin and hung it over the front door and the men had had a "christening" party and they didn't jist christen it in the customary way of pouring liquor over it either. They christened it by having a competition to see who could urinate all over it from a standing position. All five of them tried and all failed but that didn't matter, the camp was secretly called the "Bash the Bitches Club" from that day on.

When the men were at home and another came for a visit and the club's name was mentioned, the wife, upon hearin the words the "B.T.B. Club," would immediately ask the visitor what the letters stood for. The two men would eye each other covertly, take a long swig of beer and blow her question off. They never blabbed because they all knew that if one of the wives learned what the initials stood for, they were all gonna die, that's for sure! And they knew that if the news got out to the other wives the actual meaning of the letters, they'd never be allowed to return to the cabin again.

Unbeknownst to the husbands, the wives had some meetins of their own and the guys would have been surprised to learn that some mighty fine food and drinks were consumed at these impromptu meetings at one another's homes while they were off in the woods.

Some delicious liquor like, Jack Daniels, Jim Beams, Seagram's and Chivas Regal to name jist a few were downed by their better halves. The wives didn't lie on the dirty floors next to their flea-bitten dogs and whine about the friggin roads their lives had taken like the men did either. They mixed their drinks with ginger ale and loaded the glasses with ice and they were golden! And their dinner wasn't jist a piece of over-cooked venison or some under-cooked chunks of porcupine or beaver. Theirs was a five course meal of prime western beef, a Caesar's salad, hot dinner rolls and fresh apple pie ah-la-mode for dessert. All the wives agreed that it was wonderful to have the bed completely to themselves and not to have to answer to anyone for two whole days.

The men had a solidarity about the camp that would have put most unions to shame. They'd agreed on many different rules when they'd first built the cabin and one was followed specifically. That was, that the first man to get home at the end of the weekend was to set up the scenario for all the other men before they returned.

Upon arriving home, filthy, unshaven, smelling of body odor, dead animals and still hung over, he'd grab his few belongings, straggle out of his vehicle and head for the house. Upon entering the kitchen, his wife would slide her eyes over his filthy self and ask how his weekend had gone? The kids would gather around excitedly clamoring to be heard and ply him with questions. "Did yah see any deer dad?" "Did yah kilt any bears?" "Did yah see any bigfoots dad?" "Gee dad, you smell!"

The guilty husbands would then carefully recite a memorized litany of excuses like, "the weather was too hot," "the lumber companies had scared the deer away," "his gun had misfired," "the bullets were too weak," "the sun was too bright," "it had rained too much" or "there were too many hunters "from away" in the area. They always had an excuse why they didn't bring home any game.

Then the father would rumple his kid's hair, pat them on the cheek and head for the shower and bed. If his wife followed him to the bathroom and made a comment about how filthy his clothing was, or how badly he needed to bathe, he'd turn in the bathroom door, and say, "Well, I woulda changed my underwear if you'd remembered to pack some for me!"

Outraged by the blatant lies, his wife, with temper flaring and eyes snapping, would eye the fool for a long, cold moment and reply, "For your information mister man, I did pack you extra underwear. I tucked it in your gun case where I was one hundred percent sure you'd find it!" With that final volley from his better half, settin the mood for the rest of the evening, he'd slide the shower door shut with a bang and his wife would hurry downstairs to call the other wives to report the latest homecoming.

The years slid by one into another and very little changed with the guys except for the fact that they were growing older. Everyday life in rural Aroostook County was as slow moving as the seasons and everything was ruled by potatoes, it was either spring and time to plant the prolific spud, or midsummer and time to cultivate or spray the bastids or it was fall and it was time to dig the bastids up! The inhabitants of Aroostook County and their everyday lives never seemed to be very far from that particular tuber. And once the spuds had been harvested, the long ordeal at the potato houses would begin with the dumping of the potatoes into holding bins and then the culling, bagging and selling of them. Next came the loading of the bagged potatoes onto the waiting railroad cars, to the hiring of the crew who would come to the potato houses early every morning to cut them into seed stock that would be stored for the upcoming spring and planting. Potatoes had made Aroostook County and nobody could ever really forget that.

But nothing ever remains the same, no matter how much we want it too and the camp was the same. As the kids grew and got older, the boys would beg their fathers to "take them up to tha camp" with them and the wives, upon hearin this oft repeated request, would stop whatever they were doing, give the husband a strong look that said; "Whatever do you all do up there that you can't take one of these kids off my hands for a day or a weekend?" And the husband, feeling more than a little guilty, would finally capitulate and the whiner would soon find himself happily ensconced on the front seat of his father's vehicle, headin for the north woods, while the trapped father would be swearing under his breath and tryin to figure out a way to explain, why his kid was there to the other fathers.

As soon as the truck carryin the kid pulled up to the cabin, the father would send the inquisitive boy off on as many "wild goose" chases as he could think up and once the kid was out of sight, he'd head for the cabin to hide all the Playboy and "girlie" magazines, pick up the empty beer and liquor bottles and any other questionable items that the kid might see and blab about to his mother when he returned home.

Days slid into weeks, weeks into months and months into years and the men began looking jist as ratty as the cabin they loved. Oh, there had been some changes over the ensuing years, like an old shag carpet on the cabin floor, a portable television and a gas cook stove, but that was about it. Jake had secretly installed a shower by the back door and the men all agreed that that had been a brilliant idea. But none of them would use it until jist before they were scheduled to return home. To them, staying rumpled, unshaven and smelly was part of the lure of the weekend at the cabin.

Then came the day that finally signaled the demise of the cabin and the "B.T.B." club too and it was Walt's wife that caused it all. She'd called all the other guy's wives only to find that they already had plans for the weekend and she couldn't think what she should do to make the time pass quicker. She walked from room to room in her home and she couldn't think of a single thing that she needed to do and as she was stirring the cream into her coffee, the thought came to her. "I'll jist hop in the car and drive on up to the cabin and surprise Walt!" she thought to herself.

Having driven there with Walt, a couple of times over the years, she had a pretty good idea about how to get there and after driving for nearly an hour, she finally pulled up behind the pickup-filled yard. As she parked the car behind the last truck and slid out the door, a mangy looking dog suddenly appeared on the top step of the porch and it began the long, drawn out call that the Bluetick Hound is known for. The dog, smelling a stranger, bayed at full force and this brought the men running out the front door to see what tha hell was bothering the mutt. They all came to a screeching halt at the sight of Walt's wife standing there by the porch steps. Walt, having been the last one out the door, slid his bottle of home brew behind his shirt and gaped at his wife. "Jaysus honey, what are yuh doin here?" "Is everything alright at home?" "Well, I was home all alone and I thought that you jist might like some company."She replied.

Upon hearin her words, Walt swallowed hard and looked beseechingly at the other men before he answered his wife. Jake grabbed his still wailing dog and drug him off the porch and out behind the shed. Leo and Billy, headed for the woods with mumbled excuses about checking out the new deer blind and Leroy, suddenly remembered that his wife needed him back at home and he took off hell bent for home in his pickup.

Jist as his wife set her foot on tha front step, Walt remembered something. He remembered that when he'd left home that morning, he'd been pissed off with his wife's whining and he'd pinned up her picture to the back wall of the cabin and it was still hanging there, filled with darts! Sweat rolled off Walt's brow like rain on tha face of Mount Katahdin and he dropped the hidden bottle of home brew onto tha floor behind him. As he turned, he tripped on the bottle and stumbled and his wife, mistaking his clumsiness for drunkenness, pushed him aside, kicked the bottle down the steps and stepped into the cabin.

Given the darkness of the interior, the overwhelming smell of home brew and cigarettes, it took her exactly ten seconds to realize what was sticking into her picture that was pinned up on the back wall and she never said a word. She turned, glared into her husband's dumbfounded face and slid on past him and out the door. Walt's face was turning blue before he was able to draw some air into his tortured lungs and trembling a little, he groped for a chair to sit down. He heard the car door slam and the gravel shoot through the yard as his wife spun the car around and down the dirt road. And his mind began wondering if he'd ever get the nerve to go home again!

One by one, the cowards slunk back to the cabin, jist waiting to hear about the explosion that never came and upon seeing Walt, slumped in his favorite chair; they carried on as though nothing had happened. Finally, long about midnight and after a lot of brews, Jake asked Walt what had happened to his wife. Walt, bleary eyed and drunk, looked at his lifelong friend and replied; "Jaysus Jake, I've faced wild animals, tha Viet Kong in the jungles of Viet Nam, angry boyfriends and vicious mother-in-laws, but I've never seen anyone as angry as my wife was today! I don't know what I'm going to find when I git home tomorrow!" "In that case Walt, have another brew!" and Jake handed Walt another bottle of beer.

And as life is want to do, even the hardest times are eased by the memory of the good times and Walt returned home to a wife who was as cold as the north side of Mount Katahdin, but being the smart man he is, the promise of a lovely diamond bracelet and a grand trip to Prince Edward Island, did a lot to thaw her out.

THA SUBSTITUTE

The third grade brought a whole new dimension into my life in the form of Lizzie Wallop. Lizzie had already retired as a Latin teacher after teaching some thirty-odd years in the high school and she only occasionally accepted substitute teaching jobs. She must have been at least seventy years old by the time she substituted for my class and she was more than a little senile. When Mr. Bolestridge, the principal announced that she was coming, we waited for her arrival with a mixture of fear and excitement because her extensive reputation at the high school had preceded her.

Little did we know, but all the horror stories our older cousins and brothers and sisters had told us about Lizzie and how she conducted her classroom, weren't exaggerations, they were all true! We'd heard the story about the poor little French kid from Sheridan who'd been mangled by Lizzie when he'd failed to do as she commanded.

His parents had migrated over the Canadian border into our area of Aroostook County and his first language was French. French was always spoken at home so by the time he'd gotten to the eighth grade; he still didn't understand or speak English all that well. He stumbled into her class one day and slunk into a seat in the back of the room. Mrs. Wallop, cast a rheumy, brown eye on him and issued a guttural command in his general direction that he didn't understand at all.

She waited impatiently for the kid to stand up and tell her his name, but he jist sat where he was, hoping against hope that she would move on to some other sorry specimen.

Outraged by his lack of response and what she deemed disrespect, she threw her attendance book onto the floor, shoved her chair away from the desk and strode down the aisle to where he was still sitting. She reached out her gnarled hand and grabbed him by the ear.

Surprised by her attack, the poor kid didn't know what to do and he pulled his head back hoping that she'd let go of his ear. But Mrs. Wallop had been down that road a good many times before and she gripped the offending cartilage harder. She snapped his head forward and tore part of his earlobe away from his head when she drug him out of his chair into a standing position. Then she hauled him over to the door and chucked him out into the hallway and slammed the door. Another time, when a high school kid had the nerve to mock her behind his book, she threw him right out a class room window! She didn't suffer fools gladly and she wasn't afraid to be challenged either!

Lizzie was a large woman with coarse features. She had heavy dark, connected eyebrows that overhung her bloodshot brown eyes and she wore her greasy, gray hair pulled straight back in an unkempt bun at the nape of her neck. Lizzie had the habit of taking a lead pencil out of her bun and used it to scratch her head whenever the impulse came over her. She weighed about two hundred plus pounds and she always dressed in black and no matter what she wore, there was always a streak of what appeared to be dried-on food running down the front of her dress or blouse. Her husband had been a small town editor when they'd married and they were considered quite cultured and well-to-do by most people's standards, at least in our neck of the woods anyway.

Lizzie drove around town in a large, white Cadillac like she owned the place. If she wanted to get anything at the local A & P Grocery Store, she simply stopped her car anywhere she damn-well pleased and walked off to do her errands. She didn't care if it was in the middle of the street, behind someone else's car or right in front of the fire station. Where she decided to stop was where she left it. It got so that folks, upon seeing her car occupying an odd place, would simply jump in and repark it in a better spot and Lizzie was never the wiser. Folks all agreed that this was much easier than having to confront her about her piss poor driving.

She was always in the company of two large, white, Maine Coon Cats who, she didn't hesitate to tell all her students, were much smarter than they could ever be. It was probably the truth too, but we didn't like hearing it. It was rumored around town that these cats were trained to attack on command and no one ever wanted to go to her house for anything.

The morning that I most remember was one that will stay with me the rest of my days. Mrs. Bartlett, our regular beloved teacher, had called in sick and desperate for a substitute, the principal called his favorite teacher substitute, Lizzie Wallop.

Lizzie strode into our classroom like a general on a mission and on a mission she was. She was going to show us, one and all, jist how stupid and uneducated we really were. With her lunch bag clutched in one large hand and a scruffy, cloth bag in the other, she cast a scornful glance around the room, her gaze scalding across each of us in one swift glance. We knew that one bag was for her lunch, but we were never quite certain what she carried in the other.

She dropped the heavy bags onto the floor beneath her desk, kicked them aside with her foot and sat down. She didn't bother to introduce herself. We all knew only too well who she was by her well-deserved reputation. She jist sat there in her creaking wooden chair for the longest time, letting her muddy, brown eyes roam over the entire classroom. It seemed as though she could tell by jist looking at us, how smart we were and what we were going to accomplish in life.

She'd glance at the list of names on the paper on the desk in front of her and then upon recognizing our parent's names; she'd curl her lip and make random comments about our parentage to no one, in particular. Things like, "Robinson, I knew your grandfather very well. I hope you're smarter than he was." or "Alcott, I always thought your mother had more sense than to marry your father." "Michaud, I hope you have the good sense to stay away from alcohol better than your grandfather did." Nice comments like that.

Finally, she looked in my direction and roared, "Stevens, stand up!" I arose and stood there mute, with my heart pounding in my throat, waiting to hear what nice things she was going to say about me, my siblings or my parents. She examined me with a yellow-tinged critical eye from head to toe and then she announced to the class at large that "Little girls with blond hair should know better than to wear white blouses!" My classmates snickered at her comments and thinking that she had moved on, I quickly sat down. She looked up to find me sitting and she bellowed in my direction once again, "Get up Stevens, get up and read!" When I finished reading the paragraph from the English book in front of me, she stared at me for a long moment and said, "Well, well,

well, there is a gem in this old sack of rocks after all." I didn't know what that meant but my reading sure saved me. After that, whenever she was asked to sub, she always called on me to read to her.

She next cast a jaundiced eye on Timmy Levesque and she commanded him to stand up. Well, Timmy wasn't very tall. His whole family didn't stand over five feet, but she didn't notice that fact or if she did, she didn't even care. She thought that he was only half-standing or that he was slouching or that he hadn't stood-up at all, so she yelled at him again in her grating voice, "Stand up!" "I said, stand up!" Timmy merely looked back at her and very meekly replied, "I am!"

Feeling that somehow she had been challenged, Lizzie's sweaty face became suffused with anger and her eyes bulged out of her head. She shoved her chair aside so violently that it fell back against the chalkboard with a loud crash. She scrabbled into a standing position and grabbed the huge Webster's Dictionary from the row of books on the desk in front of her, drew it back over her head and heaved it directly at Timmy. He ducked jist in time and it sailed by his head and hit the back wall with a loud thud, leaving a good sized dent in the wall. If it had connected, it surely would have decapitated poor little Timmy. The class held its breath to see what carnage she was going to cause next.

Lizzie placed her hands on her ample hips and demanded that Timmy come up to where she was standing. As the poor little kid rounded the corner of her desk, her right hand snaked out and she grabbed him by her favorite appendage, the right ear and she used it to propel him forward. With a vicious twist to his ear, she forced him to kneel down in front of her and with a swift kick in Timmy's small backside, pushed him forward under her desk. Then she retrieved her wayward chair, plumped herself down in it, cast a jaundiced eye once again in our direction and commenced berating the rest of our class.

The front of her desk had an oval opening and we could see poor Timmy imprisoned between Lizzie's knees and her lunch bag. With a satisfied look on her face that her latest prisoner couldn't cause any further distractions, Lizzie announced that we would now proceed with our reading lesson.

As time and the day wore on, Timmy became restless and began exploring his surroundings. It didn't take too long before he spied

Lizzie's lunch bag and he gingerly opened it and began examining its contents. He reached inside and withdrew a banana which he held out the front hole of the desk for everyone to see. Then, to everyone's delight, Timmy proceeded to eat it! He rummaged around in the bag a little more and he came up with her sandwich. He ate that too! Timmy ate everything she had brought for her lunch! Finally, there was nothing left for him to eat and he pushed the lunch bag away.

Then Timmy spied the other, larger bag. Being careful not to make a sound, he pulled it over in front of him and looked inside. Then he reached into the bag and withdrew a piece of flesh-colored material. When he's finally deciphered what it was that he was holding, he laughed quietly and held it out the front of the desk for all of us to see. It was a huge pair of ladies cotton bloomers! Knowing full well what would happen to us if we laughed out loud, Timmy pulled the old pair of bloomers over his head and we all hid our red faces behind our books and pretended to study our reading. Finally, Timmy tired of this game and with a full belly, leaned against the side of the desk and fell asleep. Every now and then, he'd give a little snore, emit a loud burp and sleep on.

After what seemed like an eternity, the lunch bell rang and we were dismissed with the warning that in the afternoon classes, if anyone dared to defy her, they would meet the same fate as had befallen Timmy. She nudged Timmy awake with a swift kick into the small of his back and pulled him by the nape of his neck out from under her desk. Jist for good measure, she cuffed him once or twice across the back of his small head, then she yelled into his ear for him to go home and tell his parents how he'd misbehaved that morning.

Then, she gave him a strong shove in the general direction of the door and that was all the impetus that he needed. Timmy shot out of that room and down the hall to the front stairs. He couldn't wait to tell everyone how he had outsmarted Lizzie. Need-less-to-say, he didn't return to school for the rest of that week and by the time he did return, she had moved on to bigger challenges.

Lizzie's reputation for violence in the classroom did more to purge the Ashland School system of lazy students than all of World War II and the Korean conflict put together. She is long gone now but, never, never forgotten!

ANGEL

Every once in a while, all the Gods in the universe get together and create a child that is so beautiful, so talented that it's almost as though they tried too hard. A child such as this was born in our small town of Ashland to a poor, French Canadian family. From the very moment of her birth, everyone was drawn to her by her beauty and goodness. She was indeed a child of the Angels.

She had large, almond shaped eyes, and her dark lashes were tipped with gold. Her hair was the color of burnished copper, and it hung down her back in long, flowing ringlets. Her skin was the color of amber, and sunlight danced on her arms as she walked down the street. You could easily picture her on a faraway tropical island with bright red flowers in her hair. Folks kept looking at her to find a flaw, but there wasn't any that you could easily see anyway.

She had the gift of laughter too, and it drew you to her jist to hear that magical sound again. It sounded like small bells swaying gently in the wind. The local priest tried to persuade her parents to send her off to a convent in Fort Kent, a town located up along the Canadian border, but her parents wouldn't be parted from the only beauty in their otherwise dismal lives. Her given name was Ange Marie, but it wasn't too long before she acquired the name "Angel" because that was the name that so aptly described her.

Time passed and before you knew it, she'd grown from a lovely girl-child into a stunning young woman. It seemed as though the Gods didn't know when to stop. She was almost too beautiful and too much woman. At fifteen, when she walked down the street, sexuality oozed from her very being, and every male between six and sixty responded with an eagerness that would have put a pack of dogs to shame.

In a small town like ours, people are often judgmental without cause, and in Angel's case, they were even more so. It seems that when one person is extremely blessed, this brings out the worst in others, and it wasn't long before the love affair between Angel, and the town came to an end.

In a town of fifteen hundred people, everyone knows everyone else, and before long, small bits of gossip began filtering about town concerning Angel. She drew people, mainly men, to her simply by being. The women of the town, who felt threatened by her, began turning on her with a vengeance. Angel couldn't go to a dance or on a date. She couldn't do the simplest, most innocent thing without it being blown all out of proportion.

There was no way she could remain untouched, when every male in the county was lusting after her. And it wasn't long before she was doing exactly what everyone had already accused her of. She didn't discriminate; she took on all comers, and she didn't charge either. The better part of the male population of Aroostook County beat a path to Angel's door.

The years passed, and her liaisons became shorter and less passionate. The beauty that had once shown so brightly began to fade. The old crones and gossips gathered on their doorsteps as Angel passed by. They gloried in the fact that her cheeks didn't seem as pink as they used to and her hair didn't have that shine, or bounce anymore. Life had taken its share of her, along with everyone else.

Angel knew what she was, and it didn't seem to bother her. She didn't care whom she shared her bed with. When one lover left, there was always another willing and eager to take his place. She loved them, and they left her and that's the way her life was, day in and day out, year after year. Folks used to drive by her house late at night jist to see which "happily" married man was now occupying her bed.

Then Angel met a man who came, loved her for who she was, and stayed. To the town's astonishment, they married and had three children together. Angel seemed to have renounced her old life and now there were younger, prettier girls eager to pick up where she had left off. Men still followed her with their eyes, but that was all. Angel was out of the business simply by the fact that she now had a husband and children.

Things seemed to go well during the next few years, until Angel's husband took a job with a paper company, that sent him to cut logs in the woods along the Canadian border, and he had to stay at the camp for weeks at a time.

Things being what they were and people being what they are, it wasn't long before Angel's name was making the rounds again, but this time, it was different. She had a husband, even if he wasn't around, and folks began speculating who would be the first to tell her husband when he got back to town, about Angel's fall from grace.

It was an evening that folks in our small town would never forget. They still talk about it late at night, when a cold, north wind stirs the trees and there is a hint of frost in the air. The first and only murder in our town took place on a Saturday night in November, and Angel was the catalyst that caused it.

On that fatal night, as she lay curled in her newest lover's arms, she didn't hear her husband drive into the yard and enter the house. Her lover never knew what hit him, as the bullet entered his head and splattered his brains all over the bedroom wall. Police arrested Angel's husband, and the court tried him for a "crime of passion." Found guilty, they sent him down state to the Thomaston State Prison to serve a life sentence for murder in the second degree.

Everything about Angel faded after that. Her beauty, which had been on the wane, disappeared altogether. Folks commented that it was almost as though she had grown old overnight. She was often seen, at all hours of the day and night, walking along the streets and country roads, but the only thing that chased her now was an occasional stray dog.

Angel died not too long ago and was buried along the edge of St. Mark's Cemetery in Sheridan. The few who attended her hasty funeral, still talk in hushed voices, about the strange thing that happened that day. As they lowered Angel's casket into the cold, damp ground, a golden mist rose from the gaping, black hole. It hovered over her casket for a brief moment, and then it ever so slowly, wound its way upwards through the trees toward Heaven....

THA APPLE TREE

Hughy slid out of bed and shuffled over to the window that looked out into the back pasture and was surprised to see that there was jist a hint of frost on the ground. Fall had arrived overnight in Aroostook County. The wind was out of the north and it bent the apple trees in his orchard as it passed through the heavily laden branches, down over the empty potato fields and across the road.

He yawned and pulled his work clothes on over his threadbare union suit and headed down the stairs. His wife was busy in the kitchen and Hughy slid past her and out the door without a word. Hearin the backdoor slam, she turned with a question and was jist in time to see the back of his head as he went through the shed into the barn.

"Well." She said angrily to herself, "Yah git up early, cook a nice breakfast and what do you git? If he's too stupid to eat his breakfast, that's his problem!" She slid a well-cooked egg and two toast onto her plate and headed for the living room and her favorite television gospel hour. If he didn't give a damn, she didn't give a damn either!

As the preaching ended and the singing began, she turned the television up and began to sing along with the program. Then the spirit of the gospel, combined with the rhythm of the music, moved her and she began to dance around the living room, lost in a spiritual world of her own. She didn't stop to think about how she sounded or how she looked. She'd done this every morning, everyday, for the past forty years.

As she danced around the coffee table, she felt, rather than heard, another presence in the room and when she opened her eyes, she saw her husband standing in the doorway watchin her. "I thought you'd gone and killed yourself." He said. "I could hear tha caterwaulin all tha way out to tha barn and I was tryin to milk. Your singin was makin tha cows jumpy."

Stung by the candor of his unflattering remarks, she brushed past him into the kitchen. "Your food is on tha stove and tha coffee's ready if you're goin tah eat." She dumped her dishes into the sink, squirted some detergent on them and turned on the hot water.

The phone rang and he shoved past her to grab it. It was her mother-in-law and she heard him say that he'd be goin into town later in the day and that he'd stop by and pick up her grocery list. He hung up and walked over to the stove, scooped up his dried eggs and toast and turned and sat down at the table. Angered at what she'd heard him say to his mother, she turned to him. "I thought that we'd agreed to take a ride up tha Realty Road and have a look at all the trees and all them pretty leaves." He continued eatin and didn't meet her eyes. "Well." He said finally. "You've lived in "Tha County" all your life and I don't see why you want tah go and look at all them friggin leaves anyway! I'da thought that you'd seen enough of them as they go flittin past tha house every day!"

With that, he shoved back his chair and headed once more for the barn. Jist before the door slammed behind him, he turned, stuck his head back through the doorway and said. "You know, winter will be here before we know it and them apples ain't goin tah keep much longer. If the birds or crows peck them full of holes, they won't be good for nothin! There was a frost on the ground this mornin and we'd best be gettin to them today!" Not waiting for her reply, he slammed the door and disappeared around the corner of the house.

She grabbed his dishes off the table, threw them on top of hers in the dishpan and walked over to the window that overlooked the front porch and pushed the curtains aside. As she looked out across the road at the mountains in the distance she wondered for the millionth time why things had come to be this way. "There must be something better out there." She thought. "But, I don't know where it is and I don't even know if I'd recognize it if I friggin saw it! Give a man forty years, two kids and this is all it comes down to. A lot of back-breakin work, work that never ends. Life's ah bitch and then yah die! There's more truth to that than poetry!" She said to herself and let the curtain fall back over the window. "Might as well git my glad rags on and go pick them apples or I won't be hearin the last of it for tha next two months!"

She heard the truck shift into gear jist as she came around the corner of the barn. "Thanks a friggin lot!" She screamed into the frigid air as she watched him drive away across the field. She stood for a moment and cussed some more as she saw the truck disappear through the tall grass, headed for the apple orchard. She wiped her hand across her hot face and started down the road behind him. "Oh well," she thought. "I guess I could use tha exercise. A couple of miles ain't that much and tha day really is lovely."

By the time she'd reached the edge of the pasture, she could see him. He'd backed the pickup up under his favorite tree, the Golden Delicious. His grandfather had planted that tree nearly a hundred years ago and even though it was beginnin to show its age, it was still bearin wonderful fragrant apples. The pale yellow fruit was perfectly round and its flesh was a crisp white with small threads of red running through it at the core. The apples had an aroma that made you think of vanilla and cinnamon mixed together and they made the best pies and applesauce. They'd never seen another tree like this one and he tended it with loving care from year to year. "Friggin tree gits more attention than I do," She thought jealously. "If he ever gave me that much attention, I might jist blossom too!"

By the time she reached the truck, he was halfway up the tree. She shielded her eyes from the sun and looked up at him. "Don't yah think that you're a little too high? You're not as young as you used to be yah know." He grunted as he pulled himself a little higher. Sliding his foot into a fork in the tree, he began pullin the ripe, yellow apples off the branches. He turned slightly and looked down in her direction. "Git that bag off tha pickup," He ordered. "En I'll throw them down to you."

She drug the large burlap bag off the truck and walked over to the tree. She waited expectantly and he began tossin handfuls of apples down to her, but he didn't wait to see if she'd caught the ones he'd thrown, he jist continued throwin them down to her. "Jaysus! Give me a minute will yah! I've only gut two hands!" She dropped a couple and they rolled under the tree directly beneath him. She bent down and retrieved the apples and jist as she was about to move back, she looked up to where he was. The next thing she heard was the sound of wood breaking as a large limb broke off the tree and came plummeting to the ground right next to her.

Suddenly, she saw her husband swinging wildly in the air because there was nothing left for him to stand on. The fork of the ancient tree where he'd placed his foot had broken off. He scrabbled for the tree and a foothold and another branch came plummeting to the ground. Hughy quickly saw that he had two distinct choices. It was either the tailgate of the pickup that he was going to hit or his wife and he chose his wife. "She'd be a hell of a lot softer!" He thought to himself as he began the abrupt descent.

He saw the surprised look on his wife's face as she realized where he was headed. He gained momentum as his two hundred plus pounds fell the fifteen feet in a heartbeat and he hit his wife head on.

There was no time for her to do anything! She screamed when she felt the full impact of her husband's body as he slammed into her and her legs buckled under the force of the fall. The impact drove her shoulder into the ground and she felt her neck snap as she fell backwards. They lay there in a jumbled heap until he was able to catch his breath.

Finally, when he'd stopped trembling and his breathing had somewhat returned to normal, Hughy slid off his wife and pulled himself up against the pickup. He leaned against the tailgate until he was sure that he hadn't broken anything and then he looked over to where she still lay.

He watched as her eyes rolled back into their normal position and she began to come around. She groaned as she tried to turn over and he finally walked over and helped her into a sitting position on the ground. "Are yah alright?" He asked. She reached up, brushed her hair out of her eyes and then she winced in pain as she brought her right arm back down. "Don't know, but I guess I'll live. I sure as hell don't want tah go through that again!" She said in a slurred voice.

She pulled herself up into a sitting position and tried to stand. He reached out to help her and she knocked his hand away. "Don't be doin me no more favors!" She snarled. "I never thought that I'd see tha day that I'd nearly be killed by my own husband!"

Her right eye had swollen shut and was already turning black. A trickle of blood from her nose had run down over her top lip. She brought her good arm up and drug her old coat sleeve across her nose, leaving a bright red smear across her left cheek.

Stung by her anger and her harsh words, he turned on his heel and started for the cab of the truck. "It isn't like I meant for it to happen for Christ's sake! I did fall fifteen feet out of that friggin apple tree, yah know! Besides, couldn't yah see that I was fallin? Yah coulda moved yah know!" She watched him stalk away. "Hey, where you goin?" She asked. "I'm goin to tha barn to git my ladder. We still have tah pick them friggin apples yah know!"

She scrabbled into a standing position and leaned against the rusty fender to catch her breath. Then she walked unsteadily around to the other side of the truck, opened the door and slowly drew herself up into the seat. She looked over at him and said, "Yah know somethin, when I was layin there half dead; tha only thing runnin through my mind was a newspaper headline." "Wife Killed When Husband Falls From Tree."

"Well, it coulda been worse," He snapped. "I coulda hit tha tailgate and been really hurt or even killed!" "Yes," She replied. "I coulda been killed too! The only question is, did you miss tha tailgate by accident or did you aim for me on purpose?"

His ruddy, weather beaten face colored slightly and he avoided her direct gaze and didn't answer. He shifted the truck into gear and drove slowly across the bumpy pasture towards the house. Groaning as she felt each jolt hit her body, she said, "Oh, I git it, tha answer is in tha question!" Hearin her angry remark, his face reddened even more and he floored the old rattletrap and headed for the barn.

Martha Stevens-David

GREAT AUNT CASSIE

She was really our great aunt, but us Stevens' kids always called her Aunt Cassie. She only stood about five feet tall in her stocking feet, but she had more drive and energy in her little finger than most people had in their whole body. There wasn't anything that she couldn't or wouldn't do if she put her mind to it. To me, she was the epitome of the true American pioneer spirit.

The word impossible jist wasn't in her vocabulary. If the old Farmall tractor needed a new part that wasn't available at the local Ashland parts store, she could always be relied upon to know where one could be found, bought or borrowed.

Long after Uncle Hal, had thrown down his wrenches in disgust and stormed off, swearing at the top of his lungs, Aunt Cassie would calmly come out of the house, wipe her hands on her flour sack apron, pick up the abandoned tools and proceed to repair the tractor.

Aunt Cassie was a woman who not only loved Uncle Hal, she also loved life but the thing she loved the most was a good dose of gossip. From time to time, she'd go to visit all the neighbors and after downing numerous cups of tea and ferreting out the latest, juicy story, she'd return home, anticipating the first chance she'd have to pass on the slightly embellished stories.

Aunt Cassie was an inveterate pack rat. She never threw anything away and she couldn't stand for anyone else to throw anything away either. She often made secret, furtive excursions to the local dumps where she'd joyfully spend the entire morning sorting thru other people's trash.

She never came home disappointed either. She'd immediately cart everything she'd found up to her attic that was located directly over her kitchen. Year after year, as Aunt Cassie slowly but surely accumulated more and more "treasures," the kitchen ceiling began to curve noticeably downwards. Everyone who knew her began making side bets as to when the ceiling would finally cave in.

By the time we were born, Aunt Cassie's three kids were all grown up and on their own. So, we, her great nieces and nephews became the ones to replace her own kids in helping, from time to time, with chores around their farm.

Aunt Cassie missed her true calling when she became an Aroostook County farmer's wife at the age of fifteen. She really should have gone to work for the Federal Bureau of Investigation or the Central Intelligence Agency. She had an uncanny way with a chocolate chip cookie that would make you spill your guts about all the gossip you'd ever heard and even some you haven't. If you told her some story that she hadn't previously heard before, her eyes would light up and she'd hastily shove another cookie into your grubby hand. Then, she'd lean a little closer and with her voice scarcely above a whisper, ask, "And then Tooter, what happened?"

Then came a day when Aunt Cassie thought she'd died and gone to gossip heaven. She'd finally acquired what Uncle Hal commonly referred to as "That God-Damned thing," the telephone. She finally got the phone by begging and pleading with Uncle Hal about how it would save them so much time and money not to have to run into town every time they needed a new part for the tractor or for the other farm equipment. She finally convinced him when she said that she'd call over to Presque Isle and have the parts they needed mailed out to them.

From the first day it was installed, Aunt Cassie was beside herself with joy. From the very beginning, she had been connected to a six family "party-line." Each family was assigned a certain number of rings and when the phone rang for any family on the line, it also rang at all the other houses too.

It wasn't too long before she'd memorized all the neighbor's rings and upon hearing the phone begin to ring, she'd quickly count the rings, immediately drop whatever she was doing and run into the parlor and pick it up. She could be found most anytime of the day or night, leaning over her old desk, with the telephone receiver cupped under her chin, listening in on someone else's conversation. Uncle Hal constantly complained that her cooking had gone to hell in a wheelbarrow ever since she'd gotten that God-damned thing!

She got into trouble quite a few times when she overheard some real juicy gossip and forgot that she was the rubberee and not the callee and she'd joined right in on the conversation before she realized what she was doing.

Over the years, the habit of holding the receiver cupped under her chin while she listened in on other's phone calls, began to take its toll. She took to holding her head at a slight angle as though she had a crick in her neck. Whenever anyone asked her about her health, she'd gingerly rub her neck and complain of a touch of arthritis here and there. Hearing this, Uncle Hal would snort and laugh that it wasn't "arthritis" but "telephoneitis." She certainly wasn't going to get any sympathy from him!

Aunt Cassie had a way of getting you to do something terrible by making it seem like a great big adventure. One day, when I went for a visit, she was happily washing her breakfast dishes when suddenly she knelt down and began rummaging through the cabinets under the sink. When she stood up, she was holding two small, empty lard pails in each hand. She spun around, looked me right in the eye, lowered her voice to a whisper and said, "Tooter, I found the biggest patch of strawberries yestiday morning... Let's go!" With a big smile on her face, she handed me the two dainty lard pails, grabbed a huge milking pail for herself and off we went to the secret place where the wild strawberries were calling her name.

Or, she'd sit you down in her cluttered kitchen, with the wood stove stoked to the brim, hand you a couple of freshly baked molasses cookies and ask you how you'd like to earn a quarter. In nineteen fifty-two, that was a lot of money to most people, and especially for us Stevens' kids, so we usually said yes. It certainly didn't take us long to catch on to her ways.

She was a master of suspense too. She'd never tell you right away what the job really was. She'd hand you a hat, boots, gloves and an old jacket and then she'd take off at a fast clip towards the barn and you'd have to run to keep up with her. Before you knew it, you'd rounded the corner of the building, past the outhouse and you were out behind the barn. It didn't take overly long to get the gist of her plan, what with a huge smelly pile of cow manure staring you in the face!

After you'd swallowed deeply several times, to keep all those cookies down that she'd jist fed you, she'd thrust a three pronged pitchfork into your hands and say, "I jist need, oh maybe three or four trailer loads of manure for the flower beds and my garden. And oh yes, I nearly forgot, I guess we can't forget the lawn, now can we?" You knew right then that this was going to be an all day affair! God! How I hated that smelly, disgusting job, but Aunt Cassie would work right alongside you and she sang all the while she was slinging forkful after forkful of "poor man's fertilizer" into the manure spreader. You can't say all this stuff wasn't "educational" though. To this very day, I know how to grow a pretty mean garden and my flowers are to die for and oh yes, I can still sing "Mockingbird Hill" all the way through.

After the garden had been thoroughly covered with rich, black manure and the earth turned over, then the lawn and flower beds had to be covered. Then everything had to have a good dose of water and she'd move on to another important task.

For the next couple of weeks, we'd be extremely careful not to visit Aunt Cassie unless we absolutely had to. If the Aroostook River had receded off Uncle Hal's flats on the island, we'd take the long way around to go fishin down to the island. Instead of going straight down the road past her house, we'd run down over Mr. Beaulier's property to the Bangor & Aroostook Railroad tracks and cross them and go down thru the woods to get to the river. It took us a great deal longer and added miles of walking to our fishing trip, but going that way, we knew that she couldn't see us.

If her "eagle" eyes happened to catch us slinking past her house to go fishing or strawberrying, she'd thrust her curtains aside and shout from her kitchen window, "Jake!" "Tooter!" "Bub!" "Helen!" And we'd all have to go and see what it was that she wanted. God!, didn't the weeds grow huge in Aunt Cassie's garden what with all that good rich cow manure on it and Lord!, didn't the grass grow fast on her huge lawn!

Aunt Cassie considered herself an "expert" in givin home permanents. All any of her female relatives had to do was to mention that they "needed" a new perm and Aunt Cassie would whip out her old Marcel waving kit and begin.

279

It was fascinating for us kids to sit in her kitchen and watch this mysterious, malodorous event take place. Aunt Cassie would saturate each clump of hair with a poisonous, smelling liquid then she'd wind the hair up in a rusty roller and clamp the roller into place with an aluminum clip. Once the victim's entire head was rolled up, a kind of chemical reaction would take place and blue, sulfur-smelling smoke would drift into the air and we'd hold our breath, half expecting the victim's head to burst into flames or for them to be electrocuted!

God forbid that Aunt Cassie received a telephone call at that moment of if she heard the phone ring on the party line for someone else, because she'd be gone. She'd abandon the unwitting person in a heartbeat, leaving them sitting in her kitchen with blue smoke rolling off their head, while she rubbered in on the latest news.

After an indeterminate amount of time, she'd reappear as though she hadn't ever left and begin removing the perming paraphernalia. Sometimes, only half of the hair had taken properly and the other half had been fried to a crisp. Upon seeing the look of horror on her latest victim's face, Aunt Cassie would grasp the dead hair in her hand, laugh and say, "Ain't that jist like the fashions in gay Paree!" Usually, it took at least a year before anyone's hair had grown in enough for them to need another perm. Few were ever foolish enough to mention that they "needed" another perm in front of Aunt Cassie again.

When things got too boring at our house, we'd always sneak off down the Goding Road to Aunt Cassie's house to see what was going on there. Usually, we were never disappointed. The farm was always filled with new and exciting creatures and experiences.

When spring finally rolled around, off we'd go to see all the new piglets, baby calves and chickens. The new calves were so cute, especially the ones that had jist been born and were trying to stand on their wobbly legs. Aunt Cassie would allow us to pet them and brush their coats only after we'd agreed that the stalls would be so much "nicer" without all that smelly old cow shit all over the place! The deal was, that we could pet and brush the calves to our heart's content, after we'd cleaned out all the stalls. It sounded like a fair deal to us at the time.

We also loved to look at and hold the soft yellow chicks and this was okay with Aunt Cassie too if we agreed to pound up a few old crockery jars into feed for the hens. We'd sit down on the ground around a large rock that she called her "chicken" rock. It had a deep indentation in it from all the years of pounding bits of broken crockery on it. We'd always fight over who got to use the hammer first and hearing us argue, she'd chide us from her kitchen window, "Kids!" "Kids!" "I've got more than enough broken dishes from the dump to go around. Now don't be fightin over that old stuff!"

As Mark, her oldest grandson grew; he often came to visit his grandparent's farm. When we knew that Mark was there visiting, we'd drop everything and head down over the hill to play with him. We used to call him the "city" kid because he lived in Ashland which was about five miles from our house.

To say that Aunt Cassie doted on her grandson was putting it mildly. We knew that if Mark was with us when we took it into our heads to chop down a "few" trees or if we jist "happened" to pull up some of Uncle Hal's potatoes, then we wouldn't get into too much trouble. Mark was our "insurance" policy, so to speak.

Mark didn't get to visit his grandparents too often because his parents thought that Uncle Hal's swearin and other vices might have a bad influence on him. When he did get to visit, Mark would act like a kid let out of jail. He'd want to do everything that he wasn't allowed to do at home. He wouldn't take a bath unless Grampy Sutherland took one too and he'd imitate his grandfather in every possible way.

Uncle Hal knew that Mark wasn't allowed to swear and he'd wait with baited breath until Mark's next visit and then he'd purposely try out every cuss word that he knew and a few that he'd made up. Mark soaked up all these new and different experiences like a sponge. All the while, Uncle Hal would smile to himself and he'd wait to hear the explosions that were sure to come from the direction of Station Hill after Mark had gone home.

Mark's last name was Michaud, but as soon as he got to the farm, he'd insist that we call him "Sutherland." He'd always tell us that if we didn't call him that, he'd blame everything that we'd done on us. Being a bunch of kids, we didn't care what we called him. If he wanted to be called Sutherland, that was fine with us.

I'll never forget that fine summer's morning when Jake, Bub, Helen and I were down to Aunt Cassie's. Mark had jist arrived the night before and he was going to stay for a week. We were sitting in the grass on Aunt Cassie's lawn arguin about what we were going to do for the day. Jake wanted to go down to the island, steal dad's boat and take it on a fast trip around the island. Bub wanted to go out to the back fields and smoke some Indian tobacco. Helen and I wanted to go strawberrying in the overgrown hay fields across the road. Mark wanted to go down to the railroad siding and find some snakes to put on the tracks before the next train came through.

Aunt Cassie looked out her kitchen window where she was washin dishes and yelled out to us to ask us what was wrong. Jake lied to her and said that we were thinkin of goin down in the woods to chop down some trees to build a log cabin. Hearing this, Aunt Cassie stopped what she was doing and looked at us for a couple of seconds, then with a shrewd look on her face, she said, "I don't know about you, but if it was me, I wouldn't go down in them woods right now, what with all those skeeters and mingies around. And it's God-awful hot today too!" We all looked at each other and waited. "Why don't you play right here?" "Where?" We all yelled. She looked out through the screened in window with a big smile on her face and she knew that she had us.

"Well," She said. "You know that I've gut that old chicken coop right over there behind you and it's empty right now. I think that it would make a perfectly fine playhouse, don't you?" We turned and looked where she had pointed and sure enough, there it was! Reeling us a little closer into her trap, she continued. "There's only one problem though kids. It really ought to be cleaned out before you play in there. It ain't been cleaned in years!" "No problem!" We all yelled. Jake ran to get the wheelbarrow, Bub and I ran to get the shovels, Mark ran to get some gloves and Helen went to get us some drinking water from the hose. We scurried up the small incline to the shit-filled chicken coop like an anxious husband on his honeymoon.

We pushed open the sagging chicken coop door and gagged at the sight that awaited us. The walls and floor were covered with chicken droppings and the smell was horrendous! We each grabbed a tool and we shoveled, we swept, we carted and we cleaned all morning and after about five hours, the "play house" was beginning to look pretty good. Well, we could finally see the floor anyway.

Suddenly, through the dust that hung in the air, I looked over at Jake. His red hair and face were completely covered with a fine, white dust. Beads of sweat ran down the side of his face like small rivers and he was thoroughly and systematically scratching himself. I looked at him for a moment and then I felt the sudden urge to scratch too. Mark, watching us, began to scratch and whine about feeling all itchy. Bub and Helen were standing in a corner and they looked jist like the rest of us. We dropped everything and got the hell out of that hen house.

Mark ran screeching down the hill to where Aunt Cassie was watchin from her kitchen window. She looked out to where we were standin, scratchin and itchin and asked. "What, tired of playin already?" She asked and she seemed to be laughing a little as she said it. "Grammy," Mark whined. "Do chickens have lice?" "God yes!" She replied. "But don't worry, chicken lice don't stay too long on kids!" And she burst out laughing.

Jake looked up at her face in the screen window and asked, "Well, how long do they stay?" "Oh, not more than two or three days," She replied. We all looked at each other in horror and Mark shot into the house.

As we tiredly rounded the corner of her house, headed for home, we heard this parting shot from the direction of her window. "By the way kids, anytime you want to come and play in the other chicken coop, jist let me know. It ain't been cleaned in a long, long time neither!" To this day, I swear that I could hear her laughter in the still afternoon air behind us as we straggled, filthy, itching and scratching, up the long hill towards home.

Note: I hurriedly finished this story so that I could present it to Aunt Cassie in honor of her ninetieth birthday on March 18, 2001. After she'd read it, a relative asked her how she'd liked the story. She mulled the question over for a couple of seconds and then she said. "I don't mind that Tooter said that I liked to dig in the dump, because I do! I don't mind that she said that I liked to gossip because that's true too! And I don't even mind that she wrote that I liked to rubber in on my neighbor's telephone calls because I did! But I don't like it that she wrote that I had a crick in my neck because I don't!"

Note: July 7, 2004, as of this writing, Aunt Cassie is still alive and well and still living alone in her old house on the Goding Road and she turned ninety-four on March 18, 2004. May God Bless you Aunt Cassie. I will always love you.

Note: March 21, 2007. As of this writing, Aunt Cassie is still alive and well but she has moved into what she calls "Wrinkle Village" a (euphemism for the Home for the Elderly) in Ashland for the winter. I spoke with her yesterday and after a long and happy conversation, she asked, "Is there anything I can do for you Tooter?" "God no!" I replied. "You did more for me when I was a kid that I can ever repay you for." "Well," she said. "What were a few cookies? When I close my eyes, I can still see your little blond head as you walked by my house, goin fishin or you seated on Uncle Hal's lap as you helped him cultivate the potatoes. You know Tooter, I hope I can move back to my old shack when warm weather comes and have a little garden. I want to plant a potato plant for Hal." I hope you can move back too Aunt Cassie and plant a potato plant for Uncle Hal for me too. I will always love you, Aunt Cassie.

Note: May 15, 2007. As of this writing, Aunt Cassie is still doing well but she still had a little problem when I spoke with her last week. It seems that after having gone a lifetime without actually knowin what her age really was, she finally found her birth certificate and she called me in a state of panic. ""Tooter," she said. "I finally found my birth certificate!" "Well," Aunt Cass, that's good news." "No," she replied, "It ain't." "Why not, Aunt Cass?" I asked. "Well, you know, these fools went and gave me a big birthday party because they thought I was ninety-seven and I'm not!" "Well, how old are you?" I asked. "I'm younger than I thought I was, I'm only ninety-six!" I had to laugh at that and then I asked, "Well, isn't that good news?" "No," she replied, "It ain't!" "Why?" "Well," these fools will think I lied and now I'll have to give back all tha presents!" "Oh" Aunt Cass, you may only be ninety-six but you're still tha oldest person in Ashland." She had a think about it and then she said, "I guess you're right."

Note: During the Ashland Days Celebration on the Fourth of July, 2007, Aunt Cassie was honored again. She was awarded a cane and a plaque and after all the uproar had died down, she called me to tell me the news. "Tooter," she said. "These fools went and made a big deal over me agin and they had a ceremony and they gave me a beautiful cane and a plaque with my name and age engraved on it." "Oh," Aunt Cass, that's wonderful!" "No it ain't!" she replied. "Why not?" I asked. "Well," she replied. "Tha damn fools gave me a beautiful cane and then the sons-ah-whores took it back!" "En if that wasn't bad enough," she went on, "They gave me a plaque and then they asked me where I was goin to hang it in my apartment. I looked that old fool right in the eye and said, "I'm not goin to hang it anywhere, I'm goin to put it under my bed!" She wasn't at all impressed with the plaque but she sure did want that cane!

She went on to say that her family had "surprised" her and hadn't told her about the ceremony in her honor and when they'd come to pick her up, they hadn't even allowed her to change her clothes. Then they'd taken her uptown and put her in a buggy that was hooked to a horse and it had pulled her all over to hell and gone. She wasn't happy or impressed with that ceremony either. She said that a newspaper reporter had come up to her and had taken her picture for the Presque Isle Star Herald and he'd asked her how she'd liked the buggy ride. She said that she had told him that at age fourteen, her father, Old Ock Bragdon, had told her that she was grown now and that she'd best be lookin for a husband to support her. So, he'd put her in his horse cart and they'd driven the long ride from Buffalo into Ashland. She said that she hadn't liked the buggy ride with her father eighty-three years ago and she didn't like this one either! Aunt Cassie went on to tell me that she sure hoped that they'd gotten this "honorin" thing out of their systems and that she sure to God hoped that she didn't make it to one hundred because she dreaded to think what them friggin fools might do to her then! But I sure hope you do make it to you hundredth birthday Aunt Cass.

Note: February 18, 2008   Aunt Cass began losing ground right after Christmas and is now in a nursing home in Caribou. Today is her 97th birthday and she is going softly into her good night. I'm sorry to lose you, Aunt Cass but I certainly don't want you to suffer. May God bless and keep you till we meet again.

Note: March 13, 2008   Great Aunt Cass left this earthly realm last night at 6:15. She's not suffering anymore and I'm certain Heaven is a much brighter and busier place now. I wrote the following poem jist for her:

For Aunt Cass

I haven't come to say goodbye
Because you didn't really die...

You're in the sky and in the trees
And all my lifelong memories...

You are in all the things that grow
And in the very winds that blow...

I'm not sad now that you've gone
My memories of you go on and on...

So wait for me now that you sleep
For I have promises to keep....

In Loving Memory of
my great Aunt Cassie Sutherland
03-13-08

Her House

Her house stands lonely on the hill,
no birds are singing, all is still
The grass has grown, her flowers droop,
there are no chickens in the coop...

The cows are gone, the fire is cold,
the house is sagging, it's grown old
Her spirit lingers, just out of sight,
it comes around most every night...

At fifteen she came to stay and live,
so much hard work, so much to give
She started young, her family,
a little girl, two boys, make three...

Some eighty years upon this hill,
and then to spend no more
Every time I look for her,
she's gone thru Heaven's door....

Martha Stevens-David

SNOOKY LONG

By tha time Snooky was born, his parents were well into their forties and after trying for years, they'd finally given up on ever having a child of their own. At birth, he didn't look at all like most other newborn babies. His skin had a slightly olive cast and he had a profusion of pitch black hair which stood straight up on his little round head. His face was oval and he had his father's decidedly pointed chin. His nose had a slightly angular look which gave him a fox-like appearance, but it was his eyes that one really paid attention to. They were jet black and there was a shine to them that most people's eyes didn't have. Even when he was real little, he had a way of fixing his dark, shiny eyes on a person that made folks feel very uncomfortable, because he never seemed to blink

When folks stopped Mrs. Long to have a look at tha new baby, they were at a loss as to how to react or what to say. The baby lay in his stroller and gazed back at them as directly as they gazed at him. He never took his eyes off them as he took their measure. Disconcerted, folks would back away; turn to his mother and mumble, "What an interesting baby!" Or "Where did you get this little tyke?" Folks hated to be mean or admit it, but there was something about that Long baby that didn't sit quite right with them. They couldn't put their feelings into words, but tha feelings were there all the same.

Even as an infant, Snooky was demanding. When nursed, he'd suckle at one breast jist long enough to get tha milk flowing and then he'd pull his head back and howl at tha top of his lungs. Afraid that he wasn't getting enough milk, Mrs. Long would hastily switch him to tha other breast. He didn't eat, he didn't sleep and it wasn't too long before Snooky had worn his poor, doting mother's nerves to a complete frazzle.

Snooky wasn't easy to please at all. If they picked him up for a cuddle, he'd let out cries that pierced their ears until they quickly dropped him back into his crib. If he was in his crib, he'd thrash around until he'd taken his sheet right off tha mattress and then he'd howl until they picked him up. If they sat down to rock, he'd squirm and wriggle until he'd worked himself up into a rage and then he'd scream all over again. There was jist no way of pleasing him. People, his father in particular, jist left him tha hell alone.

Old Mr. Long was a simple, honest, hardworking man and when folks asked him how tha boy was doing, his dad would look at them with a dazed look on his face and whisper, "Fine, jist fine." His father didn't know what to make of this new addition that had sprung from his withered loins so late in life. He only knew that things had changed a great deal since that friggin kid had arrived and it looked like things were only going to get worse from here on in.

If his father attempted to play with him, Snooky would look back at him with his cold, beady eyes and let out a screech that brought everyone within hearin distance, running. If his father walked over to tha crib and smiled down at him, tha kid would look up at his father with such a mean look on his cunning, little face that Mr. Long could feel the hair rise up on tha back of his neck. It was akin to starin into tha face of a wild animal.

As Snooky grew, he was quick of wit and deed. He did everything early. As soon as he could talk, he learned to lie and he quickly progressed from lying to stealing. He was never content with what he had; he had to have it all. If he played with tha other kids in the neighborhood, which wasn't often, he was soon sent home for fighting, stealing, lying or all of the above. There was many tha time that Mrs. Long would come around the corner of tha house to find Snooky smoking from someone's cast-off cigarette butt. By tha time he was six years old, his reputation as a "little Christer" had spread to all tha surrounding towns in "Tha County."

As tha kid got older, Snooky's father stayed away from him as much as possible. He made damn sure that he left home in the morning long before Snooky woke up and he never went home until he was absolutely certain that tha kid was fast asleep.

It wasn't too long before Snooky learned that money was power. If relatives came for a visit, Snooky would wait until they'd settled on a chair and then he'd sidle up to them, lean against their knees and fix his mean, little eyes on them. If they tried to shoo him away, he'd jist press a little harder against their knees with his small, pointy elbows and stay where he was. His mother, seeing Snooky leaning up against folk's knees, would smile and say, "He's such a friendly little bugger. Isn't he tha cutest little thing?" He'd stay there and stare at the visitors until they were so unsettled that they didn't know what to do. Finally, jist to get rid of tha little conniver, they'd grope around in their pockets for a fistful of change and they'd shove tha money into Snooky's hot little hands. Satisfied, he'd take off to hide tha loot in his room. His mother laughingly told folks that "Little Snooky" had more money in his bank than she did! People, who'd unwillingly contributed to tha little bastard's savings, didn't doubt her for a minute. Need-less-to-say, tha Longs didn't have too many unannounced visitors dropping by.

It was when Snooky went off to school that things really got bad. He was a royal pain in the ass to say tha least. He terrorized tha other kids until he got what he wanted. If he happened to be caught by a teacher doing something that he wasn't supposed to, he wouldn't even apologize. He'd jist look back at tha teacher with his little shit-eating grin on his face. He was never kept after school because tha teachers had all they could stand of him during tha day. It wasn't uncommon to see Snooky skipping down tha road towards home long before school let out at tha end of tha day. Tha elementary school teachers used to offer each other bribes to take him in their class tha next year. Poor Mr. and Mrs. Long spent so much time at tha school, that folks around town laughingly joked that they must be tha new "substitute" teachers.

Being a small town, in those days, folks didn't run to child behaviorists or child psychologists if they were experiencing a problem with their kid. Generally, if a kid misbehaved, the parents simply "warmed his ass until it glowed a bright red," and that was that. Back then, no one thought of it as child abuse. Parents didn't have tha time nor the energy to worry about long reaching side effects on their kid's psyche.

At about tha fifth grade, the principal called Mr. and Mrs. Long into his office and explained that there was a problem with Snooky's antisocial behavior. His parents looked at each other in bewilderment, what was the principal trying to say? They had no idea what "antisocial" meant. Did it mean something good or bad? What had they done wrong?

There were no answers. Snooky was Snooky. He'd been born that way and that was that. They were told that all tha tests showed that Snooky was bright, very bright. He could do any work he was given, but he jist didn't want to. He only came to school each day to harass tha teachers and get what he could from tha other children.

Mr. Michaud, tha principal, explained that after much testing and discussion it had been determined that Snooky was a "sociopath." For a moment or two Mr. Long thought that that must be a good thing, but as tha principal explained in greater detail, Mr. Long's tired old heart sank lower and lower in his old chest. Tha principal told them that it was tha general consensus among Snooky's teachers that he didn't belong in a "regular" school and perhaps his parents should consider sending Snooky to another kind of school. "What kind of school is that?" His father asked. "I, frankly, don't know," tha principal replied. "Snooky is only ten years old and if he continues on tha way he is, I can only see reform school in his future." His parents thanked tha principal and dejectedly left his office.

At home that night, his parents tried to talk to Snooky about what tha principal had said, but he wasn't interested. He announced that he didn't need that friggin old school anyway and that he was already smarter than his teachers. For some reason, his father believed him. So, at tha ripe old age of ten, Snooky no longer went to school.

For a while, it seemed that Snooky had turned over a new leaf. He took to getting up early with his father and before you knew it, not only was he working in his father's garage, he was runnin it! He took to motor vehicle repairs with a passion and skill that his father never had. Customers were often astounded to learn that their short, foul mouthed, chain smoking, grease covered, auto mechanic wasn't a midget, he was really only ten years old!

Snooky's reputation soon grew as a mechanic and folks began telling each other that maybe there was hope for him yet. But they quickly realized that a lcopard really doesn't change his spots. They learned that if they left anything of value in their vehicle, then it certainly wouldn't be there when they went back to get it. So folks made sure that their vehicles were given a through going over long before they dropped them off at Long's garage.

Snooky had tha uncanny ability to take an old worn out engine and with very little work, make it run like new. He had more business than he could repair all by himself. He kept his father busy running to the junkyard in Presque Isle, looking for spare parts. If tha parts couldn't be found at tha junkyard, Snooky found other ways or means to get them. Farmers soon learned that if they left their farm machinery out in tha field for a few days, then tha machines didn't always work tha same as they had when they'd left them there.

It wasn't uncommon to have a farmer pull up in tha garage driveway complaining that his "new" muffler had suddenly turned "rusty" overnight or that tha spark plugs he'd had put in jist last week were corroded and misfiring. Now, no one was stupid enough to come right out and blame Snooky for all these problems, but everyone had their suspicions jist the same.

In tha corner of tha smoky, grease-filled garage, Snooky posted a sign which read in big red letters, "Not Responsible for Items Left in Vehicles." On tha rare occasions that Snooky did close his garage, he bolted tha doors with tha largest chain and padlock he could find. Folks, around Ashland, often joked that "wouldn't you know it, only a thief would have tha biggest padlock and chain around" or things like, "Jeesus Jake, your old truck sure sounds better with my new muffler." Or "Does your truck handle better with my new shocks on it?"

Time went by and tha garage remained pretty much tha same, only a little more dilapidated. Snooky had only one real interest and that was repairing vehicles. Because his garage was located jist outside of Ashland on tha Masardis Road, it was in a prime location for tourists and Canadian log trucks that were experiencing mechanical problems.

About half a mile down tha Masardis Road from Snooky's garage, there was a pot hole in tha road that had been there for at least a hundred years. Every so often, the men from tha Ashland Town Garage would go out and half-heartedly make a big production out of filling in tha sink hole and repairing it. However, due to all tha heavy log trucks going back and forth daily to Levesque's Mill in Masardis, tha pot hole always returned each year, bigger than ever.

Tha pot hole was located at tha bottom of Pike's Hill and as a vehicle approached the crest of tha hill and began slowing down, Snooky would grin widely and begin counting tha minutes until tha vehicle hit tha hole. Once he heard tha resounding sound of metal being wrenched from its base, Snooky would smile to himself and say "Ka-ching!" "Ka-ching!" Snooky had made quite a business out of all tha wheel alignments, wheel balancing and shock replacements from that pot hole, not to mention tha very lucrative business of hub cap replacements.

It was rumored by folks around town that tha reason Snooky kept that back hoe out behind his garage all tha time was so he could dig out that pothole every few months or so. All of tha local folks knew of tha pothole hazard so, they always drove on tha other side of tha road to avoid it. But at tha start of fishing season in May through tha hunting season in November, Snooky's garage was a very busy place.

Folks knew that Snooky was a little "light fingered" to say tha least, but that didn't bother them too much because he never over-charged them for their repair work. This odd quirk to his character was an oft discussed fact around town. Well, folks reasoned amongst themselves, with so many other bad habits, it was good that tha Devil had missed that one.

Snooky didn't bother to chase girls like all tha other young fellers around town either. He didn't have time for all that; he was too busy fixing things. But, tha girls always found a way to Snooky anyway. Jist tha fact that he was so very different was what drew them to him. He always looked tha same whenever and wherever you saw him. From his faded Ford cap right down to his boots, there was only one word to describe him and that was greasy! Tha girls chased after him all tha same and he never took them out. Well, not that anyone noticed anyway. But, every once in a while, a baby would turn up in one family or another and pretty soon folks were hinting that tha poor fatherless baby certainly had tha "Long" look to it, especially around tha eyes and nose.

Snooky's garage seldom closed. He could be found there twenty-four hours a day, seven days a week. On a slow evening, Snooky would sit out in front of tha old garage with his chair tipped back on two legs against tha wall. His greasy Ford cap was tilted at jist tha right angle to keep tha setting sun out of one eye while his dank, black hair fell over his other one. An ever-present Camel cigarette dangled out of tha corner of his mouth. Every now and then, a long hunk of glowing ash fell off his cigarette and tumbled down tha greasy bib front of his pants. "Jaysus, Snooky," folks warned him. "If yah don't change your clothes once in a while or take a bath, you're goin to blow yourself up one of these days." When one cigarette went out, he'd immediately tap another one out of his pack and light it by striking a match against tha thumbnail of his grease stained hands.

One year slid into another without much notice except for tha years changing on tha calendar. Snooky became tha owner of a much mangled bulldozer when one of his customers couldn't pay for his truck repairs. Pretty soon Snooky had that scarred up old piece of junk runnin jist like new.

Snooky spent all his free time learnin how to run it. He'd drop tha heavy blade along tha side of tha weather beaten building and push all tha grease soaked dirt back into tha woods behind tha garage. He began building a road down into tha back woods and when anyone asked Snooky jist what he was doing, he'd look back at them with his bright, black eyes, but he never gave them an answer.

Then came nineteen fifty-two, tha year of the snow-less winter and elderly folks around town began whispering to one another that this winter wasn't "seemly" and something bad was going to happen. They could feel it in their dry old bones and tha predictions became more and more dire. Tha weeks went by and tha elderly, whose mind was still sound, searched back in their memory to try and recall a year that had been like this one.

It turned the fifteenth of January and there was still no snow on tha barren ground. Tha temperature hovered around thirty-two degrees and influenza ran rampant through tha scattered settlements of "Tha County." Young and old alike, began dropping like flies. Folks cursed, prayed and cried and blamed everyone and everything that they could think of. Tha illness took old Mr. Long first and it wasn't too long before Mrs. Long joined her husband in tha cold, damp ground of tha Ashland Cemetery. Finally, tha dyin and tha cryin ceased and folks picked up tha tattered remnants of their lives and went on.

Snooky quickly sold tha old family home on Main Street and moved tha rest of his belongings into tha back room of his dilapidated garage.

He threw his clothes, which were all tha same hue of black, onto a pile of retread tires and that was that.

With tha death of his parents and tha opening of Stacy's garage on tha Frenchville Road, Snooky's life took a decided turn for tha worse. Competition for used car parts became decidedly fierce. It was becoming necessary to range further and further afield to check out tha junkyards and abandoned vehicles in tha surrounding towns. If Snooky's manner of obtaining replacement parts was questionable before, it was now tha latest topic around town. Folks began commenting that they had been awakened at odd hours of tha night by tha sounds of a tow truck dragging vehicles around tha back of Snooky's garage. Other folks living along tha Presque Isle Road commented that they'd heard Snooky's bulldozer working late at night in tha woods behind his garage. "What tha hell could he be doing at that time of night?" They kept asking each other.

In most small towns, folks generally tend to mind their own business especially if it's in their own best interest. But, all these strange happenings, especially at such odd hours, only served to pique their interest. It wasn't too long before tha local law enforcement began to hear all tha rumors too. Folks in Presque Isle, Caribou and Houlton began reporting stolen vehicles. Tha police were even more confused when they discovered that tha "stolen" vehicles were older vehicles, farm equipment or even old abandoned vehicles. "Who in hell would go to all that trouble to steal old vehicles?" They wondered. This mystery caused tha troopers at tha Houlton State Police Barracks many a sleepless night discussing tha strange happenings.

It was on a cold and starlight night that they finally discovered tha truth. Tha local game warden, Sonny Campbell, was flying back to Presque Isle from Eagle Lake one night and his flight path happened to take him over tha property behind Snooky's garage. As he passed over tha area, tha warden looked down and thought he saw a light moving in tha woods. He banked his plane and decided that he'd have another look at tha spot where he'd seen tha light. As he came in low over tha trees, he was startled to see a man on an old bulldozer pushing dirt over a freshly dug hole. As tha warden looked more carefully around tha area, he was surprised to see that there were more than twenty other mounds identical to tha one the man had been bulldozing. "Well, well,

well, what do we have here?" thought tha warden as he banked tha plane for home.

Bright and early tha next morning, tha warden paid a visit to his old friend Captain Crocker who lived on the Goding Road. After much discussion, they decided that perhaps they'd better take another look at tha land behind Snooky's garage. As they flew over tha area, it became apparent that Snooky had been a very busy boy.

Snooky was arrested and found guilty of auto theft, farm machinery theft and conspiracy and was sent down to Thomaston State Prison to serve a sentence of three and a half years. Folks around town weren't really too shocked by this sudden turn of events because most of them really didn't expect people to be much better than they really were.

It was oft heard around town that since Snooky had been sent away and his garage closed, there wasn't a good repair shop around anymore. More than one resident was heard to mutter that they'd sure as hell be glad when Snooky was released from tha slammer because they certainly weren't going to take any more vehicles out to that God-damned crook Stacy on tha Frenchville Road.

Folks, when asked by people from away, if we have any things of interest in our small Maine town, tell visitors that there's a Logging Museum on the Garfield Road and oh yes, there's an "engine burial ground" on your left, behind tha old garage, jist down tha Masardis Road.

WINTER KING

On the death of his father in nineteen fifty, Les McCormack, our neighbor to the north, inherited the small family farm. Some years, if the drink wasn't calling him more than the potatoes, Les would plant a few crops here and there around his hundred or so acres.

There was a small apple orchard located jist down over the hill from the homestead and his father had taken great pains to nurture the trees so that by the time Les was old enough to farm, the trees were mature and were producing a variety of wonderful apples.

Les didn't particularly love apples or farming but there were several things that he loved and those were horses, horse racing, womanizing and drinking and not necessarily in that order. Every spring, his trainers used to hook the lovely, sleek animals to their sulky carts and race them up and down the Goding Road that ran in front of our house, for their daily exercise. We used to sit in the tall grass by the side of the dirt road and watch as the well-groomed horses responded to the touch of a whip or a softly spoken word.

Les came from a long line of drinkers, womanizers and avid horsemen and when his father died, he simply picked-up where his father had left off in regard to horse racing. He took some of his large inheritance and drove all the way to Louisville, Kentucky, the city that was famous for breeding Kentucky Derby winners. Les had the money and he didn't care how much it was going to cost. If he had to, he was going to buy himself a winner!

Les took his own sweet time and made the rounds of all the well-known horse breeding farms in and around Louisville, not only checking out all the horses and foals, but also sampling a lot of Kentucky bourbon and quite a few of the local fillies as well. Finally, jist as he was about to give up and come home, he found the foal that he was looking for.

297

The young horse was from full-blooded Arabian stock and Les, the first time he saw him, felt something that he later described as a bolt of lightning, go through his old, quiverin heart. The stallion had a sleek look to him and a stance that proved his great breeding lines. His legs were long and slim, but powerful and though he was young and still untrained, he already had a commanding presence.

He'd stand stock-still while all the would-be buyers from around the world touched and examined him. He didn't even whinny or snort or shy away when his owner pried open his mouth to show the on-lookers that his teeth were in first class condition jist like the rest of him. He had class and breeding and it was there for all the world to see.

The horse, aware that people were watching, gamboled up to the white painted fence and as though trained, bowed his lovely head in Les' direction. This was all it took and it wasn't too long before the seller had a check clutched tightly in his hand and Les had the stallion's reins clutched jist as tightly in his.

It was a beautiful sunny, spring day in Aroostook County, Maine when Les finally returned with his prize. Upon hearing the news of his latest acquisition, we hurried up the dusty, dirt road to have a look at his latest treasure.

The young horse was quickly installed in the new pasture that Les had built nearest the house. From his kitchen windows, old Les would sit with his ever-present drink in hand and gaze at the lovely creature as it cavorted and wheeled around the dandelion-filled pasture.

Over the ensuing months, as the horse matured, he developed a long streak of white in the hair of his forelock, but the rest of him was a glossy chestnut red. After much discussion and rejection, Les finally named the horse, "Winter King" and the name seemed to fit him perfectly.

Through our regular weekly visits, Winter King quickly grew to recognize us whenever we made the short trip across the potato fields to his pasture. Jake, me, Bub and Helen would scurry up to the fence, climb up a couple of rails and wait for him to come to us.

When we called his name, he'd raise his beautiful head, lift his velvety top lip over his perfect white teeth and whinny long and loud, jist as though he was trying to tell us how happy he was to see us again. Every time we heard him make that long whinny of recognition, my older brother Jake would turn with a big smile plastered across his freckled-face and say to the rest of us, "Didja hear that? He jist said helloooooooooooo to us in horse talk." We all nodded our heads in agreement; we knew that Jake was right.

By the time spring strolled into "Tha County" the next year, Winter King was a yearling and nearly full-grown and Les called down to Scarborough Downs for his favorite jockey to come up to Aroostook and train him.

Winter King's training began in earnest and we'd hold our breath as he came gamboling down the road. His hooves made little puffs of dust rise up from the dirt as his flying feet barely touched the ground. He didn't need too much training; his pace was so well-coordinated that he appeared to be dancing on air as he flashed by with the sulky flying along behind him.

Les had many loves in his life, after horses and liquor came wimmin. He'd been married a number of times throughout his long life and had "shacked-up" a lot more times than folks could rightly remember.

The local gossips had it that after his first marriage ended, he'd taken to carving all the wimmin's names, who had spent time in his bed, on the inside of the closet door of his bedroom.

There were many discussions, by suspicious husbands in the county, especially over a good bottle of brew late at night, about how they could get a look at all the names carved on the inside of that closet door in Les' bedroom.

Les ordered a horse van specially designed for Winter King from a custom van place down in Tennessee. Winter King wasn't to be bundled in with all the other horses; he wasn't common and he deserved a van all his own, to Les' way of thinking anyway.

On the day that it finally arrived, we ran across the newly planted potato fields to see it. The van was a thing of beauty too. It was a glossy black with brass accents and Winter King's name was painted in bright gold letters across the front. Les bragged to everyone for miles around that it had cost him twenty-five thousand dollars and worth every penny too, he'd said.

Winter King had a "special" harness too. Les sent to Ireland for a custom hand-made one. When it finally arrived, we watched excitedly as it was unwrapped. It was made of soft, black leather and the metal rings and studs that held it together were coated with real gold. Les held the horse's head while his trainer slipped the gold-plated bit into his mouth. Winter King accepted the new mouth piece with dignity. He shook his head and pranced a little and then he stood stock still and looked at all of us with his large amber-colored eyes. We could see our reflection in his eyes as he stood there. He knew he was beautiful too.

It was lonely and quiet for us kids after Winter King left in July. Les had a lengthy racing itinerary that included all the racing circuits from Canada and the Maritime Provinces down to New York and finally, Scarborough Downs in Maine at the close of the racing season in September. We waited with baited breath for any news about Winter King and how many races he'd won in his first season.

Winter King was everything he'd been rumored to be and everything Les had paid for and more. Year in and year out, he won race after race and it was rumored that by the time his racing career was through, he'd won well over a million dollars for his old, drunken owner.

When Winter King came home for any length of time, we used to run across the neglected potato fields to Les' house to gaze at this beautiful horse as he grazed peacefully in the pasture next to the house. Sometimes, if his racing season was past and the apples were on the ground, Les would let us feed the apples to Winter King. He'd walk up to us, stick his head over the fence and pick the apples out of our grubby hands jist like an elegant person eating dinner in a five star restaurant.

One year, when Les returned to the county at the end of the racing circuit, not only did he bring home Winter King, he also brought another young filly with him. She was about twenty years old and the only name we ever heard him call her was "Sweeta."

She was a beauty in herself. She had long flowing, naturally blond hair that reached nearly to her waist and her skin was the color and texture of fine porcelain. Her deep blue eyes were edged with long, dark lashes that swept across her cheeks when she closed her eyes.

She didn't wear makeup that one could easily see and her lips were a natural red that made all the other women envy her. She only stood about five feet tall even in her cow girl boots, but her figure was very well-proportioned. Yes sir! She was one fine lookin woman.

Les was mesmerized. There wasn't anything he wouldn't and didn't do for her. Now Les may or may not, have been "in love" or even "in like," but he certainly was "in lust." Whenever Sweeta came into a room or into his sight, his rummy old blood-shot eyes would light up and you could easily see how he felt about her.

Soon after Sweeta moved in, Les began remodeling his old farmhouse with a passion that was usually reserved for his horses. Whatever Sweeta wanted, Sweeta got! She redecorated the entire house and then she left, jist as suddenly as she'd arrived.

Folks said that the last time Sweeta was seen, she was at the Greyhound Station in Presque Isle, waiting for any bus leaving Aroostook County for all points south. Finally, one of the more nosey folks sidled over to where she was sitting on the bus station bench and asked her why she was leaving.

She looked the inquisitive old gossip directly in the face. "Well," she finally replied. "Les was awful good to me and tha money was wonderful and all that. But gitting up each morning and seeing his family jewels hanging down his leg like baseballs in an old sock, well, that was jist too much for me to take. But tha worst part was that after we'd finish making love, he'd kick his heels in the air and whinny jist like a damn horse!"

Les didn't mourn the loss of his latest woman too long and it wasn't long before he'd quickly installed another to take her place.

The years slipped quickly by and as the end of Winter King's racing days grew near, Les was approached by other horse breeders to farm him out to stud, but Les was adamant. He wouldn't even consider it. When asked why, Les would look at the lovely horse and say, "He's earned his keep and then some en he don't owe me nothin!"

The day finally came and we heard that Winter King was sick and Les, sobbing like a baby, had the vet put him down. Les buried the lovely horse right behind his house, in the same pasture that he'd grazed in for so many years, and he had a special bronze marker laid at the head of his final resting place. It read,

"REST IN PEACE – WINTER KING."

We used to go up to the farm, climb over the dilapidated fence and sit on Winter King's grave. We'd polish his headstone with our grubby hands and talk to him, as though he was still there.

Old Les wasn't the same after Winter King was gone. He continued racing for a while longer, but he never did reach the heights with the other horses that he'd attained with Winter King.

Folks said that when Winter King died, a lot of Les had died along with him. They sometimes joked that "Les was already dead and embalmed, he jist wasn't buried."

By the time Les was seventy-five, horses, booze, broads and cigars had taken the best of him and he finally retired from horse racing altogether. He sold off his remaining racing stable, piled all his racing junk up in his old barn and closed the doors. Folks said that he never again ventured inside that barn.

Sometimes, stupid people, hoping for a good deal, approached Les wanting to buy Winter King's van and other racing accoutrements, but Les would get that gleam in his rummy old eyes and wobble off into the house for his shotgun.

Some days, when he'd drunk too much, his mind was set in yesteryear, and his flabby old legs couldn't chase us off his property, we'd sneak inside his barn and sit in the sulky that Winter King had used when he'd won all his races.

We spent long, happy hours polishing and dusting that aging contraption, sitting in the driver's seat, pretending that we were the jockeys and that Winter King had jist won another race.

Old Les spent the remainder of his days in a drunken stupor, reliving in his memory, his days with Winter King and the reflected glory.

When Les finally passed away, people came for miles around to pay their last respects. The funeral was said to be the largest ever attended in our part of Aroostook County.

Folks came for many different reasons. Some came simply to pay their last respects to an old friend and fellow horseman. Others came because they'd grown up with him and they'd know him all their lives. Still others came because they thought they'd finally have a chance to sneak upstairs and have a look at the names written behind the bedroom closet door.

Folks talked about the large funeral for many months thereafter, and it was said that the rug leading up the stairs to Les' bedroom was worn thin by all the snoopers who wanted a firsthand look at all his lover's names carved into the closet door.

Folks said that when the door was opened, there were gasps of shock, surprise and relief when they finally read with their own eyes all that was written there. It said:

WINTER KING   1-1-53 - 7-2-63   MY ONLY LOVE...

About the Author

Martha Stevens-David, having grown up in Ashland in Aroostook County, Maine, desired to be a "writer" since the age of nine and she began putting her words to paper nearly thirty years ago. She writes in the "northern Maine dialect" and along with her short story collection, she also writes children's stories and poetry.

She is proud to say that among her list of publications, she is the most published writer on the official Maine website, www.Maine.gov.

Made in the USA
Charleston, SC
17 January 2012